Exquisite Desire

Exquisite Desire

Religion, the Erotic, and the Song of Songs

CAREY ELLEN WALSH

FORTRESS PRESS
Minneapolis

EXQUISITE DESIRE
Religion, the Erotic, and the Song of Songs

All biblical translations are by the author.

Cover image: *An Odalisque,* Joseph Douglas. Copyright © 2000 Christie's
    Images/SuperStock. Used by permission.
Lyrics (preface): "Badlands" © 1978 Bruce Springsteen. (ASCAP). All rights
    reserved. Used by permission.
Figures: Othmar Keel, *The Song of Songs.* Trans. Frederick J. Gaiser.
    Continental Commentary (Minneapolis: Fortress Press, 1994). Used by
    permission.
Cover design: Joseph Bonyata
Book design: Ann Delgehausen

Library of Congress Cataloging-in-Publication Data
Walsh, Carey Ellen
  Exquisite desire : religion, the erotic, and the Song of songs / Carey Ellen
Walsh.
      p. cm.
  Includes bibliographical references and index.
  ISBN 0-8006-3249-4 (alk. paper)
      1. Erotica—Biblical teaching. 2. Bible. O.T. Song of Solomon—
Criticism, interpretation, etc. I. Title.

BS1485.6.E73 W35 2000
221.8'3067—dc21   00-041721

Manufactured in the U.S.A.   AF 1-3249
04   03   02   01   00   1   2   3   4   5   6   7   8   9   10

For Brownie Ketcham

my wise mentor,
spiritual advisor,
beloved friend.

You showed me loving-kindness
and through it I glimpsed God's.
Encounter is all. You saved my life.

Contents

Figures

Frontispiece: A reclining singer supports her head with her left hand; her right hand rests on a lute. (Sketch on a limestone shard from Deir el-Medina; twelfth century B.C.E.)

Chapter 1: A couple on a bed. (Old Babylonian terra-cotta; ca. 1750 B.C.E.)

Chapter 2: King Akhenaton and Queen Nefertiti kissing. (Unfinished carnelian plaque; ca. 1340 B.C.E.)

Chapter 3: Two large birds, probably doves, sit on the rim of a large vessel; a small drinking bowl is in front of each. (Clay vessel from Vounos, Cypress; ca. 2000 B.C.E.)

Chapter 4: Ashurbanipal celebrates in an arbor with his wife after his victory over the Elamites. The bed is decorated with erotic motifs. (Relief from the palace of Ashurbanipal in Nineveh; ca. 640 B.C.E.)

Chapter 5: A woman drinks beer through a straw while a man approaches her from behind. (Old Babylonian terra-cotta relief; ca. 1750 B.C.E.)

Chapter 6: An Egyptian queen holds two love apples and a lotus bud under the nose of her husband. Her robe, which emphasizes her lower abdomen, makes the meaning of her gesture unmistakable. (Painted relief from Tell el-Amarna; ca. 1340 B.C.E.)

Chapter 7: A naked goddess standing on a warhorse holds four gigantic lotus blossoms. (Gold foil from Lachish; thirteenth/twelfth century B.C.E.)

Chapter 8: A goddess with naked upper body feeds two goats. She is seated on a mountain. (Carving on a small ivory box from Ugarit; fourteenth/thirteenth century B.C.E.)

Preface

The Song of Songs is a depth charge into the nature of desire itself, one that modern readers can learn from as much as the ancient Israelites must have. I have written this book to show you the Song's beauty, and, if read carefully, your own.

For better or worse, I have always listened to my curiosity, even when it attracted unwanted attention and I'd hear often about the killed cat. I suppose it was meant as cautionary, but all I felt was sadness for the little being who couldn't *not* discover just one bit more about its world. This is obviously, then, a pro-desire book. I know that there are dangers to desire, so does the woman in the Song of Songs. This is why the Song offers such profound wisdom. We have desires in us, in our makeup, and rather than squash what is irrepressible anyway, the Song teaches us how to reflect on and hone them for joy.

I wrote this book out of curiosity. I was researching Israelite vineyards for another book and devoted a good two days to the vineyard references in the Song of Songs. I left after the two days, but felt dazzled and confused by what I had read. Dazzled enough to go stand in vineyards in Napa Valley California for a week and discover that, sure enough, grapevines were highly erotic, as the Song easily displayed. Something snagged me about the Song and I returned to it. I have had nagging sensations before, some small, irritant inside that tells me to take another look, and I always honor it. I felt it when I first fell in love with my former spouse, when I met an enchanting Israeli who spoke the language I loved, when I first felt kindness, when I saw the desert, when I heard Mozart and Bruce Springsteen.

I felt it in my late, embarrassing curiosity with the Hebrew Bible. This is the key example, since I have written this book for people who may not know how to access the gifts of the Hebrew Bible. These include Religious Studies professors, by the way, and other inquisitive types who like literature. My students at Rhodes College have helped so much with their inevitable, plaintive query: "Why do we have to read this?" I hope this book helps people actually *want* to. I had never read the Bible and at twenty-two years old, thought that I should just take a class on it. I was there, basically, to run my culture's background check.

It was one messy, outrageous story after another, assaulting my assumptions that the Bible was about neat, calm, white people praying and having a white, clean sheep always next to them when they were greeting each other in something sounding pretty Amish. At Yale, I got to the end of the Moses story and was . . . blown away. I gasped and was haunted by that tale. Years later, I studied and became a Hebrew Bible professor. Then, I wished that I had grown up with the Bible and even felt robbed that my parents hadn't sent me to Hebrew day school when I was little, so that I could have had a leg up in the field. Since they are Irish Catholics, I've come to see that my expectations were a tad unrealistic. But now, I am glad that I can come to the Hebrew Bible *as if* it is brand new. I still feel assaulted by its audacity and yearn to know what these ancient wizards of storytelling meant. If there is a heaven and if I could meet two people, they are the J writer responsible for so much of Genesis, and Jeremiah, the depressed prophet. Then, if God were feeling particularly gracious that day, I'd like to chat with some of the people who first heard these tales, how stories of wild family fun and Jeremiah's ranting actually played to the Jerusalem crowd.

I also wrote this for two specific reasons. First, the Song of Songs has suffered from a unique interpretive history, where it was considered either too sensual, and so it was made an allegory about religion, or merely sexual and it was left at that. The scholarly literature on the Song has vacillated from one extreme to the other and betrays an interpretive confusion that I wanted to address. The Song is intensely sexual, yet biblical scholars tend to ignore the gains offered by theorists of sexuality, and by so doing, mute some of its wisdom. I use the theories of sex, gender, and desire as tools to understand the themes in the Song, but do not, I hope, impose them.

Second, I believe that academic writing should not be restricted to the guild of specialists in a field, but that it can be, at times, accessible to all. I have tried to keep the writing jargon-free, accessible to anyone with interest in desire, sexuality, meaning in life, or this Song. Again, my students have helped, brutally, since they always want the material quick and lean. This book is not quick, but I do hope it is lean, with the thematic issues kept always at the forefront. So, you need not be religious, or an academic, a Christian, Jew, or woman, to grasp the ideas in this book. I have written it for all out there who are like me, simply:

> The ones who had a notion,
> a notion deep inside, that it ain't
> no sin to be glad you're alive.
> —BRUCE SPRINGSTEEN, SAGE

Lastly, a word about publication. This book was originally under contract with another publisher, who, when he saw the actual manuscript, broke the contract since the book was "prurient." I looked that up, because I am a text person, and it means, "arousing an unwholesome desire." This is wrong. We all have desires, sexual and otherwise, and they cannot be "unwholesome." Nor should they go ignored. If we want to understand ourselves, our lives, and any faith we muster, we must become literate about desire. If we deny or giggle, we choke off the one avenue where, as Rilke says, God does speak, in our longings. The irony is a deep one. I became the (temporarily) muzzled woman I wrote about, whose voice had been ignored or dismissed by terming it, "prurient." And so, the woman in the Song, who never loses her voice, despite obstacles, became my guide again after the manuscript was done.

I am grateful, therefore, to Linda Maloney of Liturgical Press, and to Michael West and K. C. Hanson of Fortress Press for their belief in this project. And I am grateful to Hal Rast and Ann Delgehausen for their able, kind editing. It has been a pleasure to work with them all and be heard. This book is all about voicing desire and they let me.

1

A Question of Desire

Is There Some Accounting for Biblical Taste?

Let him kiss me with kisses of his mouth
for better is your love than wine,
   your anointing oils are fragrant,
your name is better than perfume poured out.
   Therefore women love you!
Draw me after you, let us run!
   Let the king bring me into his chambers.

   —SONG 1:2-4

God bless the feisty ancient woman who felt this fierce passion
and excitement and somehow saw to it that it got preserved in
the Bible. Without any introduction of characters or context, we
glimpse a bald declaration of sexual want as the book's opening.
We are startled by what this biblical woman wants—kisses and
plenty of them—but why is a biblical book jumping right in, de-
voting itself to sexual desire? These opening verses are not even
just the racy, preliminary lines meant to entice readers into the
book—this biblical Song writhes for eight enjoyable, unnerving
chapters on a woman's desire and arousal. What does this Song
tell us about ancient wants, and which of those wants persist
today for readers of the Bible?

Canonical Setting

What is a book of erotica (that is, descriptions of sexual yearning between two lovers) doing in the Bible anyway? And how are we to cope—in embarrassed silence or in glee, essentially mimicking the very pleasure described in the Song? How can modern readers feast on this biblical treat and gain nourishment for their lives today? There is much that we still share with the ancient spirit, even though our means of expression have changed over the centuries. In this instance, what we share with the author(s) of the Song of Songs is a furtive fascination with desire. Desire fuels the motives behind many of our actions. In fact, a good part of our socialization process involves our desires, which often get scripted by the media through an onslaught of advertisements, movies, and cultural messages. What we see and hear over and over again in a culture becomes what we desire, yet in large measure, we never give our full consent to this external shaping of our desires. The power of desire in our individual lives has never been examined.

But there is definitely interest. We like to see desire acted out or taken to the extreme in works of fiction, film, and television. How else can we explain the popularity of soap operas, fatal attractions, and the tragic romances from *Romeo and Juliet* to *Titanic*? There is comfort and safety, a vicarious thrill, gained from watching how desire propels an individual to act. We also, perhaps, hope to learn something about how to manage or even admit to our own desires. Art and popular culture offer a way to try on perspectives about desire. We awaken and then hone our own desires by reacting with a variety of expressions, from "I would never do that!" to "I bet I would do that," to the starker expression "God, I want that." What looks at first outrageous begins to elicit our own desires. The Song of Songs partly offers a vicarious journey of an ancient woman and man in a crush. But it does more than enact a desire. It lays bare desire's impact on the individual and probes its complexity as a force in life. It offers a depth charge into the nature of desire itself, one that the modern can learn from as much as the ancient Israelite must have. If, as Freud contended, desire drives everything or nearly everything we do, then coming to understand its force is certainly worth the effort and is easily worth an entire biblical book.

The Song of Songs is worth reading for its exploration of desire, not because of some blind adherence to an established tradition of biblical authority. Today, if we are to get anywhere with understanding the Bible or being open to its world, it has to *earn* our respect. The days are gone when it held authoritarian power in people's lives, and the change is for the best. The options for responding to the Bible become real ones: dismissal or rediscovery. The Song offers insight into the nature of human desire, not just more biblical legislation with the force of the Ten Commandments or the Sermon on the Mount. Instead, it is investigative, probing, and wholly experiential. Impressively, it holds its own with current postmodern theoreticians of desire such as Michel Foucault, Georges Bataille, and Julia Kristeva. My intent in this book is to demonstrate just what this ancient Hebrew Song can teach us about desire.

The desire in the Song of Songs has long taxed and excited the interpretive skills of biblical scholars over the centuries. Its canonicity or authoritative sacredness was disputed early on by the rabbis (*Mishnah Yadayim* 3:5), since it was unclear what specifically religious, legal, or wisdom material it contained. There is no mention of God in the eight chapters of this book of the Hebrew Bible, no clear moral instruction, and nothing about the nationhood of Israel. The book lacked, in other words, much of what was identifiably "biblical" about the other writings already collected in the canon. And it contained much that was *not* in the other biblical books as well, namely, sexual desire, fantasies of coupling, and descriptions of bodily arousal. In its plain sense, the book describes longing and ancient lust. This topic undoubtedly interests the historian bent on constructing a history of pleasure for the biblical world, but it also snags the curiosity of just about anyone who experiences lust today, a good two thousand years after the Song was written.

For most of its postbiblical history, however, the Song of Songs was read not as a book of *erotica*—which it is—but as an allegory of Israel's love for God, or for Christians, of Christ's love for the church.[1] The sexual excitement was read in effect as a symbol of spiritual anticipation. Yet spiritual allegory does not really tame or domesticate the Song, or reduce it to a merely pious devotional. The metaphors of desire still provoke and excite response from the reader, who then has to remind himself or herself that all this fevered lust is really about God and us. The erotic passion expressed in this Song is definitely all-consuming, erotic, on the brink of bodily orgasm. And it is most often expressed from the viewpoint of an aroused woman. It is this lust, particularly *female* lust, which must first be understood before the pious allegory—of an Israel ready and willing for its God—could even work. The metaphor's vehicle, that is, the image used, must be grasped before the possibilities of its tenor—that is, what idea that image can represent—become apparent.[2]

It is, first of all, shocking that an entire biblical book is devoted to a woman's desire. At a minimum, the Song offers a counterbalance to the other, terse biblical descriptions of sex that are discussed in the next chapter. At a maximum, it is truly subversive, offering a dissonant voice of the canon, that of a woman in command of and enjoying her own sexuality. It is startling, as we shall see, especially in contrast to the other biblical texts about women and sex, for in the Song, whatever lessons are offered about desire come from the (quite active) lips of an aroused woman.

In the Christian Old Testament, the Song of Songs comes after Ecclesiastes and before the books of the prophets. It is variously called Song of Songs or Canticle of Canticles, from the Latin, or Song of Solomon, all based on the book's beginning line: "the Song of Songs, which is Solomon's." This line does not signal authorship, however, but reflects a custom to accredit the ancient heroic kings with various texts of the Bible. It was a way to legitimize biblical materials subsequent to the kings' lives. Hence, Proverbs, Ecclesiastes, and the Song of Songs, all wisdom books, are accredited to Solomon, based on the tradition that he was Israel's wisest king.[3] David, for his part, was credited with roughly half the psalms, since he played the lyre and so often prayed and talked to his God.

The order of biblical books in the Hebrew Bible varies from that in Christian Bibles that include both Old and New Testaments. In the Hebrew Bible, used primarily by Jews, the Song falls before Ecclesiastes and after Ruth in the final third section called the Writings. The Torah (or Pentateuch), the first five books of the Bible, is the first part, with the Prophets comprising the middle portion. None of this has bearing on our interpretation of the Song, but with both title variations and switches in the biblical lineup, it is often difficult to locate in Bibles.

The Song of Songs was originally subject to debate over whether it belonged in the Bible, largely due to its salacious content. Controversy surrounded the inclusion of one other book too, Ecclesiastes, also attributed to Solomon. In fact, it is probable that dropping Solomon's name in these controversial texts was a strategy to ensure their inclusion in the Bible. Ecclesiastes was suspect because of its thoroughgoing skepticism about the point of life. In the end, both texts made the canonical cut and the Bible as we have it today is all the stronger for offering such divergent perspectives. These two books represent alternate voices to the traditional or dominant theologies in the Bible, and so add to its rich multivocality. In other words, the presence of many voices is assurance that we are not simply getting one powerful man's view of ancient life and faith. For those interested in the Bible, there is enough here for everyone. A modern, just as an ancient, could lean toward, say, Deuteronomy and away from Job, or away from Paul and toward Luke. There is room for preference in biblical reading, which the collection itself encourages.

And there is room for varying responses, from wonder and humility to repulsion, shock, and boredom. Just because the Bible is an intimidating icon in a culture deeply ambivalent about religion shouldn't make us feel that we're not allowed to just pick the thing up and see for ourselves what's in it.

I began this project essentially as a reading exercise, asking what could be gained if I plumbed the biblical texts for their views on pleasure. Would I, first of all, find what I was looking for, and would their pleasures be at all similar to what I consider pleasures? Could an ancient text and the desires it encodes still speak to our own desires and how we manage them today? My intent was to jump in, think hard, read even harder, and be willing to go where the text led. And so I abandoned myself to the text, and not in docile submission to something overbearingly called Scripture for two thousand years. Instead, it was an almost defiant gesture of wanting a place to stand, of wanting so famous and so leather-bound a text to earn its place for once, to earn its status right before my eyes.

I sense that this kind of reading experiment on the Bible does not happen much anymore or that it is certainly not a given. So I meant this as a kind of athletic reading to discover truths, not assume them, to find the "inspiration" in this text. The ardor and pleasure of reading come into play, with lips and heart and spittle as in the ancient days when texts were read aloud. Since this is a Song about pleasure, why not be a good sport and approach it with a spirit of delight? Biblical scholars, and I am one, at times jump too quickly to the historical context of a biblical book or passage and forget to pursue the worldviews or perspectives offered. We tally up a list of pertinent facts that illumine a text's meaning. But we still leave something wanting in the heart. Most people are not reading the Bible to learn about the ancient world, nor were the writers aiming to bequeath only historical information. The Bible is not famous or potent because it talks of ancient Israelites who loved their God and often tripped up famously. It is potent because it talks so profoundly of these likable, tough people and their love that something in its pages scrapes at our own souls and desires. It has the antiquated, embarrassing nerve to have something to teach us, to even go where we have not been able to go yet. The Bible taps my emotions, and that is why it is worth its salt. When I put away the defensiveness and discomfort, the stories awaken and stretch my emotions. My soul grows just a little on the horizon of life, and I need not cave in to the false gods of today—cynicism and indifference. I am dead in the water if left with only those options: trendy, okay, but dead. What this Song does, and unabashedly, is champion a passion for life itself.

The Song of Songs is itself notorious for not giving an inch on its historical context, its date of composition, its precise situation, the identity of its characters, and the location of their meetings. The *whatness* of what is happening in any kind of plot or narrative is so far inscrutable. The Song toys with certainties and is a challenge to comprehension. In fact, it is sort of the Zen koan for biblical studies, meant to frustrate the tried accesses to meaning and open up others. But how fitting given its topic, love! Time, place, and names end up not mattering all that much when desire itself is timeless, private, and potent, rendering humans silly, confused, exasperated, triumphant, giddy, heartbroken, at once small and very large. Who really cares about the names of the protagonists in erotic literature, about *who* is writhing in desire in this Song, when it is the writhing and the desire themselves that are so tantalizing? Who cares finally if it is Solomon in the Song or some later writer pining for a lover just out of reach, yet whose taste still lingers in memory, body, and soul? We care about the pining and that taste. Let's hear more about that. Desire is emotional spectacle, not documentary. The Song provides at points some details on location and identity, but only noncommittally. Its real interest lies in mining the mysteries of desire itself. Detail, plot, even clarity, all otherwise salient features in a text, are burdens here, shirked in the trade-off for *feeling* desire, a bargain brave and well worth it.

The Song compels us out of our compartmentalizations: of the rational and affective, the public and private, the sexual and chaste, and today's favorite, the appropriate and the inappropriate.[4] These serve pragmatic functions in life, helping to ensure our competencies as citizens, but they also hinder and stall our desire. They function, too, to police desires. Desire burns within each human heart, then and now. We are bombarded with suggestions of what we should desire and how much, and at the same time, are instructed to keep these desires to ourselves. The consumerist culture has it both ways. First it inundates us with products and lures, subliminally feeding our desires, and then it ropes those desires off as either private or inappropriate. That speaking on desire might itself be deemed inappropriate in culture or in, say, a church, is a way to silence a voice and is a stodgy, last-ditch attempt to stay the course of convention. The woman in the Song is censored by her culture when she goes public with her desire. She runs into the streets of Jerusalem, the capital, with her want laid bare, and the city guards beat her up (5:7). Our guards today are more subtle, but they are there, keeping watch over the trafficking of desire, feeding it, bludgeoning it with consumerism and titillation, and shaming it off the streets with veiled threats, subtle and powerful. The woman in the Song does what I want to do now, get up and keep searching, keep speaking of one's yearnings.

This book is about desire because it is the subject of this Song, and because it is the subject of life when we get right down to it. Spirituality, for example, is no hedged bet to soften the edges of a stressful life; still less is it marked solely by a lazy obedience to a tradition we just ended up inheriting. Instead, the spiritual quest is precisely—no more, and nothing less than—the yearning for meaning, the hungry desire for it, and, just as important, the painful coping with its periodic absence. That we all search and work for more meaning, for fuller lives during the course of our lives, makes of us all spiritual beings.

And there are books that nourish because they satisfy the yearning for meaning on some fundamental level. *Moby Dick,* for example, had that effect on me. The same has been true for me with the Song, and I hope to demonstrate that impact not by becoming confessional and cloying, a scary Bible-thumper, but through my interaction with this ancient, daring little text. This Song is worth the effort. It probes: the limits of both language and the body; the assertion of identity, in a self-ownership that ultimately redeems desire from mere stalking—yearning having taken a hostage; and the terrible, delicious ache of waiting, the ecstasy and the danger. This, I presume, would pique the interests of anyone conscious of the force of desire.

SOCIAL HISTORY

> Your love is better than wine.
> —SONG 1:2

Social historians of ancient Israel are able to reconstruct facets of Israelite daily life such as livelihood, marital customs, rituals, dining habits, religious and legal beliefs, and the like. We do this in large part by analyzing and comparing the biblical materials with other ancient cultural records and archaeological data. But in addition to these features of daily life, fears, dreams, and desires also constitute the makeup of any culture. These are much harder to reconstruct for an ancient culture because they are often the products of the inner worlds of a people. The silence in historical scholarship about the dreams, fears, and desires of an ancient culture can be deafening and sad. It gives the impression that these ancient people did not really live in the sense that we mean it, but of course they did.

We know, for example, that water was valued because it was scarce in the semiarid region of Israel, and we can reasonably infer that it was desired and that its lack would have been a source of fear for the Israelite. The archaeology of the cistern, the tunnel, and pool constructions of the Iron Age (1200–586 B.C.E.) shows the importance of preserving the water supply.[5] In addition, biblical stories of collecting water from wells and gifts of rain from the deity attest to the value with which water was held, just as the prophetic threats of drought attest to the fear of a lack of water. And, too, the fortification systems of Iron II (1000–586) cities indicate that attack from enemies or intruders was likely feared by the society, worth the labor and attention of citywide architectural planning. Protection, then, was desired for the peace of mind it encouraged.

I wish to explore precisely the discourse in the Song for desire, how pleasures are described and longed for, and how these pleasures may offer at least a glimpse into a culture's attitudes and values toward sensual desire. It is the task of the social historian to interpret and reconstruct what daily life was for a given society— in my case, that of ancient Israel. So, in addition to livelihood, customs, and religious and political contexts, pleasure was also, one presumes, a part of ancient life. We can picture the ancient Israelites as procreating because God told them to according to the Bible, but is this not a distortion, made by a reliance, even unconsciously, on biblical theology or ideology? One wonders what the Israelites did for fun when they weren't dutifully procreating, sowing grain, battling, offering sacrifices, and just overall being so earnestly biblical about their lives. Understanding biblical culture also means understanding the pleasures and joys of these past lives and grasping that these were more varied than simple adherence to God.

In a sense, then, we are concerned with cultural history. We are also concerned with demonstrating how human the biblical texts are and how similar these characters really are to us today, even as we have become more sophisticated—or, at least, toy-dependent—with our pleasures. We may have upped the number of available pleasures or structured time so that we may pursue them during leisure hours, but we may be left just as wanting, just as hungry and yearning as are the biblical characters. In fact, I think this is the case. We have cluttered our lives with toys, amusement parks, and clubs, and allowed for multiple sexual partners and practices, but we have not yet gotten a sturdy grasp of enjoyment or of pleasure. We even demonstrate an insecurity or disillusionment around our pleasures, and we lack ways to address this beyond the therapeutic. Mining the rich thought in the Hebrew Bible about desire gets us to think about why pleasure is important in existence, and so offers us a lifeline, a renewal of our sexual and spiritual energies.

The ancient Israelite's world spelled want more often than not, so desires and longings must have loomed large at times, if only through exhaustion and as a sorry replacement for any immediate gratification. How did these people yearn? Was it a process of what we now term sublimation, making do with what one had? In the farm and dusty life of ancient Israel, did desire more often than not come down simply to adequate food and more water for drinking, or did it extend to loftier appetites of gleeful enjoyment, of satiation rather than adequacy? Did desires sublimate into religious ideology itself, a clustering of daily wants caught up and projected onto a god who might or might not satisfy them? If so, then it would have been nearly impossible to be an atheist. The pain of privation alone could explain the maxim that "there are no atheists in antiquity." Does want, then, birth desire and then birth the idea of a god, or, as we might say, the notion of a higher power that can contain our desires? Desire is an impulse and emotion for more in life at any given moment. God is a belief that there is something more to life. Can't these be the same?

Dreams are sometimes expressed in biblical materials, as of a restored community or time of prosperity and faith after a pending destruction forecast by various prophets. For instance, Isaiah dreams of a day when people

> will beat their swords into plowshares,
>   and their spears into pruning hooks;
> nation will not lift up sword against nation,
>   neither will they learn war anymore.
>   —Isa 2:4

And when

> the wolf will dwell with the lamb,
>> the leopard will crouch down with the kid.
>
> —Isa 11:6-7

The prophet evidently was dreaming, as the predatory fierceness of nations and animals alike has not yet abated. Dreams or visions of a future day without the fears or hardships of the present day testify to a culture's values—to what it finds comforting in a vision of the future. The utopian images we build say much about our present conditions.

But how is sensual desire constructed in the Hebrew Bible? What did the ancient Israelite want, yearn for so achingly that traces remained in the cultural record of the Bible, either overtly proclaimed or etched in frustration, perhaps even unconscious? What were the sorts of pleasures that brought relief and joy into ancient life? We tend to assume that Israelite life must have been rather bleak, consisting of subsistence farming and domestic routine, with trust bargained for and risked only on the village level through strategies of endogamous marriage, legal customs, and military defense. But surely in all the preoccupations of daily agrarian life, there was a time for joy (Eccles 3:4), a time for yearning, and moments simply of wishing for something else or for something more. These moments are private, left to the inner worlds of the ancient Israelites. But they have to have been there. For a culture to produce such complex literature as the Bible there had to have been much more than just a whole lot of farming going on. Can we catch the desires in biblical materials? Our yields would not tell us with certainty what any individual yearned for, but through glimpsing what the culture valued as pleasurable, they might include individual desires as well. And what rocked the Israelites' world may just have the power to rock ours still, if we are attentive to them.

The statement of the Song quoted above, that "your love is better than wine," is at first glance a rather straightforward, touching compliment offered by a lover to her beloved, in a book that contains their extended flirtation. What interests me is that it is an assertion of a preference, of love over wine. It demonstrates a choice or preference of pleasures. In terms of Israelite culture, what would it take or mean for that to be true, for love to be, in fact or in flirtation, better than wine? How, in other words, did the ancient Israelite construct desire? How did he or she make value judgments such as this and thereby reveal preferences about pleasures? Pleasures are simply the available activities and objects that we consider pleasant, that we would choose to repeat often, and that bring us joy. Desire is a response to available pleasure and comprises, eventually, a choice. It is desire that zooms in on love and wine and then prefers one to the other, from someone who has enjoyed both.

This question of pleasure in history is a broad study under which drinking, dining, joke telling, storytelling, and dancing all fall. The Song of Songs gives direct and sustained testimony to an Israelite pleasure of love. Love is the central theme, or rather, wanting the lover is the central theme. Desire is not oblique or strangled by any competing theme such as faithlessness, but remains overt. Its predominance in the Song of Songs is striking. In fact, its prominence in this book, coupled with its absence in the rest of the canon, is an important issue to which we shall return.

PLEASURE AND HARDSHIP

Pleasures are made all the more sweet by their occurring infrequently or within a life that is often taxing. Hardship, the making do without, tends to both simplify what we consider pleasures and polish our desire for them. Deprivation, if intermittent and not constant, heightens our appreciation of the pleasures of life. Sleep, water, food, and warmth: all become exquisite pleasures if we have been deprived of them for a period of time beyond our comfort levels. A culture such as ours, bent by excess, has trouble imagining this edge between pleasure and its absence, but this edge is where want is born. Instead, we offer best-selling instruction manuals on how to enjoy the simple pleasures of life without having to endure the discomfort of want. Even these manuals can become just more unsatisfying stuff. No one wants to count the self-help books on their shelves.

For the ancient Israelites, desire was born in the divide between pleasure and its absence, but deprivation was no experiment.[6] Instead, it was a daily intruder into life. What is remarkable—and endearing, really—is that joy could be expressed so often in the Hebrew Bible. Rejoicing, celebration, and laughter occur far more than one might expect. These ancients did have a good time, and their literature reflects a vigorous capacity for joy.

As a response to life's pleasures, joy reaches beyond satisfaction and even contentment. It is triumphant and noticeable—indeed, flamboyant—elevating pleasure to glee. In fact, in Hebrew, the term for delight, *haphes̟*, is a primary verb for desire. The pleasures of life are there not just to satisfy longings or even bring contentment, but to relish and delight in. Joy, then, becomes a clue for where desires lie for a person or a culture. For what brings momentary joy will be sought out again, and we really do not even need Freud to point to this pleasure principle operating in our lives. To secure more moments of joy, we will gladly concede any principle. We each get a life and the choice about how to spend it. We instinctively work to maximize the pleasure and minimize the pain. In the lab of life, then, we experiment and find the pleasures, and learn to avoid the pains even though they are inevitable.

What, then, did biblical human beings desire? It may, first of all, be refreshing to realize that human desire is inscribed throughout the biblical texts; that these were not dour, ascetic nomads, but a people who both enjoyed the pleasures of life and lamented and yearned when they went without them. They had gumption. There were pleasures in the biblical world, such as (from the perspective of male authorship) women, wine, God, song, laughter, and dancing. These were some of the sheer perks of being alive.

In general, the ancient Israelites, like us, yearned for specific things in their lives or for a quality of life. These are often pedestrian pleasures, such as a harvest (Mic 7:1), a good woman (Ps 45:11), or enough to eat (Ps 145:16). Or they yearned more broadly for ways to enhance their life, as when the Psalmist asks:

> Would you like to enjoy life,
>> do you want long life and happiness?
> —Ps 34:12

The question is surely rhetorical, with no one sanely answering in the negative, yet it also illumines the Israelite pursuit of happiness. Enjoyment and the desire for it were present in ancient Israel, and I stress this, since I am not sure that our images of biblical life—of dust, camels, massive legal prohibitions, wars, "smiting," prophecies of doom, a crucifixion—allow for it. Too, I am not sure that we today consciously think of enjoyment as a value, as what the Benedictines call "holy leisure," the activity that nourishes our souls. Religion can consist of lots of "shoulds," and leisure can be off-limits for spiritual discussion. We might place a value on success, security, or some unnamed future goal, but then easily and frequently neglect the daily joys. The attention the ancients gave to daily pleasure may instruct us in some holy leisure.

The Bible reveals some tidy self-selection of desires: good people end up wanting the good (Prov 11:23); mockers want only some more mockery (Prov 1:22); and the wicked want just the plunder of some more wickedness (Prov 12:12). Hence Proverbs would seem to be making a case for like desires attracting like. In addition, the ancients could on occasion share in a national desire, such as for their first king (1 Sam 9:20). And, bitterly, in Jeremiah, they could long together for what they had lost, namely, the freedom and pleasure of living in Jerusalem (Jer 44:14).

Some objects of desire are, of course, deemed more worthy than others. So, for example, desiring wisdom is better than desiring jewels (Prov 3:15), and, not surprisingly, wanting to worship God is seen as the best desire of all (e.g., 2 Sam 23:5, Pss 21:2; 34:12ff; 37:4; 145:19; Prov 10:24; 11:23; 13:12, 19; Isa 26:8-9; Job 13:3; 2 Chron 15:15). The sheer frequency of this particular religious desire indicates that true fulfillment of all human desires is met in God, which is an essential theological agenda of the biblical authors. They were writing, after all, to make the case for worshipping and remembering this God, yet here I will take it seriously as an object of desire.

In fact, even God is presented as having desire in the Hebrew Bible. God's desires, of course, will not be portrayed as complicated or as drawn out as human ones: "What he desires, he does" (Job 23:13). God desires, for example, to live on a mountain (Pss 68:17; 132:13-14), and as creator of the world, he can pretty much name his preferred real estate. He desires Jerusalem (as a female) again in her renewal (Isa 62:4). Elsewhere, God desires simply to enjoy his people (Ps 149:4) or their faithful love rather than sacrifices (Hos 6:6). This shows the human side of God, with emotions and responses to various features of life. At the same time, it gives divine sanction for desire on the human plane.

The attested joys in the Bible are those occasions of sly, ancient victories over hardship and of bragging over found pleasures. The Psalmist, for example, says:

> This is the day the LORD made,
>   let us rejoice and be happy in it. (118:24)

This is not merely a formulaic call to worship. It likely became formulaic first by being so pure an expression of where joy lies, namely, in every single, dazzling day. The joy over this simple view is even exuberant, worthy of two verbs denoting glee. And there is even a confident optimism in rejoicing, for as sure as each next day comes, so does the pleasure worthy of joy.

The pleasures that bring joy are certainly worth the effort of discovering and returning to them. This is why we *enjoy* pleasures;

we gravitate by experience toward those pleasures that enhance and nourish our capacity for joy. In essence, then, desire is for things once enjoyed and then yearned for again. The objects of desire are realistic in the sense that they have already been enjoyed: they come from life and bring it further pleasure. And the Hebrew Bible is full of desires in this sense. The pleasures of ancient life, however, are typically oblique in the biblical materials, because they are not germane to the intent and messages of the texts. Several humans hit the jackpot of contentment as all their desires are met. David gets his heart's desire from the Lord (2 Sam 23:5), Solomon gets to build everything he desires in Jerusalem (1 Kgs 9:1), and Jeroboam as the new king gets to rule over all he desires (1 Kgs 11:37). Such satisfaction is not the privilege only of kings. Individuals in the Psalms are described as getting their hearts' desires, but again without these desires being spelled out (Pss 13:12; 21:2; 37:4).

Hence, desires have to be detected in the texts. For example, the story of the Exodus from Egypt is a foundational story of oppression under slavery, of a migration out from such bondage, and of the dawning of a new religious consciousness in one saving God. Life in Egypt is portrayed as harsh and impossible: all male Hebrew babies are being drowned in the Nile; the slaves have to make bricks without even straw to act as a cohesive; and the pharaoh is unsympathetic and ignorant of the God of the Hebrews. Life in Egypt, in other words, is really no life at all and so is worth escaping. Yet later, in the desert wanderings, we catch a glimpse of what the people nevertheless miss about Egypt, what they *desire* in nostalgia born of duress and fear in that desert.

What the newly emancipated Israelites end up missing about slavery are the meat, fish, cucumbers, melons, leeks, onions, and garlic (Num 11:4-6). The manna that God rained down from heaven to feed them was like coriander seed and was apparently not desired, either because it was what they had, because God sent it, or because it was all they had. It proved, at any rate, not to be what the people really desired, the familiar tastes of Egypt.

Perhaps they would not have traded it all—freedom, God, and manna—to return to Egypt for these taste treats, but nevertheless the choice occurred to them: the preference of leeks and meat over coriander seed bread and freedom asserted itself. This desire is obviated when we recall that the story primarily illustrates the people's fear and lack of faith in God as provider. Therefore, one can imagine a scenario in which God would rain down meat, fish, leeks, and garlic, and the people would have been just as petulant. They might have even whined then for *Egyptian* coriander seed bread! Still, the story illustrates desires operating, even blocking, their spiritual willingness to follow God to freedom.

In prophetic literature, pleasures are often glimpsed in backhanded ways as well. They arise in the prophet's condemnation of what he deems excessive pleasure or pleasure that results in neglecting one's religious fidelity. For example, Amos rails against indulging in pleasures:

> Alas to those who lie on beds of ivory . . .
> eating lambs, singing, and drinking wine from bowls,
>   and anointing themselves with washed oil.
>   —Amos 6:4-6

Much about pleasure is contained in such dismissive judgments. The people remain deserving of judgment and are not faithful enough—the point of this passage—yet their pleasures are nevertheless seen through the prophet's very disappointment. We can learn much about prophecy and what Yahwistic faith entailed, but we can also catch at least a glimpse of what gave Israelites pleasure—what, in other words, was fun about their lives. Here, finely made beds for lounging, lamb meat, singing, drinking, and the best olive oils, what we would today term "extra virgin," all signify a basking in life's enjoyments.

Since the biblical world was a peasant economy where most people made enough to survive on, plus some amenities for trade or enjoyment, the pleasures might well have stayed fundamental, hardened into basics. But we ought not to presume that their lives, with their fewer competing pleasures, were less pleasurable than our own, or that their desires were less intense. It is entirely possible that the desires for a bountiful harvest, a wife to love, and children were seared into the Israelite heart with a greater intensity than our own desires, which suffer under the dissipation of so many options for purchase, for sexual partners, for religions. Our pleasures have become commodities and this affects the strength of felt desire.

The desires felt in the Hebrew Bible, overall, tend to revolve, hungrily at times, around three elements vital to life, then and now, and sometimes costing death. They all come into play in the Song and so are worth noting here. First, the ancient farmers of the biblical world yearned for plentiful, fruit-filled harvests. Each year, the threat of famine, drought, and crop failure kept them anxious and prayerful, first for a good yield, and then for an abundance of the delectables of fruit, none necessary to subsistence living, but a delightful, anticipated addition to it. Pomegranates, figs, olives and their oil, and the most esteemed fruit of them all, grapes, were treats for the too frequently dry mouths of ancient Israel. This is why all of these products are mentioned in the description of the promised land (Deut 8:8). Second, they were also hungry with desire for love when they felt it. Sex, then, did go considerably beyond the procreative commandment "to be fruitful and multiply" first uttered to Adam and Eve (Gen 1:28). And it went well beyond some sort of demographic duty for building up a people of faith.

Third, throughout the Hebrew Bible, the yearning so frequently and wrenchingly chimed is for the other, whom no one gets to see and too few get to hear, namely, the elusive God. Jack Miles has noted that God increasingly vanishes from the scene as one reads through the Hebrew Bible.[7] With God's retreat, the descriptions of human yearning intensify to prophetic decibels or philosophical rationalizations in wisdom literature as a kind of defiant or disgusted "who needs him anyway?" The wisdom literature is trying to ask that question in all seriousness. In the Song of Songs, God is not even mentioned; in Ecclesiastes, he is, but is almost useless to the author. The biblical people, in a sense, literally do try to love this God with all their heart, soul, and might as they were instructed to (Deut 6:5), and the degree of this difficulty manifests itself in the biblical texts with the repeated suspicions that their love is one-sided.

Georges Bataille defined eroticism simply as the "assenting of life up to the point of death."[8] If we can leave aside for the moment the obvious sexual meanings of the term "eroticism," the Bible is chock-full of such gestures of assent, of stark and ardent want. Spirituality, sexuality, and work are not viewed as far apart in the Bible, for the same fire, human desire, fuels them. Indeed, the Song shares Bataille's existential view of erotic passion when it declares love to be "strong as death" (8:6). For this biblical book, love, then, is both better than wine and stronger than death, a complex desire, to be sure! In fact, these two disparate views frame the book, with the wine equation first asserted in the beginning chapter (1:2) and death in its final one (8:6). More important, they frame the topic, providing the range of the feeling of love: more potent, sweet, dizzying, and delicious than wine, as well as threatening, overwhelming, inescapable, and final as death itself. Desire can both intoxicate and ignite the human soul and take it on a lifelong search, a yearning quelled only by death. If desire, eroticism, is the assenting of life up to the point of death, then this particular book assents. But so too do the rest of the books of the Hebrew Bible. They are packed with assenting to life up to death; many characters simply go there, many prophets threaten it. Biblical characters, including God, yearn, fight, scratch, hunger, and thirst in their assenting to life.[9] This eroticism, quite simply, is what makes it a testimony of the spirit.

This assent toward life is essentially what notions of spirituality are all about. Spirituality itself comes through ardor, in the willingness to assent when it involves risk. It does not get more clear-cut than Moses' hardy speech to the people poised to finally enter their Promised Land. They must commit first:

> I put before you life and death, blessing and curse.
> Choose life so that you and your descendants may live.
> —DEUT 30:19

All substantial, loving relationships come through effort, not under threats of early dismissal or attention deficit. You have to want to stay through the muck and the absurdities. The time to park it is when reason is telling you to leave. Spirituality is not immediate gratification. It is more the ardor of patience, a willingness to put oneself in God's way in case he shows. This is no facile enterprise for a bunch of post-traumatic stressed Hebrews coming out of the desert into their land, or for us, steeped in secular worlds. But what else are you really going to do with life but try to assent fully? So much will thwart that desire—busyness, pain, exhaustion, boredom. So much of living will drain off our passion for life. This is, in fact, the counter to Freud's pleasure principle, what he dourly termed the reality principle. There will be considerable interference with our love of life, and the reality principle is about delaying gratification as a means to cope.

The Hebrew Bible is full of a reality principle, on the ground with its famine, drought, wars, pestilence, and high mortality rates, and in a more rarefied sphere with its continued delaying of a present God. The New Testament, of course, lacks that tension of absence—Jesus is on the scene. For much of the Hebrew Bible, God is not present but is yearned for, spoken about. For Freud and the Hebrew Bible, and I hope my own life, these principles of reality and of pleasure come toward a harmony, neither squelching the other. I want to breathe, love, bleed, write, pray, wrest meaning from life *even if it is not there,* and this is a solo journey of the spirit. I cast my life's meaning somehow there, assenting to life to the point of death. As it is, we may live on a spiritual edge somewhere between gratitude for the pleasures and joys we experience and a restlessness or yearning for something more. Contentment, because it lacks impetus, does not propel a spiritual quest. The desires are satisfied just enough. Full contentment with life would not have produced the biblical materials either, for yearning is what fuels faith itself. Rather, skating as we do somewhere between gratitude for life and a yearning for more—whether that more is God, forgiveness, peace, or sensual pleasures—sparks desire and the spiritual quest.

Desire is about *wanting* more than it is about *getting*. It is the hunger that highlights the food; the patience that highlights the faith; the arousal that anticipates the sex. It commands a shift in perspective. The salt of a lover's lips or the sweet juice of grapes is not just pleasurable anymore; with desire, they become exquisite. Desire is the discipline to live on that edge between wanting and satisfaction. It is not for the timid or the fickle.

A DEFINITION OF YEARNING

Before turning to sensual desire in the next chapter, I want first to define in broad strokes what yearning is. Desire, or yearning, differs from fantasy or pipe dreams. The latter are unrealistic, escapist journeys with little or no chance of being enjoyed within the parameters of one's life. A desire, by contrast, is feasible in historical time, but missing in the here and now of a life. The desired object is wanted, and is out there somewhere, but is lacking at the present time. This absence fuels the desire. We say, for example, that it makes the heart grow fonder for a loved one. Exactly. Absence inflames desire as selective memory forgets all unpleasantness and longing grows pure. Desire is memory of an experienced pleasure. Without the previous taste, it is wish or curiosity: it is out of focus.

Desire has a focus and specificity typically beyond that of mere wish fulfillment. For example, one can wish today to win the lottery, or a teenage girl may wish to get married even if she has never dated. Such wishes remain rather vague fantasies even if they are insistent. But once in love, that teenager's wish clarifies and gains in intensity. Or alternately, it subsides with the dawning awareness that there may be no Prince Charming; and anyway, the reality of love seems to involve the legwork of dating a lot of frogs before it can be realized. The taste of first love and its loss generates a kind of determination. The girl can then get behind the cultural expectation that she marry and can now actively want it. She has entered a state of wanting rather than dreaming. Desire has content, and therefore pain to it, in the acute knowledge of just what is missing. Desire, unlike fantasy, is born in the previous enjoyment of a pleasure and then is honed by the absence of that pleasure. Indeed, part of the continued pleasure may stem simply from the replay of a bodily sensation, the familiarity of it.[10]

Yearning for more in life or for a replay of experienced pleasure need not signify an act of ingratitude. It could just as easily be a ritualized celebration of life's enjoyments, a zestful wish to return to life's greatest offerings. Desiring pleasure and repeated joy need not betray existential disappointment at all. Gratitude is a deeply felt acceptance of life's pleasures, so that wanting them is a gesture of appreciation. Yearning itself may even come to be experienced as a pleasure. The Song is concerned with the provocative question of whether the exquisite sensation of wanting another could surpass in any realistic sense the pleasure of sexual consummation. The surprising claim that it can does seem to be the premise of the Song, which stays focused on the experience of yearning, not its relief.

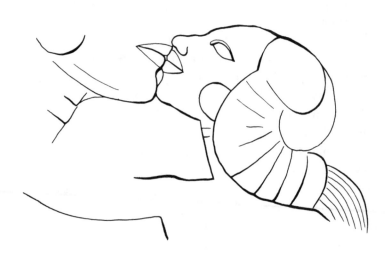

2

Erotics in the Bible

"Faint with Love"

DESIRE'S TENSION

Human desires are evident throughout the Hebrew Bible and tend to revolve around the three central elements discussed in chapter 1: harvests with fruit, love, and God. All three areas of human interest and desire are evident, too, in the Song of Songs through the creative play of metaphors, as I shall demonstrate in the following three chapters. In this chapter, I want to discuss more generally how biblical texts represent human desire, so that the Song's unique contribution to the canon will be evident.

Biblical Hebrew, like English, has no one term for "desire," but instead employs a variety of verbs to convey want, such as "ask for," "seek," "delight in," "want," "yearn," and "long for."[1] These terms do not comprise, though, a precise scale for rating biblical passions, so that, for example, "ask for" always denotes a timid desire, while "long for" denotes an urgent one. But they do suggest desire's diversity or range. Today we have a similar range of feeling entailed in our different words for wanting. To "ask for" a date or job can signify either a mild or intense desire. To "seek" can signify a haphazard or urgent intent. Overall, it is safe to assume that the terms "yearn" and "long for," then and now, do denote a strong affective state in an individual, while "ask" or "seek" may do so but need not. The range of emotional force in desire would have varied in antiquity, as it does today. There is an obvious difference, for example, between saying "I want a Coke" and "I want you," even though nothing in the grammar itself betrays that difference. The various terms for desire in the Bible denote human want but not the emotional intensity carried by that want.

Biblical people *were* full of wants and yearnings, and religion was not merely their killjoy. Biblical characters are alive and kicking, emoting, and taking pleasure in their lives, or wanting to. Asceticism—the denial of desire and pleasure as an act of religious devotion—is not really a pronounced biblical theme. There are a few biblical traditions involving abstention from pleasurable elements. For example, the Nazirites, men such as Samson, are people who neither cut their hair nor eat anything from the grapevine (Num 6:2-6; Judg 13:4), and the Rechabites are a group who remained nomadic as a stance against settled urban life and its pleasures (Jer 35:1-19). And the prophet Jeremiah is the only celibate in the Hebrew Bible, yet this status is not so much devotional as it is practical. Jerusalem is on the eve of its destruction, Jeremiah is the prophet tapped to bring that news, and so he does not have the time or leisure for starting a family and enjoying domestic life (Jeremiah 16).[2]

Asceticism really develops after the biblical period in the third century C.E., mostly with the desert hermits, who renounced worldly affairs for a desert of silence and hardship in service to God, and then with monastic orders beginning in the fourth century.[3] For the Hebrew Bible, wants are not seen as occasions for renunciation as they are for asceticism. Desire is not something to be suppressed, discarded, or channeled strictly into religious devotion, but is presented as simply a facet of human life.

This is true even in the wisdom and legal materials, in which there are strict sanctions about pleasurable behavior. Desire itself is nowhere prohibited, just redirected or schooled. Proverbs, a wisdom book, offers instructions on how to live the best life through management of one's self and household, and overall moderation is viewed as the best course. In the legal materials, there are clear prohibitions involving desire, but these entail a restriction of object choices, not the emotion itself. Leviticus 18, for example, lists the various people one cannot sleep with as a way to circumscribe incest, but it is worth noting that the text does not deny the desire for incest. In fact, the need for legislation suggests its reality as a desire in ancient Israel.

The last of the Ten Commandments is perhaps the best-known law about desire in the Bible:

> Do not desire another man's house; or his wife, his slaves, his cattle, his donkeys or anything else he owns.
> —Exod 20:17

This, too, is not a prohibition against desire itself. The Tenth Commandment differs from the other commandments by its specification of objects. The others stand as principled sanctions, without the need for such delineation. Six through nine, for example, forbid murder, adultery, theft, and lying, respectively.[4] These prohibitions are short and to the point. The Tenth Commandment is by contrast a qualified prohibition. It prohibits not the emotion—desire—but the forbidden routes it might take, namely, into a neighbor's domain.[5] In fact, the translation in some Bibles is already interpreting this directional sense for the reader, when it renders the phrase, "Thou shalt not covet."

There is no Hebrew term for "covet." The verb here is *hamad*, one of the verbs for desire. "Covet" is desire for something already owned by another. So, the final commandment is an injunction against the desire for objects already spoken for, namely, someone else's house, wife, slave, and farm animals.[6] In this sense, the Tenth Commandment serves as extra insurance for honoring the Eighth Commandment against theft. It nips theft in the bud by catching it at the level of desire. Incidentally, when Jesus later stresses that even *thoughts* of adultery or murderous anger are prohibited by the law (Matt 5:21-28), he is not really innovating.

Instead, the reflex toward one's intention behind an action is already implicit in the Tenth Commandment itself.

As a counterpart to both these legal circumspections of desire's objects and the proverbial cautions for moderation, the Song of Songs offers book-length testimony to the emotion of desire itself. It probes the force and feeling of desire within the human breast to the extent that even the objects of desire become secondary, allowed to stay blurry in the Song. For we do not even know who the main lovers are meant to be, and we come to suspect that identification may not matter. There is, too, the fast, confusing changes of venue, which make it hard—impossible, really—to keep up with the lovers. They are at home, out in the street, alone, together, in a pasture, atop a mountain, talking with others, in Jerusalem, near En-gedi, talking to themselves, in a vineyard—all seemingly in a matter of seconds.

The Song is full of various geographic and flora name-droppings that send biblical scholars running on wild chases for clarity, when the heated murkiness of desire may just be the point. For in the grip of desire, you often feel as if you aren't sure where you are, and you care even less. Time speeds and slows without your consent, locations shift, details are lustfully ignored under desire's influence. In a song about desire, then, the emotion quite rightly hijacks sequence and literary plausibility. Desire has just this prodigious force, to tamper even with the text that has it as its central theme.

The jumpiness of the Song is often misunderstood by those who consider it merely evidence of multiple authorship and a mediocre editing job. This undermines what may be the real thematic mastery of the Song, that it embodies the very emotion it is describing. For desire is never a clear-cut progressive journey, and the abrupt scene and voice changes testify to that truth, even if they also suggest the possibility of multiple authorship. What does seem to matter in the Song is the journey of desire through the human heart, which has its own rules and itinerary. That journey is shown in the internal talk of a woman and a man, back and forth without transitions smoothing it out for the reader. Instead, desire propels the two lovers into various actions: waiting, searching, pining, teasing, and confiding in others. Emotions run their full gamut in the want and searching that is desire, and identifications take a back seat.

The Song also stays with the emotion of desire. Desire remains the theme throughout its eight chapters. Significantly, the two lovers never end up consummating their passions. Since their desire is never satisfied, human yearning remains in tension and in focus. This aspect of the Song, that the lovers' desire is not satisfied, is crucial, yet is often overlooked. For the Song of Songs is not about sex per se, but about sexual yearning. It is not goal-oriented toward a consummation, nor does it limit its vision of sexuality to biology. Instead, the Song slows down and probes the experiential plane of sexual want. The two lovers want each other badly, achingly, and yet never do get together in the book. This is frustrating and almost unbearably erotic for the reader, who by the end wants a reprieve from the tension. The Song offers what Ilana Pardes has called a "fascinating tension between chastity and sexual freedom." It is a lust-filled book, in which the lovers' search reflects their freedom, yet a chaste quality persists nonetheless.[7]

In many ways, the Song of Songs is well ahead of its time. Although there is a long tradition of love literature in the West subsequent to the Bible,[8] there are few writings on the workings of desire in the individual. Even the Marquis de Sade, a most notorious chronicler of human lusts, only describes the sexual *acts* in his sadomasochistic romp, *120 Days of Sodom.* Earlier, the troubadours of fourteenth-century France sang of desire going unsatisfied. They kept the focus on desire's impact on the individual, as the Song of Songs does. For them, it was a necessity of the convention that the desire sung about would go unsatisfied, for they were performing for married women of the court.

The biblical Song predates the troubadour tradition by well over a millennium, and it is somewhat prescient in its attention to the psychology of desire. For it was not until Freud that questions of desire and the mind radically opened up. At least two benefits of psychoanalysis have been its attention to the mental workings of desire and its claim that sexuality is about much more than reproduction.[9] Yearnings, which are the imaginations and mental workings of how we come to know or prefer our objects of desire, are at least as instrumental to sexuality as is biological instinct. The Song demonstrates these psychological insights a good two millennia before Freud by describing the two lovers moving back and forth in their perspectives, internal or spoken, on desire. We get to see what it is like for the woman, for the man, and for her friends who are witnessing her desire. The lovers are caught coping, changing, wishing, longing, and surrendering emotionally, all without a word about consummation or procreation. Sex, wine, fruit, the pleasures of life, and even longing itself are enjoyed at times and then are absent. The Song does not trace the sexual trajectory of want to consummation or its disappointment, but rather follows longing to self-affirmed want, a sheer celebration of desire for its own sake. The woman's perspective on desire transforms throughout the book to a resolution by its end. Not consummation, but an affirmation of desire itself, of life.[10]

We saw in the first chapter how desire was a pronounced theme within the Hebrew Bible, with humans and God himself desiring more from life. One of the Bible's overarching themes, of course, is desire for a good rather than for a bad or mediocre life. The Song, then, provides the experiential linchpin for what biblical yearning as a whole is, the striving toward a good, whole life. Rabbi Aqiba, who defended the Song's inclusion in the canon, did so with the declaration that it was the Bible's inner sanctum, what he called its Holy of Holies. He saw in the book something profoundly and discretely spiritual, something related to the other biblical books, even providing their centerpiece. What did he see in a book that does not even mention God?

I suggest that it is the topic itself—desire—that is related to the holy, enough to qualify for entrance into the canon. As the poet Octavio Paz has said: "eroticism is first and foremost *a thirst for otherness*. And the supernatural is the supreme otherness."[11] This Song is devoted to the experiential side of human desire in perhaps its strongest, most visceral expression, that of sexual want. Desire for an absent lover pulsates throughout eight chapters in a heady mixture of glee, frustration, exhaustion, and surrender. Experientially, readers would be able to relate to these descriptions with the desires they themselves harbor for love, harvests, or the most absent object of all, God. In this biblical thirst for otherness, the supernatural other cannot help but be recalled, if only as a phantom memory.

It is true and significant that the spiritual object of desire, God, is not mentioned anywhere in the Song as he is, for example, in the psalms of spiritual longing (Psalms 42; 63; 143). A Song devoted to the impassioned longing for an absent lover, however, cannot help but resonate with any latent desire a reader of the Bible feels for God. The book may not even have had anything to do with spiritual desire in the minds of its authors. Nor is it a planned allegory where each figure represents a more "real" religious actor, say, where the man and woman are God and Israel, or Christ and the Church, and we can safely dispense with the Song's sexual content. No, the Song is clearly about sexual yearning between two flesh-and-blood lovers who are at once endearing and stubborn in their search. But the couple's book-length quest to find each other functions as a metaphor in which additional allusive meanings about searches, love, and limits in general get stirred.

Had this Song remained outside of the Bible, it might have been viewed simply as zesty poetic traditions of female love and longing from ancient Israel. Then it would be akin to Sappho's love poetry from ancient Greece, a serendipitous and rare remnant of a woman's voice from an ancient patriarchal culture. But its inclusion in the Bible asserts a unifying thread with biblical material that we find in desire itself, the waiting it out, and the hoping of life. God is not named, but the absent lover replicates his (seeming) absence in life, then and now. God is nowhere to be seen or felt, yet belief and yearning continue nevertheless. To reiterate, I am not suggesting that the original intention of the Song was a spiritual one. I am suggesting that by its shrewd inclusion in the Bible, its theme experientially resonates for the reader on both the sexual and spiritual planes.

What spiritual and sensual yearning share in common is that they cast us out beyond the comfort zones of our sense of self. They take us to the front line between our limited selves and what we hunger for. Audre Lorde describes the erotic as somewhere between our "sense of self and the chaos of our strongest feelings."[12] That edge is both potentially disruptive and the source of our vital energies. This is why, for Lorde, it is worth the time to explore and celebrate sexuality. It is the resource for our truest selves and our creativity. In addition, the sense of going past the limits of the self is something that both spiritual and sensual yearning require. We hunger for something just beyond us, and we lurch in that gap. Union closes the gap but can do so only temporarily. How ought we to negotiate it when union is not imminent, when we have to wait interminably for a lover or a God?

I believe that Rabbi Aqiba's intuition for the Song's inclusion in the Bible was shrewd, because the Song functions to sound out the desires latent elsewhere in the Bible. It offers some theological relief about the best-kept oddity of the Bible—that God, while seen as present, even strolling and chatting with humans in the Garden of Eden at the beginning of Genesis, will spend the rest of the Bible disappearing.[13] The God of the Bible is a God no one gets to see, so the search and struggle during a prolonged and painful absence by the loved other is, in a very real sense, *the* theme of the Bible. Belief in an unseen God, amid a life full of joys and sorrows, is about the human experience of wanting without consummation. Biblical spirituality, in large measure, learns to take pleasure in God's presence in the signs of prosperity—

a land flowing with milk and honey, a temple to call home, healthy children—and then endure or cope with the hardship of his long, lifelong absences.

Since God was an intangible presence, the full union of a lover with God could not be portrayed in the Bible. The realism of the Bible is perhaps more than we can bear, and so we choose to overlook that it is all about desire for a union that won't come. As Ilana Pardes succinctly notes:

> In the Hebrew Bible there is an urgent desire for fulfillment, but by and large—both in the characterization of God, who cannot be incarnated, and in the representations of humankind—fulfillment is denied.[14]

The Bible is really a book about promises and hopes more than their fulfillment. The faith narrated, then, is not a timid one at all. This is, if we take a minute, the Bible's asset: to speak of religious desire between a taste of the pleasure of God's presence and the hardship of long, tough absences. And this is really the Bible's merit, not its failing, for a modern world convinced that an absence of evidence is evidence of nonexistence. The Bible teaches one how to live with desire, in rigorous acceptance of nonfulfillment. The New Testament sketches a similar kind of faith. True, by then one can have God incarnate—become flesh—but even for Christians, the incarnation is still only a temporary reprieve of their yearning, since their taste of fulfillment in Jesus is also then delayed in the wait for his return.

The metaphor of sexual want in the Song teases out the spiritual want of a reader, if only by confounding the expectations of biblical reading. One expects theological material when opening a Bible. The use of a sexual metaphor for describing faith, however, is not as farfetched as it would first appear. The prophets Hosea, Jeremiah, and Ezekiel all use a sexual relationship to portray Israel's faith.[15] Since they carry messages of judgment, the metaphor is used to damning effect. They focus primarily on the negative in that intimate relationship, as Israel has violated the monogamous exclusivity required of monotheism and so must be punished.[16]

As a biblical counterpoint to these images of a punishing lover, God to his beloved, Israel, the Song works beautifully to restore just what is lovely about love, divine and human. It is a celebration of love, and it discards punishments and a shrill insistence on monogamy. It redeems the image of a woman as unapologetically proud, strong, and beautiful in her search for her lover. To ancient audiences, the Song's celebration of sexual want must have restored sexuality and spirituality from such fearful prophetic images. For modern audiences, it does that too, and offers a needed salve for our troubled exposure to gender disparity and domestic violence. The Song heals in the reading by offering soothing celebrations of the human body and heart.

The Song talks about sexual longing throughout, and it employs metaphors of fruit, especially grapes and wine, to convey and elicit that desire. The vehicle in the metaphor of sexual want is fruit, and the tenor is sexual want.[17] In another metaphoric overlay, the sexual want becomes the vehicle for the implied tenor of spiritual want. The overlay may not have been intended by the original authors. But it exists contextually by virtue of the Song's canonical inclusion and thematically by the experiential correspondence of sensual and spiritual want. Reading eight chapters of a woman in lustful, desperate yearning for her absent lover, the Bible reader cannot help but sense an additional tenor to the metaphor, especially if any of that time spent reading the Bible was in search for God.

The Song's importance as a book is in its voicing of desires unconsummated. Don't we really want to know more about this anyway—how to wade through the periods of waiting, how to survive and enjoy them since so much of life is given over to them? The standard tropes of horticulture, the natural world, architecture, and coupling pull the reader into the inner layer of desire for the unseen—an absent lover, the shepherd, the king, even the nation's God.

Not having this couple consummate is the point and the power of this book. Indeed, it is ironically the point and power of love, of desire. As delicious as consummation is, it is sweet and short-lived and inevitably changes the nature of longing. Desire becomes tamed and matured or, worse still, extinguished. It reveals object choices, and those are interesting. We see what the Israelites desired and what we do. In the process, longing tells us about ourselves: who we are is our desire, what our soul loves. It need not be ignored, downplayed, or even displaced. And even if we opt to ignore our desire, Freud's caution is that it haunts and scripts our life nevertheless in muted (or not so muted) screams of need, neuroses, and desolation. What is truest about our inner selves, our souls, is certainly worth knowing. Ecclesiastes grasped that common wisdom when he equated the end of desire with the very end of life. It is all over when one stops desiring (Eccles 12:5), for life is defined by desires.

The absence of the lover does not mean that he does not exist and that the woman is deluded. Delusion becomes one possibility, and she risks looking pathetic in her inability to just let go. But she cannot, because she is pining for someone she already and really knows and loves. Israel is, too, in its Bible. The idea that God may not exist is not even an option for ancient Israel. In the Song, then, the onlookers, whom the woman confides in, never doubt that the lover exists. Instead, they ask, "What is your beloved more than another beloved?" (5:9). And the woman can boast that he is fine; *everyone* loves him. Such esprit de corps goes well beyond monogamous love, beyond even the typical boastfulness surrounding new love. It rallies for loving this unseen lover whom she would share. It can afford to rally others, because a deity needs more than one partner. Monotheistic fidelity is not reciprocal, or it would be absurd.

In the book's last chapter, the woman dreams:

> If I met you in the street, I would kiss you,
>   and no one would despise me. (8:1)

She wants union and some public display of affection. She yearns for an open relationship, to normalize the relationship, to just plain meet already! Sexual love has the benefit of bringing periodic, tangible reassurances that sustain it, while spiritual longing has to make do in other, often frustrating ways. There is no public display of affection, just the hope that the love is mutual.

Before we examine the Song's descriptions of yearning, I want to give a brief overview of how sex is portrayed elsewhere in the Hebrew Bible. This will rather quickly illustrate the Song's unique contribution to the biblical canon.

BIBLICAL SEX DESCRIPTION

Instances of sex in the Bible occur with a brevity that often amuses readers today. The first couple's sexual scene, for example, comes down to this sole verse: "Adam knew his wife" (Gen 4:1), a phrase that employs the well-known biblical euphemism for sexual intercourse. In such galling understatement, entire worlds of feeling and personal histories of interrelating are absent from the scene. There is simply no narrative room for desire. Adam and Eve's sexual union is accomplished, as it were, almost before we have caught on that it was happening.

This, the Bible's first sex scene, gives no clues about the couple's emotional state or possible pleasure. Their sex life is provided merely to introduce the chapter's main focus, which is how the children of this union, Cain and Abel, did not get along. Sex is not exactly an aside, but it is mere prologue to the focus of narrative action. This is typical of biblical scenes; they tend to offer mere clauses on sex that provide background data for subsequent actions or peoples. Whether such biblical reticence on sex signals embarrassment, disinterest, or a pragmatic functionalism that bypasses this pleasure is an open question.[18] The following discussion of sexual description provides only the general types of treatment of sex in the Bible and is not exhaustive by any means.[19] My intent is merely to demonstrate how unique the Song of Songs is in contrast to other biblical materials on sex.

Biblical sex generally consists of four main types of description, none of which offers much, if any, insight into either male or female desire. Instead, certain stock verbs are used, generally with the male as the active subject and the woman as the grammatical object of the actions. Hence, in the above example, Adam is the agent of the verb and is named. Eve is the object of the verb, "knew," and is identified as "his wife," but is otherwise unnamed. The gender disparity is an obvious limitation for modern readers, but so is the lack of even a hint of the first couple's joy in mating, in "knowing" each other. The modern reader is left to wonder just how it was for the first couple, and further, if "know" sounded as stilted to the ancient audience as it does to us.[20] Besides "know" (see Gen 4:1; 1 Sam 1:19), the other stock terms for sex are "sleep with" (Gen 30:15; Exod 22:16; 2 Sam 11:4) and "enter, come in to" (Gen 16:2; Deut 25:5), the same verb used, for example, for entering a city gate (Gen 23:10).[21] They are all strictly pedestrian terms, evincing nothing of the emotion of desire.

The Hebrew term for "sleep with" connotes both sex and slumber, just as the English does. When King David saw Bathsheba from his rooftop, he called for her to be brought to his palace so that he could "sleep with" her (2 Sam 11:4). We can infer his desire from both the peeping and the impulsiveness, but hers is disturbingly absent. When sex is described as the male "going in to" the woman, the physical act of intercourse is expressed, and so is a territorial claim of ownership. Women are objects of this action as they are with the other verbs for sex, but here possession is overt. Once "gone in to," the woman is either owned or thereafter unmarriageable. When the mighty Samson, for example, "goes in to" his women, these are also ventures into the enemy land of the Philistines, and so his intrusions are at once sexual and political (Judg 15:1; 16:1).

With the use of these verbs for sexual union, men generally perform the actions and receive what attention there is, while the women remain the grammatical—and ideological—objects.[22] In all cases, sex is simply depicted with the use of a single verb, one that also doubles for other mundane activities ("know," "sleep," "enter"), and obviously yields no information about desire, the pleasures of lovemaking, or even a hint of the emotional condition of the participants. Sexual union is depicted primarily as the activity of the male agent of the verbs. That there may be pleasure for him goes unstated.

A second type of description of sex is only implied by the functional necessity of procreation, a prominent biblical theme. Sexual relations for the purpose of procreation are evident, of course, in the well-known biblical imperative to "be fruitful and multiply" (Gen 1:28; 9:1; 35:11), though in only one instance is the woman, whose participation would be required, even present to hear the command (Gen 1:28).[23] The functional necessity of sex for procreation is also manifest in the stories of the barren wives: Sarah (Gen 16:1), Rebekkah (Gen 25:20), Rachel (Gen 30:1), and Hannah (1 Sam 1:2). Indeed, their barrenness is the only narrative clue we have that these women have been having sex at all, and at least often enough to wonder why they are not yet pregnant.[24]

Procreation is the valued goal in these biblical passages, and so no attempt is made to describe sex from the perspective of either participant. In fact, *human* participation, both male and female, is decidedly underplayed so that the power and agency (virility?) of God can be accented. God is the true action hero in procreation, by commanding it, and by relieving all cases of barrenness.[25] Sex for procreation is, in this understanding, a mere means to an end, and so warrants no further description. It merely serves the pronatalist agenda characteristic of, but not restricted to, a biblical source known as the Priestly writer (Gen 47:27; see also Jer 3:16; Ezek 36:11).

A third type of biblical description of sex is found in the legal materials in which taboos are listed for the male about who or what he should not "go in to," namely: animals (Lev 18:23); virgin women whom he has no intention of marrying (Exod 22:16); and other men (Lev 18:22). With the exception of Exod 22:16, these are from the Priestly author writing in the postexilic period, when the people of Israel had been drastically downsized by the tragedy of the Babylonian destruction of their homeland in 586 B.C.E. Hence, this writer's pronatalist agenda is in part demographic strategy. He wishes to increase the numbers of an Israel restored after the exile by legislating where male seed should and should not go.

A fourth type of description refers not explicitly to sexual union but to the desire for it, and here, in one case at least, a woman's stance is noted, though circumscribed. In Gen 3:16, a woman's desire is yoked to her husband as part of her curse in the Garden of Eden: "to your husband is your desire, and he shall rule over you." Male desire, to recall, was also circumscribed in the tenth commandment against desiring a neighbor's wife. At another point, it is delayed in a law about confiscating enemy booty during war. Deut 22:15 legislates that when a soldier sees a captured woman whom he wants, he is to go ahead and take her into his house, but give her time to grieve for the loss of her family and town. In this instance, in a humane gesture of the law, the satisfaction of the man's desire does not come before the woman's grief.[26]

With laws and descriptions such as these about sex, it is easy to see that a woman's desire gets short shrift. Male characters typically have names and are the agents of actions, while the women remain unnamed, inactive, or absent altogether. The perspective is clearly male with a presumed male readership, and so we term such texts androcentric. This is to be expected from ancient Israelite literature and the patriarchal society from which it came. The issue of context, that of the ancient biblical world, must be faced at some point for biblical readers and the sooner the better. Doing so leads to no Sophie's choice between faith or feminism, but to an honest admission of difference. Negotiating that difference then becomes the task of biblical interpretation. The competing contexts of a biblical world and our own challenge each other in interpretation, with pertinent questions about how these ancient descriptions of sexual relations have an impact on our lives, if at all.

This is not an easy process, and many readers simply dismiss one context for the other: fundamentalists use biblical descriptions as a template for modern behavior, while more secularized readers tend to ignore the Bible because it is ancient. The interaction between the biblical world and our own is always a subtle one. It therefore takes considerable courage to be willing to go behind how the Bible has been used throughout history, in one's personal life, and try to hear it on its own terms. We can easily come to disclaim the Bible for the history of its use by unscrupulous types. But why give them such power?

The courage to go ahead and read it anyway is aided by a modern tool, our very affirmation of cultural diversity. We can use this to give the Bible a chance, to really hear characters and authors from a world much different from our own. It requires cultural sensitivity rather than anachronistic judgment of the Bible's world. By way of illustration, my students are often quick to grasp that the biblical world was patriarchal and so conclude that it is irrelevant. But by midterm, they see analogies with our world today. The Bible even helps them discern what "patriarchal" is. For example, a biblical woman is often identified with her first name plus "wife of X." That custom reflects a gender disparity of patriarchy wherein the woman is identified through her husband, and the students are quick to criticize it. But after some time, they start to notice that this custom is akin to our own where married women shed their surname in favor of their husband's. At that point, the Bible, with its sly antiquated pose, is illuminating and challenging our world.

With this combination of androcentrism and narrative reticence on matters of sex, it is impossible to wrest much about female or male desire from all these biblical passages involving sex. The woman is either ignored or defined as property for the male. Marriage in a patriarchal society was, for the most part, a matter of political and economic arrangement, with room at times for love (for example, Jacob of Rachel [Gen 29:18]; Michal of David [1 Sam 18:20]; Elkanah of Hannah [1 Sam 1:5]). Marriage for love is a fairly modern notion, becoming an expected criterion only in the nineteenth century. The man in biblical sex scenes really fares only somewhat better than the woman as his desires and wishes are collapsed into several verbal actions. Without the Song of Songs, we cannot really expect much insight into human desire in the Hebrew Bible. With it, desire is not only present, but sung for eight chapters, leaving us to wonder if the book is some anomaly to an otherwise reticent tradition on sex, or whether it sounds a pulsating undercurrent present all along.

EROTICA VERSUS PORNOGRAPHY

Before turning to the Song itself I want to address why a sexually explicit book is important to the Bible and worth reading today. Is it enough simply to read it as an entertaining literary romp, a kind of safe voyeurism that allows us to peep into ancient lust and then muster some mild sanctimony that at least it's biblical? Or do we read it out of rebellion, as a way to wreak vengeance on the sexual repression launched by early Christianity, with its splitting of the flesh and spirit in Paul, linking of sex with original sin in Augustine, and elevation of a Virgin Mother as an impossible model?

Christianity did drastically influence concepts of the body, women, and sex. By the time Paul was writing, the world was hellenized; Greek philosophy, culture, language, and art were on the scene. Ideas evolving from the thought world of Plato particularly led Paul to make distinctions between the flesh and the spirit, the ideal and the material, this world and a more perfect world. In short, Paul could effect a split or dichotomy of the world that was foreign to the Hebrew Bible. Such clean delineation is not evident in the Hebrew Bible, and that is one reason why we get so many more gruff stories of incest, men urinating on walls, drunkenness, bride switching and stealing, and more.

So, yes, reading the Song does much to correct the splitting of sexuality and spirituality occasioned with early Christianity. And since the Western world has been so influenced by Christian notions about sex, it is only good faith to read the Song in its own context. But by returning to this text, I hope to aim wider than just settling an old score, needling Christian repression. For I have found this Song to be a positive, visceral, enchanting celebration of human sexuality and have discovered that this celebration is a facet of spirituality. In other words, the Song's theology, though covert, is profoundly enriching for spirituality, and so the text warrants much more than a polite, embarrassed skim through. It deserves a hearing cleared of our hang-ups, *sexual and religious,* to sound its full potency.

The Song is essentially a book about how badly two people love and want each other. There are long descriptions of the other's body parts, graphic expressions of just what this want is doing to them, and some imaginings about when they will finally make love. It is demonstrably sexual throughout to a degree wholly unprecedented in the Bible. It is palpably erotic, startling and exciting the reader, including him or her in the narrated passions. Erotic literature will do just this. It will enlist the reader's empathy with the feelings of longing and arousal in the text. If all goes well, that is, if it is good erotica, then the longings within the reader's heart are stirred awake. A reader of erotica, then, is not disinterested, or at least does not remain so by the work's close. She or he will experience titillation, increased attention, and perhaps attendant physiological responses as well. Erotica is provocative, exciting, and pleasurable.

The Song evokes all these responses in a reader and so qualifies as erotica. But to appreciate why this is biblically significant, we should distinguish erotica from pornography. For there was a time when the Song was viewed as pornography, and that is why it originally had some trouble making it into the Bible. Both erotica and pornography are sexually explicit in content, yet their uses differ in at least three essential ways. First, erotica will tend to describe the emotions and internal worlds of at least one sexual participant, while pornography need not. Susan Sontag contrasts the "emotional flatness" of pornography by noting that this is not generally characteristic of erotica.[27] Both trade in fantasy: pornography will display and enact a fantasy, while erotica will build up to an action and mull over the idea of it.[28]

As the readers' empathy is sought in erotica, identification with the participants becomes essentially an affective one: readers bask in the emotions and excitement of the protagonists and follow through with the igniting of desire until its satisfaction. Pornography enlists readers as well, but for the goal of sexual satisfaction. The readers do not typically *empathize* with the protagonists. They are not too concerned with what the participants are thinking or feeling, but care instead about the action. You could, in other words, turn down the sound while watching pornography or skim reading until the "good parts" without missing much. But with erotica, the pleasure comes with the whole, slow quickening of desire's inevitable, skin-prickling pace. There is even a relish to the empathy, as the readers start to root for the lovers.

Second, erotica takes more time with the buildup to consummation. It can put consummation in tortuous delay and spend its time relishing the experience of waiting. In fact, for Audre Lorde, the erotic has more to do with our feelings than with any acts we may do, and that is why she sees it as such a resource for empowerment.[29] Pornography will get to the sexual acts as quickly as it can and then spend time repeating them. It is about satisfaction and a frenzy of repetition. It cuts to the chase with a speed that drains pleasure into an eventual tedium of repetitions. In fact, as Bataille noted, there is even a prophylactic function to erotica, whereby the pleasure we anticipate is spared the anxiety over what he termed the "ugliness" of the sex act.[30] In other words, erotica can keep desire pristine, even ethereal, while the movement toward sexual consummation requires facing an animalistic concreteness that can elicit some repulsion. At times, too, it can often look like pornography is more about power, while erotica is about wanting, and sex is the currency for both.[31]

In pornography, anything before the acts, such as plot or description, is really just artifice or dramatic foreplay to what is seen as the real play of sex. Pornography, then, arouses sexual excitement through the representation (and repetition) of sexual acts. Erotica arouses through the acts and through the wanting itself. Hence, it is conceivable to have erotica with only a single sex scene or even none at all, whereas with pornography it is not.

Erotica has a different agenda and tone. It elicits sexual yearning in the audience, not satisfying it in coarse displays of coitus. Erotica is devoted to the quality of the time spent waiting. It plays with the question of how lovers fill that time waiting. It asks about how we remember and picture the beloved, and what we imagine will happen when the beloved finally arrives.[32] By lingering in the want, erotica can frustrate and sharpen desire. Yearning is caught and then forged in a cauldron of emotions. We emerge not having mastered its principles, but having felt its self-transcending potential. Sexual yearning wants to disturb the self, to rip it out of its comfort zone and risk the fear and vertigo. There is something at once alluring and frightening about desire. Erotica offers a safer journey than lived experience, but it still risks igniting passions long hidden away. In a desire pursued, all the "what if" statements of fear slowly melt away in surrender to its direction. Erotica shows desire at the helm; the choice then becomes whether one will yield with exquisite pleasure, or decline the invitation altogether. If all this is a fair description of erotica, then the Song offers true testimony to how acutely and fully the ancients felt desire and can challenge us to be similarly alive and candid as well.

Finally, because erotica does invest description into areas other than the sexual act, it has more play with imagination. Erotica (and much spiritual writing) must convey that waiting by use of the imagination. It cannot simply offer strings of "I can't wait to see him," but must venture into the psyche and the vocabulary of want. Imagination is always the "invisible and ever-active participant" in erotica.³³ Erotica must convey that want and elicit it from the reader. It can do this by indirect description of all the places where the lover is absent or of how she remembers him, or through dreams, allusions, and potent metaphors. For example, the woman's invitation in the Song simply to "be drunk with love" elicits far more of the sloppy, reckless, tantalizing pleasure of love than could an explicit account of intercourse. Having invaded the heart and head, having the power even to take over, desire is not even close to having been quelled simply by the naming.

Erotic metaphors convey mystery while at the same time protecting it. As Matthew Fox notes, the Song is not trying to solve the mystery of love but rather is heightening the wonder.³⁴ Erotic metaphors are the literary equivalent of when a film shows not intercourse, but rather a vase overturning with the onset of lovemaking. This indirection stirs our imaginations awake. The sound of a dress being unzipped can have more erotic force than showing a woman naked, precisely because it stirs our imagination. The erotic plays with implied meanings—of what is under her dress, or his shirt—and calls on our imagination to supply it.³⁵ The Song will do this, too, with its own tantalizing undressings in metaphor, and it is to this erotic language that we now turn.

In short, the Song is erotica, ancient biblical lust, because it enlists the audience's imagination and desires along with its arousal. It uses allusions and metaphors that force the reader to slow down and feel them, whereas pornography cannot spare that kind of time. It is erotic because it teases; it draws the reader into the feelings of desire being described. It gets personal. At first, you were maybe reading about two lovers sketched over two millennia ago, with a halfhearted biblical or historical curiosity. But then something in the urgency and images began to ignite your own personal desires. You, reader, have just been tackled from behind by an enchanting friend. I speak from experience.

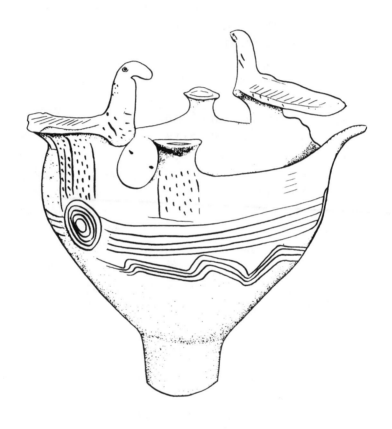

3

Biblical Flirting

INTRODUCTION

Though the Song of Songs is patently about sexual desire, it has had a rather colorful history of interpretation in which its overt meaning has gone largely ignored. That is, beginning with Origen in the mid-third century C.E., the dominant interpretation of the Song for Jews and Christians alike has been an allegorical one, whereby the human lovers depicted are understood to represent God and Israel or Christ and the church.[1] The Song's overt sexual meanings have only become commonplace with the commentaries in the twentieth century.

The reasons for the historical dominance of an allegorical interpretation of the Song are complex and for the most part beyond the scope of this work. Suffice it to say that allegorical interpretation was a legitimate and vital mode of reading Scripture from the second century C.E. on, because it could wrest religious meaning from biblical texts when it was otherwise not apparent. The Bible was assumed to be from God, and so it must be shot through with divine instruction. Hence, it was believed that *any* biblical passage must contain divine instruction, no matter how mundane or obscure it at first appeared. With the Song of Songs, divine instruction was nowhere evident, and so interpreters reasoned that it must be present in some kind of hidden form. Since God is not mentioned, they reasoned that the Song's content must then be an allegory in which the human love described really signifies or represents divine love. Interpreters of our day also, of course, look for divine or spiritual meanings in biblical texts, but we are equipped and temperamentally predisposed to view these texts with literary and historical criticism as well. We lean toward some curiosity as to the historical context of the authors and no longer assume divine authorship.

The tradition of allegorical interpretation was also aided by the sweeping changes in perspectives on sex and the body that occurred at the turn of the common era. Platonic dualism, as we noted in the last chapter, was influential in Palestine roughly at the time that the New Testament writings were being penned. Paul, whose letters comprise so much of the New Testament, could speak of a distinction in the human being between the spirit and the flesh (1 Cor 3:1-2; Rom 7:22), while in the Hebrew Bible, there was no such distinction, as the human being was viewed holistically.[2] Paul's distinction between the flesh and the spirit persisted in Christianity and helped to shape the idea of a dual or allegorical reading of texts. In other words, if the human being could be understood to have a spiritual and material dimension, then so could a text. Further, love itself could be split into notions of the noncarnal, the so-called platonic, and the carnal. Hence, the content of the Song was readily allegorized.[3]

This dualistic perspective would eventually give rise to ideas about the superiority of the spirit over the flesh. At that point, affirming views on the body, and by extension, on sexuality, desire, and woman (since mainly heterosexual men were writing), all became casualties of Christian theology. Gene McAfee asserts:

> Beginning in the later books of the Hebrew Bible, and continuing through the New Testament, there is a general decline in the value of sexuality and a tendency toward exaggerating its sinfulness. This shift in

attitude resulted . . . from the Greco-Roman cultural hegemony of the third century B.C.E. to the second century C.E.[4]

Sexuality, desire, and the body were at first devalued and then problematized as potential threats to spiritual growth in the period after the Hebrew Bible.[5] Religion naturally directed its energies toward the loftier domain of the spirit and abandoned the body, considering the body the prime locus of temptation and sin. This development has to be the low watermark for understanding sexuality and it obviously still persists today. Although the exact date of the Song of Songs is unknown, ranging anywhere from the sixth century to the fourth century B.C.E., it was written well before this attitudinal shift in sexuality occurred. But the Song's early interpreters were nevertheless influenced by this cultural disdain of sexual pleasure.

For most of its postbiblical history, then, the Song of Songs was read as an allegory of God's love for his people.[6] It is tempting to argue that the allegorical interpreters were simply repressing their own sexual longings in their search for the Song's spiritual meaning.[7] For it is true that most of the early and medieval Christian interpreters of the Song were celibate monks. They likely did find in allegorical interpretation some clandestine, sensual pleasure through working on the Song's spiritual meanings. Biblical study seemed to have its moments even then and could be titillating. Bernard of Clairvaux (1090–1153), for example, talks at length to his fellow monks on the lavish kisses in the Song. He goes into considerable, salacious detail about human kisses in order to better appreciate the allegorical kisses of Christ. This demonstrates, I suppose, the admirable homiletic sensitivity and patience of someone willing to take such time to explain a text. But certainly the erotic tones of the woman's wet and dripping lips are not all vaporized in this spiritual reading. And they were not, even for Bernard.

He was preaching to a new breed of monastics, namely, monks who had been out in the world, enjoying its pleasures before entering the order, rather than the earlier monks who had grown up cloistered in monasteries. His interpretations, then, deftly retained the Song's sexual energy instead of bypassing it. For certainly viewing Jesus as hot and bothered, offering sensuous kisses to his believers, is every bit as erotic as seeing the Song's woman wanting them. Indeed, it is almost a blasphemous homoeroticism that casts Jesus as the passionate lover, with a faint, yet inescapable, allusion to French kissing. Allegory here has done nothing to tame the Song's erotic force and has even elevated rather than assuaged sexual provocation. If repression and tittering, monkish nervousness had been the values Bernard sought to instill in his novices, he failed miserably.

The allegorical reading in Bernard's case was not sexual repression at all, or even a displacement of a celibate's sexual energies. It was instead a heuristic and adroit appropriation of the Song's sexual imagery for understanding the devotional life. When reading the allegorical interpreters of the Song, it is wise to keep in mind Michel Foucault's caution about studying sex in ancient texts. Foucault admonishes our glib assumption that earlier historical periods suffered sexual repression in contrast to our own supposedly liberated time. Allegorical interpretation simply proposed that the spirit was a more likely site for biblical meaning than was the body, in a culture that had assumed their split. To insist that early interpreters prove themselves by talking at length about sex is anachronistic and a form of cultural bullying.

Nevertheless, the early interpreters were constricted in their understanding of the Song by their assumption that the sexual and the spiritual were distinct, even competing facets in human existence. The early Christian dualism was perhaps helpful for instruction in the spiritual life, but it smuggled anti-body sentiment with it. Hence Paul counseled celibacy over marriage (1 Cor 7:1, 7-9), and Augustine eagerly declared himself celibate before he took the vows for priesthood. In the most extreme illustration of this spirit/body dualism, Origen castrated himself for the gospel. He acted on this passage in Matthew:

There are eunuchs who have made themselves eunuchs for the kingdom of heaven. Let anyone accept
this who can. (19:12)

Origen obviously could and did, and I simply know of no
better cautionary tale against the dangers of biblical literalism
than this!

I said above that all biblical books were assumed by Jew and
Christian alike to reveal some spiritual truth. Biblical interpreters
were not reading the Bible as mere literature, but as a terribly rich
source with which to grasp the divine. The Bible was not just a
book about the divine; it *provided access to it*. The Song's apparent lack of overt spiritual content meant that diligent effort went
into its interpretation, and so, ironically, it became the most frequently commented upon book in the Middle Ages.[8]

As we have seen, the allegorical interpretation is hindered by
the platonic dualism that favored the spirit over the material. But
it adds something perhaps lost in a strictly plain-sense reading,
that is, one wholly given over to sexual meanings; it brought the
experience of human yearning into the realm of the divine.
Desire tended to be split into its material and spiritual compo-
nents, but at least spiritual desire was not discarded, as it is in
plain-sense readings today. Human yearning was sacralized, not
repressed at all.

Hence, modern commentators who disdain the allegorical
method as mere signs of repression are too swift and dismissive
in their judgment. Those who champion the Song's plain erotic
sense, terming it "secular" in distinction from the "sacred" material of the rest of the Bible, are suffering under the same dualism
as their allegorical forebears. The only difference this time is that
"religious" versus "secular" has replaced "spirit" versus "flesh."[9]
Only the terms have changed in the name of progress, but the
dualism itself persists. The modern preference for only the Song's
plain sexual sense is too reductive of the Song's potency and constitutes an interpretive pendulum swing that is distortional in its
reactivity. By the same token, any attempts in the name of piety

to deny the possibility of a plain-sense, sexual meaning lose the erotic content of the Song. And denying its potential spiritual meaning for the plain sense begs the question of why the rabbis thought it did belong in the Bible and not in a tavern. We are modern and postmodern enough to insist that many meanings comprise a text—the Song of Songs and its spiritual wealth need be no exception.

Insight into the text's meaning will come instead by asking how it is that both kinds of meaning, plain-sense and allegorical, could have been generated from the Song. It is our categorizing that can reduce profound truths. The Song is not secular because it neglects to mention God and does contain descriptions of sex. That rendering is too swift, simple, and insulting to the ancients. These compartmentalizations do not work in our own world; why should they have worked for ancient Israel? Sex and death have long followed each other around, the unexpected tailing of apparent opposites.[10] And sexual intimacy, for its part, approaches levels of communion, of fullness, of ecstasy, in ways that can only be described as mystical. We decorate settings for both sex and worship with candles and incense, invitations to our senses to awaken and enjoy.

Sex and spirituality may not be disparate realities for the author(s) of the Song. My intention in the next three chapters is to demonstrate how desire is depicted in the Song of Songs. Through a cycle of metaphors, meanings are tapped, awakened, and set free to dance around each other in slippery fashion, their ambiguity and freedom left intact. Reading the Song is like making love in that there needs to be respect for mystery and allure and the arresting of any conquering impulse. The metaphoric cycles move from horticulture, farm facts about fruit cultivation, to sexual arousal (particularly in the female body), to an explosive sensual yearning for an unseen other. The language holds many meanings. These meanings are packed into daily features that at a quick glance look like Palestinian trivia, but they are not. The Song requires really multiple readings that will bother to savor a line ("let us be drunk with love" [5:1]). And, in fact, this is true of most biblical reading. Savoring can turn a book into Scripture as multiple meanings begin to jump alive, firecrackers of insight. Since the Song is erotic and focuses on the emotions of love and desire, the reader can be affected by the Song's content well before he or she can articulate that impact. The damage and pleasure have already been done before analysis can get there.

Parables in the New Testament work in a similar fashion. Something about the impossibility of a camel going through the eye of a needle registers in a heart and mind long before it is decoded. One lingers and mulls over the image, just grasping the futility in the rich man's plight. You feel for the poor rich guy, while still trying to picture a ludicrous limber camel. This ineffable quality in images is all the more potent and elusive when dealing with sexual desire. In this sense, the explication of how something is erotic is not the objective here. Grapes, wine, lips, tongues, honey, and breasts are repeated often enough in the Song, that the surprisingly heady erotic punch has landed long before an academic tells you to watch for it. I am advising instead that there is pleasure in the reading itself, so let the images and words play off the tongue and into imagination and the body. I have looked down at myself more than once while reading, vexed by the metaphor of grapes as breasts. Enjoy, then; linger over the words without hunting down their meaning, being stalled by unknown referents, skimming to get to the end of the book, or avoiding it altogether because it appears to be at variance from spirituality. It is not.

Oddly, it has taken many readings to allow the levels of meaning to filter through into my consciousness, into my heart and soul. The result has been awe at the ancient writers, still more at what they glimpsed about human desire. And I am not awed quickly or easily. So I hope you will come along on a journey through metaphors that is not only or even primarily academic, but that can yield treasures of insight and sheer beauty. You will learn something more precise and exact, sharpened, about human desire than I have seen written elsewhere, and you will glimpse the wholeness of Hebrew vision—of body and soul, sex and spirit. That holistic vision and celebration can be restorative to our severed spiritual and sexual lives. And you will learn something about reading the Bible, about entry into it with all its quaint, faintly embarrassing agrarian metaphors. I do not believe the Bible will feel so foreign and outdated to you after this, since these metaphors shape the literature. It takes courage to do this—to even want to—and a willingness to read with some might.

One reason why the Song of Songs is still worth reading today is that it lingers in desire's complexity, taking its time, being forced into metaphor. Love is arguably the most important aspect of our lives, yet we lack meaningful vocabulary to articulate its mysteries.[11] The term itself is broadened until it becomes banal, okay to use for one's beloved or just as easily for a favorite food, song, or celebrity. Anyone who has ever tried to answer a lover's playful and sincere query "why do you love me?" knows the ledge of feeling—awkward, mute, silly, frustrated—upon which the Song's writer(s) stood. Inadequate, lost, surrounded by clichés. Indeed, as Diane Ackerman notes, it is our paltry vocabulary that has led to great works of art on the subject. The lack of articulation has made a necessity of works of the imagination such as the Song of Songs, and these risk getting misunderstood or ignored, since their meaning is anything but plain.

This is the catch-22 of love—a basic, vital human issue, and an intangible. Here we hit hard the limits of language. Ackerman's study, *A Natural History of Love,* is helpful because it is not content just to name the obvious, that poets are attracted to love as their subjects. She tries to explain the attraction itself as due to the degree of difficulty. Getting love just right in expressions is daredevil tough: enter the poets, including our Hebrew poet. This difficulty, the lack of existing vocabulary rather than love's nobility, she says, has "inspired poets to create their own private vocabularies."

The writer(s) of the Song of Songs was also forced to create "private vocabularies." The Hebrew Bible is not different from culture at large in lacking a strong vocabulary for describing love. The enormity of the artistic task is felt in this Song, too. Its achievements as a poetic language of love can, by way of analogy, accrue later to our understanding of the other intangible, God. Can you really think of a more hermetically sealed, tautological, excluding command than this—that "you shall love the lord your God with all your heart, soul, and might?" (Deut 6:5). It is *the* greatest commandment, according to Jesus, yet it remains an encrypted cliché, profound if only one cared to grasp it. The spiritual goal of biblical reading is to learn how to begin to reveal this command's challenge and freedom instead of leaving it safely neutralized as a quaint platitude or tucked on the arsenal shelf of the preachy. What Diane Ackerman confesses for human love applies across the board for me, to include spiritual love:

> We have the great fortune to live on a planet abounding with humans, plants, and animals; and I often marvel at the strange task evolution sets them. Of all the errands life seems to be running, of all the mysteries that enchant us, love is my favorite.[12]

The poetry of the Hebrew Song is necessary for understanding Scripture precisely because of its description of the vital intangibles of life. It may well have been written after much of the material of the Hebrew Bible, but it provides a useful entry code back into that canon. Hence, its place is not as some last-minute entry barely qualifying as biblical. It is essential as a guide or entry into reading the Bible.

Types of Language about Love

I have isolated three major types of discourse about desire in the Song. These types are merely heuristic. I hope that they can help us navigate through the vast imagery in the Song and enable us to appreciate the nuances of human desire.

First, there are expressions of the sheer appreciation of the other's beauty; ancient declarations, basically, of how great a catch one's lover is. These expressions are mainly devoted to listing the physical characteristics of the other, and they function rhetorically as flirtation language, flattering the other with a complimentary assessment of his or her body. This type of discourse provides an aesthetic appreciation of one's lover and is obviously commonplace and still awkward today, as when we try to tell someone why she or he has the best smile, eyes, or hair. At this stage in the game of desire and arousal, the poet invites us to "observe lovers, to smile at them, to empathize with them."[13] In descriptions of that other's beauty, attention rests on the *object* of one's affections.

A second discourse of desire involves more directly the feelings of the lover. Instead of a flattering inventory of the other's physical assets, expressions of the feelings involved center on the lover as subject. This kind of language gives voice to how the lover wants, how she or he feels while wanting. It is affective description, explicitly about the emotion of desiring, and it reveals the motives of the speaker. It is a step up in intensity from flirtation, for the affective statements unmask the speaker's own vulnerability and make a claim or request of the other. Two people are now involved in the description. With flirtation, the language focused only on the other; we were left to imagine how the speaker felt. It is a difference in both kind and intensity. Compare the difference, for example, between "You have the sweetest smile" and "I want you." We intuit this difference in kind and intensity all the time, as when we can say of someone's behavior that it was just a harmless flirtation. A harmful flirtation presumably is one readied and eager to go to the next level when, for whatever reasons, one cannot or should not.

The third type of language about desire is an expression of the physical impact of yearning. It details the toll that longing for another has taken on the individual. Here again, the focus is on the speaker rather than the intended other. But now that focus has shifted away from motives and emotions. It has become a reflective self-assessment of desire's impact. The physical impact of desire itself can range from feeling faint, giddy, and sexually aroused to enjoying the pleasures themselves. It can include sexual explorations and their physiological responses. These three types of language, of course, are not exclusive of each other. Compliments and declarations of feelings occur during lovemaking as expressions of desire, and this says nothing of the physical impact pleasure is having on the couple. When it comes to ardent desire, all types of description get enlisted.

Aesthetic Appreciation and Flirtation

The beginnings of articulating desire come in the form of aesthetic appreciation of the other. The lover describes the physical attributes that make the other attractive and desirable. The litany is typically formulaic, uttered with a kind of hindsight after desire has been ignited, and so it has an idealized quality to it. In describing the other's physical beauty, sexual desire is implied but not overt.

These descriptions are often excruciating to produce for the lover unpracticed in poetry, because they insist on metaphoric expression. Since one of the functions of poetry is to bridge a social distance, it makes sense that it gets used most clearly in courtship.[14] Desire for another quickly stymies the tongue, forcing the lover to risk foolishness and frustration in language. Speech is most definitely affected by desire, and metaphors offer one of the first havens. Note the difference, for example, between something like "your eyes are pretty" and "your eyes are doves behind your veil" (4:1). The first expression is a compliment, while the second, a metaphor and also a compliment, includes ambiguity, mystery, even desire, causing you have to wonder why someone is bothering to go poetic. The image of eyes as doves resists a literal meaning about how human eyes could look like birds, suggesting instead peace, an oval shape, softness, maybe gray irises amid the white of the eyes. It is the poetic effort of such an image that signals the lover's interest and want, but it does so in covert fashion. As an expression of desire, then, compliments are ultimately limiting. For the eyes, hair, and smile of a lover are not, in the end, the sole reasons for desire's awakening. Rather, desire once awakened doubles back to these details, making them targets of lust-filled speech. Aesthetic appreciation is hindsight, with desire returning to the scene of its awakening. These details become more than the physical attributes and are now symbols of want.

In fact, there is even a touch of insincerity in flirtation. Flirts are attentive to details, to be sure, but they are also expedient, recognizing that the details really do not matter in the end. They are just the signs of one's desire and not the things desired. The lover's hair, for example, is beautiful, and it is the first to get tousled in sex. Its beauty, then, no longer matters so much, and can even obstruct the excitement of passion, as when it gets caught or hides the lips one wants to kiss. In sex, the eyes close, and poetry is dropped as communication goes on in wild, violent form. The championed beauty of the lovers is forgotten, as vision itself subsides to let the other senses take over. The woman in the Song, for example, once called her lover's thighs "alabaster columns" (5:15) in aesthetic appreciation. But if she can still remember that poetry in sexual excitement, all the more power to her. Or again, both lovers share eyes that are considered beautiful as doves, but in sex, these will hide in hair, shut, open, roll back, squint, and do all sorts of things that look nothing like doves.

The language of aesthetic appreciation funnels sexual desire toward the details and cannot in the end satisfy it, give it a full hearing. Left at these details, in fact, desire could stall to a fetish, the detail then carrying the full weight of another's desire. The lover's compliments betray an emotive urgency in desire, a longing, and so a *motive* for praising eyes and hair. Fervent desire is not dispelled with such speech but sputters around in it. Paradoxically, desire both gets a hearing in aesthetic appreciation and goes unsounded. Compliments are not enough to quell it. Hence, the language of desire must escalate to affective expression, and this further pushes imagination and poetry toward the third discourse of physical excitement.

When the lover in the Song says to his beloved, "you are stately as a palm tree" (7:7), it is a compliment of the woman's stature. *His* desire is only implied by this compliment. He has not declared his vested interest in her height; he has not yet risked his own want. He does so in the next verse by admitting that he wants to "climb the palm tree and lay hold of its branches" (7:8). Now we know why he is complimenting her. With the compliment itself, though, the focus remains on the other as object of affection. It does not implicate the speaker. Instead, complimentary description remains on the border of flattery—safe, inoffensive, desire neatly packaged.

Voiced aesthetic appreciation functions rhetorically as flattery or flirtation offered to the other who is its subject. It is typically the initial stage toward broaching intimacy, then and now. It conveys interest while keeping the two identities separate, but it means to bridge social distance. In the Song, the two lovers already know one another and have been together, so their compliments are not an introduction, but rather a renewal of their desire and intimacy.

The language the two lovers use to describe each other as objects of their affection is somewhat formulaic, polite, certainly unthreatening. And the awkwardness in courting is certainly realistic. The man here offers what he means to be a compliment to the woman, though this may not be apparent to modern readers:

> Your hair is like a flock of goats moving
> down the slopes of Gilead.
> Your teeth are like a flock of shorn ewes
> that have come up from the washing
> all of which bear twins. (4:1-2)

This is biblical flattery at work, endearing and utterly strange. The man is really trying to describe the woman's beauty. The first image conveys hair that is dark and wavy, as goats descend from mountains in a zigzag fashion, appearing as ridges from afar. Additionally, it conveys that the hair is clean enough to move, no small feat in antiquity, when olive oil was often used to clean hair in lieu of washing with scarce water.

The second image praises the condition of the woman's teeth. They are ivory, an off-white, like ewes just washed. And they are clean, with minimal fuzz, as ewes that have been shorn. It is a compliment to her general dental hygiene. Incidentally, this helps to interpret the expression "skin of my teeth," which is biblical, from the book of Job (19:20). People without toothbrushes and fluoride would have had filmy skin on their teeth. Rudimentary pastes with spices were likely used, as they were in ancient Rome. Escaping by the skin of one's teeth, as Job did, then, is one narrow margin indeed. Not having the skin on one's teeth is cause for amorous praise.

The lover forges ahead by praising that her teeth have none missing, "all of which bear twins." Again, impressive for antiquity. Both wavy clean hair and white, well-matched teeth are obvious targets of lust, since the lover eventually hopes to kiss the woman's mouth and fondle her hair. Perhaps these images are quaint and distant to us, as we can assume clean hair and teeth in romantic endeavors. Still, though, the phrases remind us that we have all been in the awkward position of proclaiming desire through wooing. It is likely that the vernacular of aesthetic appreciation we use today will sound just as distant to our successors in love.

There is something constrained by convention in aesthetic appreciation of the beloved. This is true for antiquity and for now; the lover's merits are required to be sung in the ritual of wooing with a list of attributes that are beside the point. We love someone and long to be with them not finally because they have the best hair or smile, but because our insides yearn to be with them. Aesthetic appreciation is a first step, a relief valve, a giving of praise to articulate some of the inner turmoil of desire. It is the easiest part of the Song to smile over when reading. It is honest in its awkwardness, recalling our own memories of uttering the wrong, stilted things, when underneath, we are really asking just to be as close to the lover's body as we can.

Both the man and the woman of the Song participate equally in their aesthetic appreciation of the other.[15] They are both skilled and willing to describe their lover's physical attributes. These poetic passages are similar to a convention in Arabic poetry known as the *wasf*, which contains the description of body parts through images.[16] The woman's lips, for example, are a "crimson thread" (4:3), while the man's thighs are "alabaster columns" (firm, translucent [5:15]). And they do not stop there, but proceed to detail most of their lover's body. There is overall equality shared by the male and female voice in the complimentary descriptions in the Song.

Such thorough attention to the body is wholly uncharacteristic of biblical writing, save for Jesus' eucharistic pronouncement about the bread being his body. The Bible in general is maddeningly circumspect on the body.[17] We are told in the very first chapter of Genesis that humans are made in the image of God, but we are given no clues except that that image entails male and female (Gen 1:27). We have no idea what Jesus looked like, except that blond and blue-eyed is unlikely for first-century Palestine. Nor have we any idea what Noah or Moses or Mary looked like. The physical features of characters are only occasionally noted: some, like Rachel, David, and Esther, are good-looking; others, like Samson and Absalom, have remarkably long hair; a few, like Moses and David, have striking complexions. But these details are mentioned because they prove instrumental to the plot. Samson and Absalom both die as a direct result of their long hair; Esther gains a throne because she wins the king's beauty pageant; Moses' face is shining because he has been in God's presence while receiving the law. The physical appearance of biblical characters was usually not significant for the biblical writers.

Yet physical beauty brought pleasure in the biblical world, as this Song amply demonstrates. Beauty was frequently valued in texts but seemed also to be a source of some ambivalence. There is a tension in the biblical material not to be concerned with beauty but to opt for it nonetheless. The wives of Abraham, Isaac, and Jacob, namely, Sarah, Rebekkah, and Rachel and Leah, are all good-looking, with no mention of how their husbands measured up. Wives, then, are noted as "good-looking," yet with no further hint of what constituted their attractiveness.

God, too, is ambivalent about good looks on one occasion. He sends Samuel to go and look over Jesse's sons to find which will be God's chosen king. Samuel assumes it must be one of the strapping older sons, but God protests that he is a God who looks on the inner heart, not the outer look. A chastened Samuel then meets his king to be, the handsome, ruddy, though tiny David (1 Sam 16:7, 12). God may not judge only by the outer looks, but they do seem to be a factor. David, presumably, has both inner and outer beauty covered and is, in general, irresistible to all—women, men, even God. Perhaps the prohibition against images of God in the second of the Ten Commandments (Exod 20:4) brought with it a timidity toward human beauty as well. The artwork collected by archaeology for ancient Israel is certainly poor in contrast to the treasures of ancient Egypt and Mesopotamia (modern-day Iraq).

The Song of Songs differs appreciably from the Bible's otherwise circumspect stance on the body. Here, these lovers detail each other's physical attributes as an expression of their own desire—with poems about the physical beauty of eyes, lips, thighs, and abdomens laced throughout the eight chapters. We get the details, packaged often in similes and metaphors drawn from their surrounding world. These metaphors are drawn, primarily, from three arenas of their world: (1) nature—gazelles, hills, streams, goats; (2) architecture—towers, columns, walls; and (3) horticulture—the cultivation of grapes, its product wine, and other fruits such as figs and apricots.[18]

At times, the images may strike us as odd, agrarian, and distant, yet as an honesty check, it may help to recall just how difficult it is to talk about what love is, how cute someone is, how tantalizing their breath or neck. We can quickly be reduced to winsome expressions such as "your eyes are the best." We are still stymied by our desire, left helpless, foolish, and mute at times, meaning one thing, saying another. We resort to the surrounding world and stutter with the realization that all this time, we haven't really been paying attention to it at all. It is when we fall in love that we first start noticing the world as new again. We are in this way thrust uncomfortably beyond ourselves, and that in itself serves a fledgling spiritual impulse—to pay attention to the teeming world, to say nothing of the unsolicited humility gained. Desire awakens us to our world as it propels us to another. It can even awaken in us love for that world.

Sexual attraction is inchoate and next to impossible to articulate, and so one is forced outside to look for resources in the world.[19] Ackerman considers the appeal to nature to be understandable. Love, she reminds us, is about absolute feelings, and the workings of nature, too, are the only absolutes we know that can compare.[20] We have traces of this impulse still in dated clichés about the earth moving or a cold front coming in. One needs to think big when articulating love and have a mixture of sheer bravery and poetic sophistication even to try. The poets here did, by drawing on these three metaphoric fields from the world. As readers, we need to muster a parallel courage in understanding. Poetic skill, though, does not mean that the writer must be one of the trained, elite court writers of ancient Israel. The poets can just as easily be rural farmers using the world they know to talk about the love they know or want. Everyone would have known what doves, shorn ewes, and goats coming down mountains looked like. The ineffability of love forces everyone to either poetry or silence, but it requires no specialists on the scene. Their poetic credentials could easily have come from their mundane lives, much as today's rap poets are schooled in the street and pushed into poetry.

The lovers draw from their daily world for their description of the desired other. They list features that they like in the other. As examples of aesthetic appreciation, the eyes, lips, hair, and face receive attention from both lovers. Her eyes are doves (1:15; 4:1), and so are his, though she adds that they are "bathed in milk" (5:12), that is, surrounded by the whites of the eye. Her lips are like a "crimson thread" (4:3), which means that they are red and somewhat thin. His lips, in contrast, are like lilies (5:13); they are red, too, as this is most likely the *lilium chalcedonicum,* a showy red flower native to Israel.[21] But this image suggests as well that his lips are opened like a flower, or puckered.

Her hair falls like jewels on her neck (1:10), or like a flock of goats moving down a hill (4:1; 6:5). His hair is wavy and "black as a raven" (5:11). Hair becomes a symbol of sexual yearning. It attracts the attention of the lover, perhaps because it surrounds the face or intimates the hair still unseen. Though the whole person is loved, Ackerman points out, the hair will often receive specific, poetic attention:

> Hair becomes the fetish of that love. Yielding and soft, sumptuous and colorful, decorative and dangling, it invites a lover's touch. It's fun to fondle, play with, and disarrange. Messing it up is the symbolic equivalent of undressing the other's body.[22]

Hair is mentioned three times in the Song and so was also noteworthy for these ancient lovers.

These daring lovers do not restrict themselves only to the neck up, but traverse the length of the human body. In 4:1-5, the man describes the woman from the eyes to her breasts, and in 7:1-5, he works in reverse, from her feet all the way up to her hair. In 5:10-15, the woman describes the man from head to thigh:

> My beloved is all radiant and ruddy,
> > distinguished among ten thousand.
> His head is the finest gold;
> > his locks are wavy,

black as a raven.
His eyes are like doves
 beside springs of water,
bathed in milk. . . .
His arms are rounded gold,
 set with jewels. . . .
His legs are alabaster columns . . . (5:10-14)

Their complexions, it seems, are at once healthy, sunburned, and blushed with sexual excitement. Red, healthy cheeks are noted for both; his are "ruddy," while hers are like "halves of a pomegranate" (4:3; 6:7). This signals their good complexions and hints at the physiological arousal of blushing. The use of gold and jewels above occurs for both lovers and indicates how precious and rare they each are. Genital areas and torsos are described as well, but not exclusively as aesthetic appreciation. Instead, they play a prominent role in scenes depicting sexual arousal, and so they will be discussed then. The woman's breasts, for example, figure in both types of language, aesthetic and of arousal. In terms of beauty alone, her breasts are described as "two fawns, twins of a gazelle" (4:5; 7:3), suggesting that they are bouncy, dainty, and even in size (*twins*). All these compliments are means to show aesthetic appreciation and contain desire essentially through terms of endearment.

Poetry requires that we pause long enough to taste or feel these metaphors. We have to get the feel without forcing them to be literal, or else absurdity ensues. After all, breasts look nothing like gazelles. Instead, we let the image sit in the imagination, where it was originally hatched, until it catches and makes a kind of intuitive sense. It won't always, of course, but poetry requires that we slow down enough to appreciate it. So, too, does love. And so does spiritual reality. There is no fast-food or drive-thru mentality in the languages of yearning.

Consider this from the male:

What a magnificent young woman you are!
How beautiful are your feet in sandals,
the curve of your thighs
is like the work of an artist.
Your navel is a rounded bowl
that never lacks mixed wine.
Your belly is a heap of wheat,
encircled with lilies. (7:1-2)

It is obvious that these two are lovers, for the man has been privy to seeing thigh, belly, and whatever lilies are likely to represent, with their strong scent and color darker than wheat (pubic area?). The woman too has been privy to his torso, as when she says that his "belly is ivory work, encrusted with sapphires" (5:14). To her, his abdominal muscles are apparently both precious as sapphires and carved as ivory (we might use the simile, "cut like a six-pack").

The above poem is a good, sincere, and earthy attempt by the man to sing the praises of his lover. For what else can this ancient woman be wearing on her feet but sandals? And his comparison of her thighs as perfect, from an artist's hands, is akin to our saying someone is statuesque. It is also deeply true in the biblical view, where the artist *is* her creator, God. These are better compliments than when she would be dressed up, with man-made distractions of linens and jewels (1:11; 4:9). He risks more familiarity and comments on her given, mundane beauty, just feet in sandals. It is that natural, naked beauty that is lauded rather than its accoutrements. The everydayness of the images makes this Song work. The sincerity breaks through, for we see that, clearly, he is in love; he wants to be with his beloved. Such sentiments obviously reflect his desire. He must be smitten if he is bothering to talk about the woman's feet, that they are marvelous, even while wearing the sandals everyone else wears. Nevertheless, they reflect a controlled or tamed desire, since feet are a far safer topic than the sex he wants to have. Foot praise then, is fairly harmless flirtation.

The lovers also toss out more general compliments beyond detailing specific body parts, as in this exchange:

(man)   "How beautiful you are, my love!" (1:15)
(woman) "How handsome you are, my dearest!" (1:16)

These utterances are rather bland in comparison to the compliments employing metaphors. And they are formulaic; she is almost parroting his expression in a Ping-Pong exchange of appreciation that does little or nothing for erotic desire.[23]

In conclusion, the language detailing aesthetic appreciation of the lovers is nice, tender, terribly earthy, and at times even silly or startling. Clearly, these two lovers are healthy and attractive, or they are (forgivably) blinded by love. Their lists detail not lust or sensual yearning but rather aesthetic appreciation. Desire is, undoubtedly, implied by such poetic appreciation, but it is not explicit. These expressions of physical admiration are at best cloaked invitations to further intimacy. In terms of the couple's passion, aesthetic appreciation is sincere, awkward, and endearing, but not *insistent*. They do not compel the beloved other to any course of action. The pleasure in receiving such compliments can remain aural, with the feel-good infusion of flattery, of feeling adored. We sense, in other words, that these lovers are for now content to be poets at work, that they can so far survive the separation from one another. They have not yet suffered from their love with what Julia Kristeva terms its "vertigo of identity, vertigo of words."[24] Sexual yearning, at this stage, is under flattery's control and is not going anywhere, but it will once the separation starts to chafe, and it will usher in another type of language for desire. It is to this second type of language that we turn in the next chapter.

4

A Ravished Heart

You have ravished my heart
  with a glance of your eyes.
      —Song 4:9

The Subject in Want

With this statement, the lover confesses his own condition of desire. No longer just complimenting the woman's features, he has now ventured into much scarier territory, detailing the emotional effect she has had on him. Her impact on his inner being, his subjectivity, is conveyed by these words of his, and it has been both comprehensive and devastating. This is flirtatious speech that compliments the woman's power, and it is also confession, for he is stilled, defeated, and overcome by her. This kind of utterance is more risky for the subject speaking because the feelings threaten to destabilize him. He speaks directly on the condition of yearning for another. This, then, is the second type of discourse of desire, which I have termed affective depiction. Her eyes are not simply dove-like or veiled anymore, but have now become weapons, igniting desire's inner turmoil. He is undone by those eyes and spent by her mere glance. In contemporary terms, he's a goner.

Affective depiction of want is also figurative speech. The woman's glance does not literally have such power by itself. Instead, it is devastating because of how badly the man wants her. Hence, he is not innocent in his plight, and she is not supernaturally devastating. It is no longer only the beloved that is being described. Her glance hits the target—*his* internal state of wanting. At this stage, what were physical features described with aesthetic appreciation are no longer merely the features of the other. They wound simply by exposing the inner turmoil of the lover. The desire spoken of in this type of language becomes harder both to endure and to articulate. This chapter will focus on the subjective impact of desire on the lovers. The first section discusses how the lovers view themselves in a state of sexual want. The second section examines how the metaphors have changed in descriptions of the subject in want, and a final section explores the Song's convention of separating the lovers in order to sustain the longing.

This language of desire differs from aesthetic appreciation in two essential ways. First, it is subjective, detailing the condition of being in desire rather than the object of that desire. And second, it is no longer only about pleasure. Pleasure is now laced with want and comes with the element of pain, even the violence of desire, as the above verse illustrates. "You have ravished my heart" is at first wholly complimentary of the woman's formidable presence. But it suggests also the painful turmoil, even the *abuse,* that desire has inflicted. The lover's heart has been jolted, pushed around, and even taken without his consent. The writer exercises poetic license, of course, and may simply enlist this verb for exaggeration. "Ravish" can certainly be hyperbole, meant to capture how desire feels to the lover.[1] And it does. My contention is simply that this poetry, even with its flamboyance, is nevertheless capturing some angle about desire that needs to be heeded rather than dismissed. Her glance does not literally ravish the man, of course, but emotionally it does. In poetry, in other words, there is no such thing as "just a figure of speech." Poetic speech casts a wide berth precisely to retain many meanings. "Ravish" then encodes something thematically crucial about desire's overpowering force.

Today, if we have had occasion to utter "I am undone" by another and have meant it, we are attempting to give voice to love's totalitarian disruption. We are confessing our vulnerability to desire, admitting that it threatens our very selfhood. The paradox of human sexual desire is that we simultaneously want to be undone by love and fear it. As we shall see in chapter 7, this psychological paradox is why love and death are so frequently associated in literature and art. There is pain in the pleasure of desiring, a pain that challenges the autonomy of the self. When the lover of the Song proclaims that the woman's glance has ravished him, his testimony is at once compliment and accusation. His words signal both the airy, hyperbolic giddiness of being in love and a foreboding of desire's total costs, namely, a ravished heart.

Desire courses through the languages of aesthetic appreciation and of affective want. Its effect on the lover as subject is the next, heated step, a filling out of the description of desire. The third type of language will focus on the satisfaction of want, the sexual, physical transformation of desire. Affective description makes overt the emotion that is behind the flattery anyway. For the lover's intention in trading compliments ultimately is to unite with his lover. One goes to the trouble and skill of listing all the beloved's beautiful features, after all, not out of any mere clinical attention to detail, but because it begins to voice one's desire for the other. But flattery need go no further than complimenting the desired other. Expressions of want, however, have an increased energy and intensity; they have an agenda. They too may end up going no further than a profession, but the energy is nevertheless considerable and will have to be negotiated.

Elsewhere in the Bible, Ecclesiastes offers a philosophical examination as to where in life human pleasures are to be found. Its advice on love is simple and direct: "Enjoy life with the woman whom you love" (9:9). This alerts us as to where pleasure resides, namely, in the everyday, the giving of a wife (literally, since the man negotiates with her father for her) and so what has gone un-acknowledged. Ancient men in Israel's patriarchal society may have needed that insight periodically from their wisdom material. Still, this carpe diem sentiment precludes our knowing quite a bit here: how the woman felt; what "enjoy" itself entailed, since sexual love is by no means certain here; and the subjective state of a husband in need of this advice. Is his desire even in his marriage latent or extinguished? Does he miss his wife, neglect her, or just plain forget where pleasure resides in his hardworking farm life? This Song pushes past Ecclesiastes here. It explodes all these biblical ambiguities on pleasure and desire. In essence, Hebrew pleasure is laid bare, as the Song offers an unremitting excursus of desire's intricacies. How desire feels for the one undergoing it is explored in this second kind of discourse, that of depicting the affective condition of sexual want.

The language of love in the Song, then, pushes forward to describe the subjective element involved in wanting another. This is how we know to take the desire seriously, as something more than flirtation. It is also why gender analysis is in for a rare biblical treat, for neither the male nor the female voice is rendered inert; neither subjectivity is forgotten. In this Song, both male and female voices recite their lover's assets, and both inner worlds are given attention. The beloved was more potentially objectified when she was a list of body parts in the language of aesthetic appreciation, however delightful. Now, the sexual want of both individuals is laid bare in affective description. Both partners get to this kind of description fairly fast. For her part, the woman is wanting off the bat, wasting no time. It is her want, in fact, that begins the book:

> Let him kiss me with the kisses of his mouth.
> For your love is better than wine. (1:2)

And she is quick to read her lover's desire correctly, knowing full well that "his intention toward me was love" (2:4).

The Song does not offer a progressive narrative on desire. Instead, it hits the ground running, with her voiced plea. Her urgent yearning is revealed by her speech. She wants the "kisses of his mouth." She wants, we see, nothing chaste at all: no pecks on the cheek, but his entire attentive mouth, repeating with its kisses. We can see by the use of the plural form here that she truly wants to be showered with kisses. But specifying that these come from his mouth is an odd redundancy. It betrays her excitement. And her urgency is also evident in the very slip of pronouns. She had begun by speaking about him in the third person ("him," "his"), but then switches to second person with "your love is better than wine." He has either entered the scene, which is not at all evident in the rest of her speech, or her overdone and confused language continues to signal her excitement. And her desire for his kisses and his love is an expression of a pleasure previously enjoyed, a desire ignited by experience. When she says, "your love is better than wine," we sense that she is in a position to make that call. It *is* better than wine, and so she understandably wants to repeat that rare pleasure.

The male lover is primarily quiet until chapter 4, so the woman's desire comprises most of the first three chapters of the Song. In chapter 4, after describing her physical attributes in aesthetic appreciation, the man asks her to join him, saying "You have ravished my heart with a glance of your eyes." He too agrees with her assessment of their lovemaking, adding that her love is sweet, "much better than wine" (4:9-10) as well. By sequence, then, the male lover is slower to emote, but is nevertheless able to catch up with this heartfelt cry. Desire in the Song, then, does begin in mid-excitement, with the woman beckoning the man for the kisses of his mouth, her speech slipping around precision. This is fitting, for desire is not subject to linear development. Rather, it calls its own shots. It starts whenever it wants to, regardless of time and space, and just as unnerving, it can expire erratically and inexplicably.

There is a point in wooing another, in flirtation, where praise language gives out and subjective intent must reveal itself. Compliments become no longer tenable as the sole carriers for one's desire. They even begin to look suspicious. It is the point where we start to wonder why someone is saying all these nice things about our hair. The literary conventions of moving from flattery to expressions of want differ across cultures and subcultures. But what these conventions do is signal the socially acceptable forms of moving toward increased levels of intimacy. Flattery is a first-level entry, even a petition for intimacy, while descriptions of the couple's lovemaking, whether real or imagined, can only arise or be received as appropriate when the speakers already share considerable intimacy. We cannot know from the Song what social conventions for broaching sexual intimacy were in place for ancient Israel, since the book stands as a tour de force within the Bible. Also, it is about two people who are already lovers and so can move swiftly and erratically along desire's varying discourses—from want, to compliment, to sexual pleasure, and back again. As lovers, they are free to travel the levels of intimacy in speech with a speed and improvisational zest that two people courting would not be.

With the poetry of the initial level, that of aesthetic appreciation, the intent of the language eventually uncloaks, either as the poetic, aesthetic show that it is or as an earnest, preliminary expression of yearning. That is, the beauty of poetic description could simply be replicating the woman's beauty and thereby serving mainly as an homage to love's magnanimity. Or desire could be pressing up against the limits of aesthetic appreciation, still searching for a way to reveal its hunger. In terms of the Song, we might ask it this way: are the woman's eyes really like doves, or is her lover trying to express his own physical want for her, a want earnest enough that it will trouble with such metaphors? The Song is primarily about that want in both lovers, and so it is not merely a hymn to the beauty of love. Felt want—in both sexual and emotional longing—gets articulated in the Song with a brave clarity and power unseen in the Bible, save for Psalms, which also details the affective condition of its speakers.

Affective description, as we said, turns its attention to the lover as subject. In these descriptions, in fact, the beloved is no longer the praised object, but exists in the background. The portent of speech now hangs damply on the lover's own condition. When the man says, "you have ravished me" (4:9) or that he is "overwhelmed" (6:5), he is risking more about himself than his compliments did. Expressions of want herald personal risk, for the lover speaks into a silence that can threaten to engulf him in ridicule. Yet the risk is worth it, since finally speaking one's heart, one's desire, no matter the consequences, yields a heady sense of soaring free. The lover stands free, brave, and for moments of unknowing, terribly alone.

Such expressions of want show desire's increased risk in the social sphere as well. For the man is laying bare his own want for the woman to reject or accept. At this point, we are well beyond the safe conventions of flattery. When someone compliments, say, our eyes or hair in public, it is flattery and can remain there without any response beyond polite acknowledgment, if need be. When someone says instead that they are undone by us, polite acknowledgment is no longer an option. We need to respond. The speaker has launched a proposition of sorts, a declaration of desire, which if sincere will go further, given our go-ahead.

The language of sexual longing differs from that of aesthetic appreciation in its function at precisely this edge. Rhetorically, it insists on a response from the beloved. The woman responsible for the man's ravished state is invited to ease his longing and maybe share her own. If she ignores the lover's profession of longing, then his discourse becomes a soliloquy, and a failed one at that. Intimacy will have been arrested, shaken off. This is why Bataille can claim of desire with all its force that it is an "impotent, quivering yearning."[2] The lover has taken all the risks and laid bare his desire before the boundary of its eventual satisfaction or happiness. Satisfaction and happiness would come later if they come at all. For the Song, those are delayed, so we get a virtual freeze-frame of lovers in the yearning pain of their passion. Some of the expressions of want in the Song may be uttered outside the hearing of the other and so are technically soliloquies. But they have this insistence rhetorically; the other must respond. Luckily, they each do, and so the Song is a collection of dialogues, loosely defined in all the quick shifts of time and location in the Song. The discourse of physical want has as its primary subject the lover's emotional state, but it *rhetorically* involves the beloved with its insistence on a reply. It sets the speaker up for intimacy or stalled yearning and lovesickness. There is for desire no turning back at this point. There is only the question of its direction.

Desire itself can be frightening, erupting anywhere, catching humans off guard; it is miraculously chaotic. It does not heed reason's claims, nor can it be charted. In fact, when the lover claimed his heart was ravished, he spoke of this devastation of reason. The "heart" in Hebrew thought is the organ of the intellect, not, as it is for us, of love. So his ravished heart is testimony to desire's having pinned reason. Desire darts and zigzags, lays low and then pounces without rhyme or reason. Hence, it is understandable why cultures and religions would attempt to control sexual desire through some means, be it shame, silence, legislation, or moralizing. The Song details the twists and turns, pains, and pleasures of desire and makes no attempt to force it onto a safe trajectory. Rather, desire is left in its raw form: insistent, erratic, and even mischievous. It explodes through all the senses: sight, scent, touch, taste, and hearing. The lovers' senses are stimulated and taxed by the pressure of love. Both lovers are simply bombarded with the images, smells, tastes, and sweet voice of the other and are doing their poetic best to fight back, to speak of their experience. His name is "perfume poured out" (1:3), her cheeks are "comely" (1:10), his "voice is sweet" (2:14), her scent is like henna, saffron, cinnamon, frankincense, and basically any other spice the man can recall (4:13-14). You can tell he is reaching, desperate to describe her unique, enchanting scent. And there is something maddeningly elusive about a lover's scent. Hence, even if he were to become well versed in additional spices and herbs, we intuit that her scent would still retain its mystery. Scent seems to be the sensory memory that lasts the longest.

Desire is wild. It slips out, zeroes in, circles and bandies about, retreating and erupting all over again. We pretend it is on a leash of our own design, but we are fooling ourselves. Love exposes that lie; love tells us we have been kidding ourselves all along. Desires have never been ours to control. We erect conventions, custom, laws, and morality to corral desire, but it runs free. Like the Song's gazelle, seen running, prancing on spices, slowing to enjoy lilies and a peek through our window, desire stays free in the Song, roaming at will, an undomesticated presence in life.

Desire is also subversive and furtive because it comes in with the mundane. Here in the man's desire, it erupts over a foot in a sandal:

> How beautiful are your feet in sandals,
>   O noble woman! (7:1)

Thousands of ancient toes in everyday sandals trekked past this man in a lifetime of biblically clad people. Yet he still notices hers and is subdued. Here the woman enters the rank of nobility simply for strolling past him just like everyone else. How many times, for example, has the lover seen the woman's foot in its same old sandal before its devastating uniqueness could show forth? She gets to be queen for a day in someone's loving eyes! That is desire's true miracle. It is free, unexpected. It takes the un-noticed mundane—a sandaled foot—and lights it up for the breathtaking beauty that it really is for the first time. The lover's view was simply of two feet, ten toes, leather stretching against flesh, tiny working muscles and bones, and it was enough to ignite his passion.

The rest of her body would likely have been hidden in a robe for modesty, but the feet would have been safe enough to expose in mixed company, in public, given the hot, Mediterranean climate. The woman's feet, then, offer him the chance of flesh, some nakedness against leather, and they are tantalizing. How beautiful indeed is that singular miracle of the mundane. And how fitting a symbol a sandaled foot is for desire's partial constraint within poetry—restrained by leather, yet free to the air. It is aired, muscled, sweating, and only partly harnessed by these levels of speech.

Affective description for the lover, of course, is never just a matter of getting the poetry right. Desire is felt in the soul. Hebrew uses the word "soul" to talk about the self, and this Song especially does so. The soul is what is in love. Hence, the woman refers to her lover not by name but as him "whom my soul loves" (1:6; 3:1-4). The soul is the life force in Hebrew, and so its desire, who it loves, is unmistakably attached to notions about the quality of one's existence. The woman's life force is marked through and through by her love for this man. In her case, it is not simply her romantic interest alongside other life interests. Instead, it characterizes the whole of her existence.

This notion of the soul as the life force and the seat of desire is elsewhere a key religious theme in the Bible. In Deut 6:5, the Great Commandment is to "love the Lord your God with all your heart, with all your soul, and with all your might." It is a command to direct all of one's desire and energies toward God. Love from the soul, in these texts, is understood to be comprehensive. It defines the individual's life. For Deuteronomy, then, that soul-infused love marks the individual as a lover of God. For the Song of Songs, the woman's soul is wholly invested in her lover.

Such wholesale commitment, in which one's love defines one's existence, entails considerable psychological risk. There is a risk of loss of self in love at two junctures at least: once in love, in the loosening and melding of boundaries between two people, and once in lust, as desire rips the person beyond his or her own self. Orgasm is only the most visible form of this threat. It is something we both want and fear, the self's dissolution, if only for a moment. It is at once terrifying and exhilarating.

In desire, one does not get off free, without risk, involvement, pain, or destabilization. The woman grasps desire's cost, as she is in its grip, and, as if to prepare, asks, "sustain me with raisins, refresh me with apricots, for I am faint with love" (2:5). Later, at the mere sound of his voice, her soul fails her (5:6). This is a woman who has been with him before and has languished in the waiting, in the want. For his part, her eyes continue to "overwhelm" him (6:5), and he wants that sensation. He is ravished; she is faint. These two no longer simply want to meet up or even make love. They want the furthest abandon in their union, to "be drunk with love" (5:1). They want the dissolution of autonomous selves that such all-consuming love offers. This reckless want, beyond the self's safety, is also the mark, for Bataille, of effective eroticism. He notes: "The whole business of eroticism is to destroy the self-contained character of the participators as they are in their normal lives."[3] For the lovers in the Song, this is not normal life, but a life driven by want.

A question worth posing at this point is, Why unravel human wants at all, if they can cause such explosions of emotions and pain for all to see? Why not stay busy or at least move at a clip through desire? Why does the Song linger, indulge, taste, and torment in its descriptions? Because these moments are the miracles of life, committed each day. These explosions of poignancy, smell, possibility, and seeking remind us that this is a pulsating lustful life we are living, that our senses can be guides. The very natural images of the Song remind us that miracles are not from wizards or burning bushes or even raising the dead. They are— get this—a woman's foot in a sandal, a blossoming vineyard in an oasis. She, the woman, *is* an oasis, as one's lover always is, in a desert of tedium, disappointments, frustrations, and still more hardship.

The eroticism in the Song zeroes in on a desire that does not get relieved. It has the blunt, annoying force of shaking a reader awake, compelling us to feel our own desires, to ignite them. It is a rhetorical text at its finest, that is, material meant to elicit a response. For in the end, we lose the leisure to merely sympathize with the lovers in some been-there complicity of past memories.

Instead, when the Song is finished with us (and not we with it), we have come to empathize with these people caught by want.[4]

The woman wants to go to a vineyard, where, she says to her lover, "there I will give you my love" (7:12). There is no real room for either misunderstanding or coyness here. First they must "catch . . . the little foxes that ruin the vineyards" (2:15), but even that delay does not dampen their delight. Foxes were considered pests to ancient vineyards in particular. They are no ugly scavengers desperate for any food for survival, however, like ravens and wild dogs. Instead, foxes are the tiny, feisty, quick connoisseurs of the scavenger set, who have somehow passed on the information to their species that vineyards are simply the best. We call them pests, but these little animals listen to their own desires. The animals, the gazelles and the foxes, are not present simply as charming pastoral props to the Song's poetry of love. They are not added simply for zoological flavor. They stand in as clues about desire. Grapes are simply the most valued and most enjoyed treats in the entire landscape of ancient Israel, and one thing that humans in love and foxes can agree on is "let us go into the vineyards." And certainly, we all can become pests while yearning for life's pleasure. A simple, blossoming vineyard is still a miracle of pleasure, even with its forgivable, ruffian foxes, scampering in to get their own mouth-sized stolen treasures of pleasure.

The celebration of the Song is of these vineyards, even with the knowledge that foxes can ruin them, and of desire, which is both delicious and destabilizing for the self. There is a realism about desire throughout this brave Song. It includes the costs and irritabilities of desire, all the pesky annoyances of yearning for another who is nowhere to be found. There is, too, the ever-present possibility that love can be ruined, as this fox phobia illustrates. For it acknowledges that little, unseen invasions can be dismantling love even as it is enjoyed and cherished. The end of love is the risk of desire, the sense that the ardent search and yearning and the scintillating heartache for another can just end.

The Song is a celebration of life in its quotidian pleasures, foxes and all. Desire is voluptuous, insistent, mercurial, careless, overpowering, and overwhelming. It is reckless, sincere, wild, a scavenger of sorts itself. It will not be tamed, restricted, retaught, or civilized out of its potency. It always brings with it trepidation and thrill in the irresistible chance to feel more alive for as many moments as can be grabbed.

FRUIT AND SEX

One point that still needs to be made is that when the language of aesthetic appreciation of the beloved gives way to the lover's own expressed want in the Song, the primary metaphors change. They had been zoological, agricultural, and architectural, but now shift primarily to horticulture, that is, the cultivation of fruit. Affective description of want is more urgent than aesthetic appreciation, and so it makes sense that the metaphors would somehow need to change. The complimentary equations of eyes like doves, necks sleek as towers, cheeks red like pomegranates, and thighs firm as columns, for example, no longer work for this emotional plane of desire. They say nothing overt about desire's impact on the soul. These familiar metaphors cease, while those pertaining to horticulture become prominent and telling, luscious and palpably erotic.

This shift in primary metaphors is significant to the Song's understanding of desire, yet remarkably goes unnoticed in the commentaries. We could well argue that the zoological and topographical images dwindle because they are visual images, and so are not as apt for conveying the internal emotional states, such as that of sexual longing. Leaping gazelles (2:9, 17; 8:14), goats on a mountain (4:1; 6:5), Lebanon and Carmel (7:4-5), all worked well for conjuring an image of the other as a visual object of desire, but not for the felt desire of the lover itself. And, also, one could add that architectural images such as ivory towers (3:4; 8:10), stone walls (8:10), and alabaster columns (5:15) are not much good for tracing the quickening pace of desire, precisely because they are stationary and under human design. Instead, the descriptions of felt want and of physical enjoyment entail movement—burgeoning, reaching, aching, leaning, ripening—and so require lively metaphors to match. In this respect, fruit cultivation is a particularly astute metaphoric field for depicting the slow movement and swelling of desire.

The use of agricultural imagery for description of sexual activity and desire is used throughout the ancient world, for Mesopotamia, Egypt, and Greece. Egypt even has a creation myth in which earth itself is woman and the male is a sky god coming down for intercourse. The Egyptian cosmogony, that is, the account of the world's beginning, is cast in agricultural terms, with sexual union as the horizon for creation.[5] In Greek mythology, too, agriculture figures prominently in descriptions of sex. Demeter, for example, the goddess of agriculture, is made love to by a mortal man in a "field plowed three times" (*Odyssey* 5.125-28), and agriculture comes to a halt on earth when her daughter Persephone is torn from her and bedded by Hades.[6]

Farming is a natural resource for sexual metaphors in antiquity, in part because it was nearly everyone's livelihood. And, too, farming shares some similarities with sex. The essence of agriculture is the successful manipulation of the land to yield food, while the essence of sexual congress also entails some manipulation in order to produce progeny. But the association between farming and sex functions on a much deeper level than just productivity. Because so much was at stake in ancient agriculture—namely, survival—the relationship of the farmer to his land was necessarily loving, anxious, and fraught with the emotional potentials of joy, relief, betrayal, and anger. In other words, ancient farming shared many of the same emotional qualities of an intimate relationship. The farmer's emotions were tied to his occupation, to the land, and to the elements. This was not a relationship he could ever afford to sever, and each year, his desires would be reenacted and teased by the uncertainties of farming.

With agricultural metaphors for sex, the triumph on the ground of a successful harvest and the attendant emotions were transferred to sexual procreation. The production of heirs is seen as replicating the farmer's success in the field, and a fiction is thereby created with the male being in primary control of this "harvest," even while it is the woman who gives birth. The ubiquity of these fictions in the ancient world, in fact, might, as Simone de Beauvoir argued, betray male anxiety over this fact of women giving birth.[7] Two conclusions about this construction of sexual imagery are immediately evident: (1) livelihood has provided the primary metaphoric field for sexual description in ancient texts, and (2) it has also given the full credit and initiative for sex to the farmer-male. Procreation was seen primarily as the result of male labor.

The dominant agricultural metaphor for sex in all of these ancient cultures is borrowed from the tasks of grain farming, specifically, plowing the field and depositing the seed. Mesopotamian sacred marriage songs, for example, describe sex with images of the woman as a field *in need* of plowing, and the man as the farmer who will plow and then deposit his seed in intercourse.[8] This is the case too for ancient Greece, where intercourse is depicted primarily in terms of plow agriculture.[9] And in ancient Israel, in a rather bleak moment for gender imagery, the boorish Samson accuses the Philistine men of having "plowed with my heifer," by which he means that they have slept with his wife (Judg 14:18). Here, it is true, the nameless woman gets to rise up from the level of the field, but only to serve as its work animal. The message, at any rate, is quite clear in sexual metaphors relying on grain farming: the man should be in sole control of his "plowing."

Hence, the plow metaphor works well to describe intercourse, particularly from the hardworking male's perspective. This kind of image sanctions both the goal of productivity and the relative passivity of the woman. But this may not be due simply to the sexism of the ancient mind-set. Page du Bois has noted that the association between farming and sex in antiquity resulted in a transfer of fear.[10] The farmer's fears over whether the earth was going to withhold from him in a year was added to the agricultural metaphor for sex. There was anxiety around sex with women, but it did not stem solely from misogyny.

Any feminist potential in such a metaphor, though, is nil, and we can see that it champions an androcentric viewpoint. Describing sex as a plow to the field means that the man is active, in charge, potent, and is generally representing culture as the adapting plow-endowed farmer; the woman is passive, inert, dependent, and is generally representing nature as a field that may or may not cooperate.[11] As such, the woman is also necessarily viewed as a potential difficulty, since she will have to be worked on to receive seed. The gift of life was assumed to have been within the male seed, only needing the field's cooperation. Blame for failure to conceive would naturally have gone to the field (the woman), not the diligent farmer (the man). This image presumably is not the kind of metaphor ancient women themselves would have used, at least exclusively, to describe themselves in sex, had they been writing texts. We cannot know for sure, though, since there are so few texts written by women in antiquity. With the Song of Songs, we are treated to a fresh portrayal of sex through agricultural imagery that does not render the woman as an inert field. In fact, it is so fresh and even startling a portrayal that many scholars contend that women must have written it.

The Song boldly employs agricultural metaphors drawn from fruit cultivation, with grapes, ripening, and juice, and nowhere is a field plowed. Economic context accounts for only part of this difference in figurative speech. The economies of Mesopotamia and Israel differed in that the former was largely grain-based, while the latter's was a threefold combination of grain, horticulture, and stockbreeding, characteristic of the Mediterranean lands. Still, this economic difference does not fully account for the contrasting metaphors of sexual longing: one in which intercourse is explicitly awaited, with the passivity of the woman obvious (as a field for planting); the other in which bodily female arousal is described (by means of engorged and darkened fruit). Nor does economic difference explain why Greece used primarily plow imagery in its use of agriculture for sexual metaphor, since it too shared the threefold Mediterranean economy of ancient Israel.

Hence, the Hebrew Song is clearly innovating in descriptions of sexual longing. It is mapping out a new domain for discourse on sex. In short, this discourse is about the intensifying of desire emotionally and physically, rather than its climax or consequence in reproduction.[12] Seed and procreation give way to ripening, engorgement, and taste. The lover does not say, for example, that the woman's love is "better than wheat in the sun that I have sowed," or even "your love is moister than the earth after a heavy rain." Instead, he claims that "your love is better than wine," fruit cultivation's highest gift. And the lovers' pleas for sex are not "let us be worn out by love" or "scorched by it as by the sun." They are instead the intoxicating, wet, lugubrious command: "let us be drunk with love" (5:1). The lovers want to be overwhelmed, pulled out of control, intoxicated through their lovemaking. They want to be inundated by love's gushing excitement in wine, sweet fruit (2:3), and lips "distilling liquid myrrh," (5:13); all descriptions, at least, of the increased secretions of arousal.

In one invitation or declaration of her own want, the woman invites the man to come with her to see "whether the grape blossoms have opened and the pomegranates are in bloom" (7:12). This interest in fruit is no idle curiosity for the woman, but instead helps her to decide their readiness for coupling, for "there I will give you my love" (7:12). Here the blossoms are signaling the fragile, sweet scents of sexual arousal. Again she beckons, expressing her physical want with the invitation to taste:

> I would give you spiced wine to drink,
> the juice of my pomegranates.

> Oh that his left hand were under my head
> and his right hand embrace me. (8:2-3)

Notice here the shift in pronouns, which intimates her wavering ability to concentrate under desire's spell. The surrender of the woman's juice and her yearning for the man's bodily embrace express how she asks for union with him. But there are other ways to convey the sentiment "take me!" even with grain imagery. "Plow me!" for example, would voice the woman's willing reception for lovemaking, much like Tina Turner's rendition of "Rock Me Baby" does today.[13] But here, tellingly, the woman does not enlist plow images. She speaks instead of her lust in horticultural terms. She is an active partner, the one dispensing the mixed wine and pomegranate juice.

Wine, like sex, has a dizzying, overwhelming effect. Adding spices to that wine makes it more exotic and mysterious to the taste than regular wine. Pomegranates, for their part, are a sexual symbol. Their juice is both sweet and tart, keeping the drinker poised between delight and a borderline bitter aftertaste. And the fruit itself is almost obscene upon opening. It is juicy, red, hard, and full of seeds, each of which happens to be the size and shape of a clitoris, and requires precision from the tongue. The embrace of head and torso that she longs for describes a full frontal embrace between the two, alluding, no doubt, to the sexual enjoyment allowed in such closeness. She may even be describing his gentle leading during lovemaking by recalling where his hands would be. We can be sure with her detailed description, at any rate, that the woman wants a good deal more than a bear hug. For she has yet to be convincingly coy about her desires. These images of fruit juice and fermented liquid, with added scents and tastes of spice, signify her *physiological* readiness, her longing itself. It is quite literally the woman's wetness. She is so ready for sex, in fact, that she *herself* is wine enough to drink, and delectable, enchanting, and rare as spiced wine.

Of Vineyards and Gardens

The viticultural imagery of grapes and wine aptly portrays a woman in a state of arousal and casts the male lover in a different role than that of plow farmer. The fruit images speak of the woman's desire, her longing and readiness for sex, but it nowhere renders her inert or dry like a field. Indeed, just the opposite. Her lover's role is not as plowman to a chancy, dry field. Instead, he becomes the agricultural equivalent of the vintner. Here, the farmer must work lovingly to bring the grapes to ripening, and then he will get to taste the yield. In effect, he has gotten the woman into this condition of ripening, engorging, and able to yield the most wine possible. Grapevines, by the way, only thrive with human cultivation: they yield only small, worthless berries when left untouched. Hence, the ripening fruit and vintner's anxious checking on its progress mirrors the increasing sexual excitement for both partners. This excitement takes labor, but a different sort from that of plow agriculture. These metaphors entail mutuality in the gentle cultivation of desire. Both the farmer and the grapes, as it were, have to be willing to put in the time for a successful cultivation.

Grape tending is tricky, sensitive, ongoing work. The farmer has much to do and must be attentive. If he does not act with care, consistency, love, and some luck thrown in for good measure, the resulting berries are little, hard, and sour, the very sour grapes about which biblical writers elsewhere threaten (Jer 31:29-30; Ezek 18:2). If, however, he manages to cultivate the vines with care, those same grapes become dark, soft, juicy, yielding, and delicious, and are able to produce a nectar worth drinking and fruit worth exploding in one's mouth.

Grapes, then, are the awaited delicious fruit from vineyards that will also yield wine. The pleasures they afford the ancient farmer are real and quite easily associated with the pleasures of an aroused woman. Grapes work on additional levels as well to depict sexual want in the Song. In 7:8-9, for example, the male lover desires the woman's breasts and uses grapes to convey that want. They seem to do double duty for both the sensation of touch and the delicious intoxication they can yield:

> Oh, may your breasts be like clusters of the vine
>> and the scent of your breath like apricots,
> and your mouth like the best wine,
>> flowing smoothly to me,
>> gliding over lips and teeth. (7:8-9)

Grapes, here, serve a multivalent function, as something the man yearns to hold and squeeze in their ripening tautness, and as something that yields the best wine for his lips and teeth to enjoy. The association of grapes with breasts cannot be a literal correspondence, obviously, because grapes are small and there are 8–10 grapes per vine cluster, and no one would want to crush them. Grapes function as an allusion in the Song. An allusion differs from a euphemism in that it does not offer a one-to-one substitution of two features, but instead maintains some ambiguity.[14] In other words, allusions, by their nature, do not quite fit literally. Instead, characteristics between the two features are loosely compared. Here, certain characteristics of grapes qualify them for association with a woman's breasts; namely, they are cool, smooth, darkened, ripening, and taut. Grapes signify all the man's murky desires in enjoying the woman, and may reflect as well his oral pleasure in tasting and nibbling at her breasts.

This kind of desire for the enjoyment of the woman certainly goes vastly beyond the urge to plow or procreate. It is a more egalitarian description of sexual desire in the sense that the man has had to cultivate the woman's desire to this stage of copious liquid production, and the woman's arousal has been given center stage. Given the image of plowing a field, it might not even have occured to an ancient poet that her arousal would be important. Here in the Song, it is central. The man is catering to and cultivating the woman's arousal, and the woman's excitement is privileged with the use of so many oral images. And this attention to her wet excitement is not dropped once we move to overt descriptions of sexual behavior. The woman's arousal, in other words, is not simply foreplay to actions of consummation that come later. Bluntly, the man is not just being nice to her in order to ensure his own pleasure. Instead, the pleasures of lovemaking and of sensual desire are cast as primarily oral, tactile, and olfactory delights in this Song. Lovemaking itself is cast as a complex of bodily enjoyments and is not restricted to coitus.[15] This lovemaking is a veritable feast for the senses in which both genders equally share in all its delights.

Sexuality, in antiquity and today, is about far more than genital sex, as these horticultural metaphors adroitly demonstrate.[16] It is even about more than bodily sensations. Sexuality includes the desires for genital pleasure and attractions to others, but it is also more generally about our condition as separate beings in the world. Sexuality is our sense of ourselves as sexual beings and is our urge to go outside ourselves toward another. As James B. Nelson and Sandra P. Longfellow argue in their formative work *Sexuality and the Sacred*, sexuality is the

> basic eros of our humanness that urges, invites, and lures us out of our loneliness into intimate communication and communion with God and the world.[17]

Sexuality projects us into the world as living participants and we, since we are not alone, always have to negotiate our spacing with others. From this condition stems desire, the urge to go beyond oneself. And this urge is writ large and long in the Song of Songs. It has this propulsion toward the other, bordering on obsession at times, and it uses the teeming world at hand for descriptive aids.

This display of imagery says worlds more about desire than a plow metaphor could. The lively presence of fruit can well capture desire's slow process of growing and ripening. It recalls, as well, the time put into such cultivation and the dance of waiting and hoping and fearing. This is why vintners are often in love with their vineyards, and why they often speak in relational terms about them. Isaiah's song (Isa 5:1-7) is God's song about his beloved, the vineyard. A woman as vineyard, then, would mean for a vintner-farmer that she takes that much time and care to woo. She, in other words, *must* be happy in order for there to be a bountiful harvest of pleasures.

This kind of attention or focus is not at all apparent with grain farming. Grain farming requires skill, knowledge, and a desire to take care of the land, obviously, but not the tender, ongoing passion of cultivating a vineyard. For the grain farmer, there is no love lost for the field once plowing is accomplished. What is desired is the product, the wheat. Once the ground yields that product, a farmer can all but ignore it for the half year until he needs it again for plowing. With a vineyard, the product is also desired, but the vintner cannot love it and leave it once the grapes come in. His care must continue throughout the year. The vintner must continue to tend the vines and keep them happy, as it were, so that the next year's harvest will be as good. The care of vineyards requires a continuity and patience that differs from grain farming and is an apt, even daring metaphor for arousing a woman. In modern terms, compared to a grain field, the vineyard was "high-maintenance" and worth the effort. An aroused woman, from the lover's perspective, is as well.

The use of these fruit metaphors for sex, then, is vastly different from plow imagery, both with respect to the woman's own participation and to desire's fluctuating nature. The vintner/lover has to bother to get to know what the woman wants and what arouses her. And astonishingly in this Song, he comes to even appreciate her arousal *as an end in itself,* one that eclipses any goal of penetration or procreation! Her arousal, as we noted, is not even viewed as something preparatory to later enjoyment, a mere foreplay to the real play coming. Instead, this lover gets to know how the woman works and comes to take pleasure in her very bodily arousal. Her arousal comes to stimulate his own want, which he then voices as an urgent yearning to drink of her sweet excitement.

Here, for example, he describes her mouth:

> Your lips distill nectar, my bride
> Honey and milk are under your tongue. (4:11)

This lover cannot wait to taste the harvest of love's desire. He cannot wait to drink her up, taste her salivating mouth, and exchange bodily fluids. His own sexual want is cast here completely in terms of oral enjoyment, with her lips, tongue, and the secreting treasures of her mouth.

This fluid inventory of the woman's mouth is an interesting expression of sexual want, because it is "milk and honey," rather than the ubiquitous wine of the Song. It signifies the tastes, the swirling secretions, and a startling mixture of both sweetness and nourishment. The image of milk and honey is innocent, with associations of health, motherhood, and sweetness. Yet its texture has a faintly lurid aspect as well, as it is a viscous, off-white substance akin to ejaculate. It is clear and opaque, thick and oozing; a substance that would both flow and stain. The man, of course, might not have this allusion in mind in his description. But his subconscious might. Honey is often associated with the sexual enjoyment of women even today. One thinks of Van Morrison's classic song "Tupelo Honey" as an example of a compliment to a woman and an allusion to the fierce oral enjoyment of her. If a woman truly is "as sweet as Tupelo honey," one does not need to make the pilgrimage to Mississippi to catch the salacious allusion to oral pleasure. And in the erotic film *9½ Weeks,* honey and milk are two items (along with spritzer) pulled from the fridge to douse Kim Basinger's character.

That the woman's mouth contains milk and honey is clearly meant to be a compliment. It is also an expression of the lover's own desire to taste and kiss his lover. This is inescapably an allusion to what we nowadays call French kissing, for the mouths have to be open in order to experience the taste sensations and tongue. His description, too, implies that he has been there before. His desire for her mouth is fueled by the memory of a previous experience of tasting and kissing her. He knows what is under that tongue, has experienced its sweet, chalky taste, and wants more.

But in addition to these physical qualities, the description "milk and honey" stands out as an essential biblical leitmotif for the promised land. As God declares at the beginning of Exodus:

> So I have come to rescue them from the land of the Egyptians and to bring them up out of that land into a good and spacious land, a land flowing with milk and honey.
>
> —Exod 3:8

The use of the phrase "milk and honey" is then both sexual and tied to religious memory. The poet has taken a phrase of theological promise—"a land flowing with milk and honey"— and transferred it to a description of sexual pay dirt, in the oral pleasures of kissing. Now a woman's mouth becomes what flows with milk and honey. This is a stunning overhaul of religious imagery, until we recall that both spiritual and sexual yearning can wreak a similar emotional and physiological havoc on an individual. Uncertainty, periodic torment, and lingering in the anticipation of satisfaction mark both these kinds of yearning.

It is important to remember that when the people of Israel were led out of Egypt in the book of Exodus, they were not only being rescued from harsh slavery. They were also being led into a delicious, enjoyable promised land. Pain and pleasure stood side by side in this foundational story of a people's identity. So, with milk and honey under her tongue, the beloved woman of the Song becomes the site for the lover's most cherished dreams and pleasures. The poet takes this leitmotif of natural desire—for a land promised by God, and flowing with milk and honey—and employs it for personal, sensual desire, for an intimacy close enough to describe what is under the beloved's tongue.

With that one change in perspective, the poet can suggest with this Song that there is no longer any need to travel or persist anymore toward one's dreams and pleasures. One even need no longer just hope for them, or worse, die hoping for them. Instead, the poet asserts that the task might just be to enjoy the personal, small chunks of one's promised land right here and now, under a lover's tongue. Such confident celebration is either faith or naïveté, but it is obviously not just about sexual desire anymore. For this conviction about where dreams and pleasures lie—off in the distant future or right here in the present—applies to all types of yearning, including the spiritual.

Theologically, a promised land flowing with milk and honey need not remain a dream, or worse, the lie of a god. Nor need it be somewhere out there, off in the distance. According to the poet of the Song, it can be present right here, under his lover's tongue, which he had better kiss and enjoy. The contrast with the Exodus is striking. The poet hints at a shift in attitude about yearning, in which dreams and pleasures are understood to be present in the here and now of life. The story of the Exodus was also one long tale of an arduous attitude shift for the people. They left everything they knew, even if it was slavery, and walked out into a desert with just the dream of a promised land. That promise of a future land forged their yearning, but it remained unfulfilled for all but two survivors, Joshua and Caleb. Everyone else, Moses included, died in the desert with their yearning, never having tasted of the promised land.

The bold poet of the Song has indeed sexualized Israel's most cherished national and theological leitmotif—a land flowing with milk and honey. Consider the effrontery if a poet today were to sexualize images, say, of the Lord's Prayer or maybe even "America, the Beautiful" for his lover. It would be potentially shocking, sharp, and confusing, in the way that rap lyrics often can be. This sexualization of a theological trope, however, is not necessarily reductive or offensive, especially since lust and spiritual hunger share an intensity that pushes an individual beyond his or her limits. This poetic use of the image of milk and honey is not a desecration of a theological ideal. Instead, it works to achieve a sacralizing of love. The sexual yearning of two lovers for each other can instruct about the yearning for one's dreams and pleasures in life. At the same time, it can instruct about the *meaning* of those dreams in life, and this kicks the theme onto the theological domain, even if God is nowhere named in the Song.

For a biblical woman, there can be no higher flattery than being likened to the promised land. As an expression of human desire, too, the inventiveness and association are brilliant. For the Exodus is a root tradition, fundamental to Israel's self-identity, and it is a tradition about yearning for a lifetime. The people hear this promise and go out into the desert for forty years, traveling and complaining, losing faith and gaining it again; not because they are so bad, but because the yearning between slavery and freedom is so trying. It shatters all their emotional reserves until they even moan that they would rather just get back to Egypt and enjoy the comforts of the known, even if it is slavery.

It is really a story about the journey less than it is about the arrival, since entry into the land does not occur until the book of Joshua. So it is with the Song's take on desire. It narrates the journey toward intimacy with the heightening of desire, but without ever getting there. In both biblical accounts, the participants are fundamentally changed, scorched, scoured, broken, and rebuilt by desire—for a promised land and a lover. These desires embolden the human spirit, force it out beyond its limits, comforts, and even doubts. The risk is for growth or regression. With growth, there will be ache and burn and something brand-new, unimaginable. With regression, there is a return to Egypt, or a decision that love is not worth the pain. This Song is homage to the journey itself, the miracle that humans do desire outside themselves.

Sustained Longing

Part of the power of sexual desire lies in its going unsatisfied. Left to itself, with no hope of satisfaction, desire is forged and polished, stressed to reveal its intricacies. While reading erotica that slowly works to a consummation offers a vicarious sexual satisfaction, erotica that has the diligence to remain within desire itself can offer a satisfaction beyond the sexual. It can start to get at the true and terrible mysteries lodged within the human heart, and offer insight into desire's nature.

The troubadour tradition of courtly love is similar to the Song of Songs with its focus on the sexual longing itself rather than on consummation. In this courtly love tradition, knights of eleventh- to twelfth-century France would woo estate women for small increases in intimacy, but sexual intercourse was never the goal. Rather, mining the emotions involved in sexual desire was more the point, even the linguistic game, and it seemingly offered a poetic means through which to normalize or contain desire. The poets could make overtures to married women, safely within the conventions of their love poetry. Articulating, sounding out, even relishing desire's emotions was the point, as it is in our much earlier Song. Wooing was a discipline of self-possession, about loving without possessing the beloved. For the troubadours, this was a practical necessity, since the woman was married, and adultery had severe consequences.[18] Poetry became the avenue for pushing at love's limits, its crevices, to speak of desire's internal impact.

Diane Ackerman's description of the point of courtly love can stand for that of the Song of Songs as well. It bears quoting in full since this logic of desire differs so much from our own capitalist-influenced sense of acquisition, goals, and payoffs. She notes that the

> essence of courtly love was protracted excitement, a delirium of gorgeously unbearable longing. Only by staying wholly infatuated, damp with sublimated erotic passion, could one mine one's emotions inexhaustibly.[19]

That indeed is sacrifice for art! It describes well the Song— one of "gorgeously unbearable longing." Obviously, staying in a state of perpetual arousal took what Ackerman terms a "sensuous discipline, a voluptuous rigor that took patience and skill, and it weeded out anyone who just wanted quick sex."[20] Our text in like manner weeds out anyone wanting a quick, lurid peep at ancient arousal. For the language of desire is about the mystique and power of passion more than its release.

The passion in desire means, inevitably, that there will be suffering. For the troubadours, their love was necessarily unrequited, since they were displaying their talents for wooing to married women. In the Song, the lovers are also separated throughout, but it dispenses with the illusion that were they only able to get together, their desires would be satisfied. These literary conventions for making union impossible are artificial, but they are not dishonest. These means enable the poets to speak on desire and speak on the hard truth of the impossibility of its satisfaction. They work the anticipation to its highest pitch, and then drag it around to talk it through. So this is not pornography, but it is unbearable and gorgeous wisdom, which slows down to witness right when longing becomes impossible for most of us. Bataille even argues that all love involves suffering, because it is a quest for the impossible. He notes that on some unconscious level at least, we know that even union will partly disappoint, and that dark, unspoken awareness lends "frantic intensity" to desire.[21] For Bataille, the periodic separations from one's lover act as practice sessions for coping with this larger disappointment. We grieve in both the separations and the realization that intimacy itself is intermittent. Since we prefer to romanticize love, this insight is threatening.

The Song, however, does not romanticize love or shirk from its inherent pain. It sends satisfaction to a deeper, trembling, muted realm than that of sexual congress. On the premise that desire configures everything within the human heart, not only our sexuality, but also our dreams, sentiments on life, and our spiritual curiosity, the Song gives voice to our internal worlds. Paradoxically, that is both unbiblical, since internal worlds are not generally depicted, and intensely biblical, since yearnings, the human hunger, and striving beyond one's self are what predicates belief in an unseeable God.[22] What the writers think about their God, their lives, their land, and their wives is all interwoven desire for them. Desire for God, for life, for a land they see as promised has compelled much of their biblical writing.

Most of the Hebrew Bible material is collected in the exilic period, that is, when the people were deported to Babylon and had lost the home they loved: the land, Temple, Jerusalem, their farms, the villagers, and family members. The biblical text itself, then, is in some deeply poignant way *entirely* a rebound affair. The displaced survivors were stunned and stung by the heart-wrenching loss of *everything* they held dear, and this Bible was their triumphant coping strategy, their way to resurrect their love. So, a Song about delayed or frustrated desire in the form of two lovers (one unseen) is a necessary and adroit adaptation to a subtle theological condition. It captures in part what it has felt like to live without the felt presence of their loved God.

Sexual love remains a yearning throughout the Song of Songs and is never consummated.[23] Hence, the separation of the two lovers is essential to the book's thematic design. The man's separation is achieved by his viewing the woman as *inaccessible*. For example, he describes her neck as a tower, with a necklace of a thousand shields hanging off it (4:4). This is part of his compliment to her, but it is nevertheless a revealing one. For towers were part of the fortification systems of Israelite cities, used for lookout and defense. So, too, a necklace of a thousand shields suggests a fairly strong defense system, namely, of a thousand infantry men manning the tower. In addition, it may reveal the lover's insecurity over the woman's many other suitors: a thousand armed men may have beaten him to her. On both scores, then, one thousand is certainly a formidable factor as he assesses his own chances for union. The man sees the woman as a military target, and a daunting one at that. She is, to him, heavily armed, fortified, perhaps indeed literally impenetrable.[24]

To his credit, the man nevertheless makes a pass at the woman, but does so in language that continues to reflect his belief in her inaccessibility. His odds, *in his own mind,* are not very good. He asks her to come from Lebanon, from Mount Hermon—lands outside of Israel—and to come from the dens of lions and leopards—wild animals (4:8). It is clear from his invitation to sex that foreign lands and nondomesticated animals render her inaccessible to him. An Israelite would naturally steer clear of foreign, enemy territory and the presence of dangerous carnivores. His invitation, then, is only apparently bold, for it betrays a tentative caution or even hopelessness on his part. In its spirit, it is really a confession of his own diffidence, that he simply cannot get to the woman if she is so far away and guarded by packs of wild animals. In terms of asking her out on a date, it is akin to our most resistible query, "You wouldn't want to go out with me, would you?" Although he may have meant to stress her exotic otherness, rhetorically his invitation is a self-sabotage, an inside job.

A little further on, the man describes the woman as a locked garden, full of scents, with water flowing, yet locked (4:12). Since gardens were outdoors in ancient Israel, protected, at most, from animals by a stone wall or hedge, they were unlikely to have had a lock. His description of one, then, reflects more the frustration of his pleasure than a feature of Israelite farming. The woman herself *is* a garden, an aroused woman, teeming with all kinds of scents (4:10, 14), plenty of fruits (4:13), and "waters of life" (4:15), but he cannot gain entry. *His* yearning is, then, forged—both strengthened and frustrated—by the perceived inaccessibility of his lover.

The woman's sustained yearning, for her part, is born of something else: the man's *absence.* She simply cannot find her lover. Twice she looks for him in the streets and does not find him, but only the city guards (3:2-4; 5:6-7):[25] once, when she asks where he will be, he teases that she must try and find him (2:8); and once, in a dream sequence, he vanishes before she can open the door and let him in, before they can unite (5:6). Her yearning, then, is sustained by the man's absence. Her boldness during these absences is stunning and is elsewhere matched in the Song. Indeed, her statements of yearning are overall more direct than his, she relies less on metaphoric images, or better, knows when to drop them in preference for candor. She makes such un-coy statements as, "Let me give my love to you" (7:12); "I am sick with love" (2:5; 5:8); "Oh that he were embracing me" (2:6; 8:3); "Let him kiss me with the kisses of his mouth" (1:2). Her desire is consistently voiced, repeated, vivid, and insistent.

The man also becomes direct at points, but infrequently.[26] For example, he confesses, "I am trembling, you have made me as eager for love as a chariot driver is for battle" (6:12).[27] Technically, this is direct; it is even about his subjective condition of desire. But it is still distancing. For while his own passion is unmistak-able in the chariot image, we wonder what else the woman could be but a walled city he wants to breach in battle. Twice he invites her to come with him (2:10; 4:8) with descriptions of the coun-tryside all but distracting from his proposition. In 2:10, for ex-ample, he invites her to come away with him, and then proceeds to describe the seasons, flowers, fig trees, and vines, before con-cluding, oh yes, that her face is lovely.

This is beautiful language and complimentary to the woman, but as a description of the desire that motivates the man's invita-tion, it is tame. In 4:8, geographical names of distant lands are enlisted as the woman's imagined locales: Lebanon, Amana, Senir, Hermon. Oddly, his interest in her is almost rendered secondary. He provides a descriptive itinerary that dispenses with the need to search for her. There is no initiative on his part, only a litany of distant lands. Such poetic detail adds, of course, to the overall pas-toral beauty of the Song, but it detracts from the insistence of the man's yearning. His desire ought to have propelled him to get out there and search for his lover, as the woman's desire did. Instead, he seems content to list the names of her potential sightings.

At another point, the man utters a third proposition via one of the woman's dreams: "Open to me, my love" (5:3). But that assertiveness evaporates in the dream-laden night, as he disappears before she can accept and open herself for him. Obviously, the man cannot be faulted for something that occurs in the woman's dream, yet it nevertheless reveals her perception of him as one who disappears. The Song, at times, is a frustrated game between the two lovers of He said/She said, with the woman coming out overall as the more efficient communicator.

The two lovers describe checking out their lovemaking spots as well. And this device, too, is a way to prolong and intensify their yearning. He invites her to come out from the clefts in the rock, so they can go prepare the vineyard where they would make love (2:14-15). She invites him into his garden (4:16). Together, they go to see if the vineyard flowers have blossomed, as this, she announces, will be where "I will give you my love" (7:12). Later, she invites him into her house and proceeds to describe what she will do with him there (8:2).

The scenes, with the exception of her house, are all outdoors, and center in the vineyard. Presumably, then, these sites for lovemaking would all be beyond the city walls. If so, it champions desire's resistance to being contained or domesticated, as a counter to Jerusalem and its city guards. Francis Landy argues that the Song, with its preference for rustic pleasures, may represent a subversive critique of the civilized world.[28] By describing the sites of their anticipated coupling, the lovers can further relish their want, rather than satisfy it.

The sexual longing is sustained through one other means as well, and this is in the details of their preparing to be with one another. This is similar to the scoping out of potential sites in that the anticipation of pleasure is highlighted. But now the attention is drawn to the body rather than the location. Preparing the body for an anticipated sexual encounter is a way to sustain desire and siphon off some of its urgency. Preparations, after all, give one something to do while waiting. Much time is taken with dress, perfume, and any accoutrements of lovemaking, such as oils, wine, and the like. Hence, oils and spices figure prominently in the Song. They add to the allure and summon desire in the other. She, for example, finds that his "anointing oils are fragrant, your name is perfume poured out" (1:3). This is one classy compliment on her part. The mention of his very name is a wafting fragrance. He has got to feel good hearing that, and she is clearly smitten. His very name coats her like perfumed oil. She also recalls of him that

> My beloved is to me a bag of myrrh
>   that lies between my breasts. (1:13)

He has become for her the very source of scent as she remembers being in his embrace. Myrrh does seem to be the dominant scent mentioned in the Song, and it is used for both lovers (1:13; 3:6; 4:6, 14; 5:5, 13). This may well indicate that myrrh was used in lovemaking contexts, whether it be in some oil used or on the bed, as it is in Prov 7:17.

If "his cheeks are like beds of spices, yielding fragrance" (5:13), this may evince the use of some sort of cologne for the man. Later, he notices that the woman's breath smells like apricots. The attention to scents is clearly given in order to compliment the other. At the same time, the scents are reminders of the lovers' familiarity with one another. She has been intimately close to those cheeks, enjoying the fragrance and taste. It also may reflect a practice of hygiene or beautifying. The man could well have applied some sort of scented oil to those cheeks, and the woman might have just gone ahead and eaten an apricot to keep her breath smelling fresh and sweet. We are before the time of marketed aftershave and breath mints, yet can glimpse the effort of these ancient lovers to enhance their appeal.

There is as well some evident ingenuity in these features. They have selected certain spices over others to combine with oil and/or scatter on a bed and have addressed the issue of bad breath with fruit. All of this effort to describe the eventual place and ready one's body for sex are ways to prime the anticipation of pleasure. There are surely moments in lust when the sheer anticipation is itself a pleasure too, albeit a sharp one. A lover wants union with the other; there is no doubt about that in matters of love. But at the same time, there is an exquisite dividend in the anticipation itself. The poet hones right in on that exquisite pleasure of waiting. In a sense, this chapter has done the same thing, by delaying discussion of the third type of language, that of the physical impact of desire, where it gets most sexually explicit. So let us turn now to the language of sexual arousal in the Song.

5

"Drunk with Love"

AROUSAL AND THE ANTICIPATION OF PLEASURES

The attention of the Song remains throughout on the feeling and impact of desire, rather than on any of its expected outcomes. But since sexual desire propels the two lovers toward each other as the Song keeps them apart, it is natural to wonder how the two do envision their eventual union, for this union is what fuels and tortures their desire. These imaginings constitute the third discourse of desire, that of physical arousal. This chapter, then, is devoted to a discussion of how the man and woman view their arousal and its anticipated satisfaction. This language will depict how relief and satisfaction are imagined, and so, quite naturally, will be the most sexually explicit of the types of languages about desire in the Song. The lovers imagine their sexual enjoyment and by doing so fuel their longing for each other. Also, since this language describes the anticipated enjoyment more than it does the state of wanting, we can glimpse rather directly some of the pleasures of ancient life. The first section details the bodily arousal of the lovers. A second section examines the prominence of oral pleasures in the descriptions of sexual desire, and a third concentrates on the images of vineyards and gardens as sites for sexual pleasure.

The woman's voice, as we saw, is bolder, more direct in her longing than is the man's voice. It gets bolder still in the descriptions of the physical impact of desire, that is, sexual excitement. It is a charming, almost awkward voice at times, yet daring in its raw articulation of want. Note, for example, one of her first pleas to the man: "Draw me after you, let us make haste!" (1:4, read: "take me now"). In rendering her own bodily excitement, the woman's voice takes off and truly sings. She details her arousal in far greater length than does the man and with an honesty that is still startling today:

> My beloved thrust his hand into the opening,
> > and my insides ached for him.
> I arose to open to my beloved,
> > And my hands dripped liquid myrrh. (5:4-5)

This is explicit and indicates that the woman is fully conscious about and articulate about her ardent yearnings for sex.

The man's voice, in contrast, does not match the woman's as it had earlier, when detailing aesthetic appreciation. In the language of aesthetic appreciation, the man and woman were equal; they were able to keep pace with one another. Both traded compliments in a poetic flurry of images that functioned to indicate and celebrate their mutual interest. That type of discourse of desire, then, was egalitarian, mutual, balanced, and moving, as we glimpsed the two caught up in desire's wave. As desire travels through the levels of discourse, from flirtation to physical want to excitement, however, the man cannot keep up with the woman's desire. The woman's urgency is fueled, throughout, by her wanting, and that affects her speech. Hence, as noted in the previous chapter, there were occasions when mere grammar shifts in pronouns or redundancy might have evinced the woman's shaky concentration under such passion. In fact, at this point, the woman's speech describing sexual pleasures is carrying her desire. Hence, it is no longer solely descriptive, that is, language *about* desire. It has become, in an instant, fully evocation—language filled with the desire it is seeking to describe.

This chapter focuses primarily on the descriptions of the physical impact of desire on these two lovers in the Song, while the significance of the gender difference will be addressed in chapter 6. For now, I simply note the surprising, disproportionate descriptions of a woman in a state of arousal, in contrast to her male counterpart. It could be that the man is not portrayed in a state of arousal, while the woman is, for the benefit of an intended male audience, and so the book still feeds a sexual disparity—this time at the level of audience reception, rather than text. If so, then the biblical poets have found a way to plant pornography within the canon, as a kind of Trojan horse of lascivious delight. They have managed to provide a voyeuristic close-up of an aroused woman, and added a blatant pleasure to the exercise of reading Scripture. I believe, however, that nothing quite this cynical or simple is at work, even though there is a scintillating benefit to reading this Song that is inescapable and was noticed for centuries by monks and rabbis.

From the start, this Song was meant to be much more than pornography. It aimed to arouse the entire spirit of a reader, to elicit desires and make them conscious. Yearning might most clearly be driven toward sexual pleasure, but it need never be curtailed there. So, when we are given a glimpse of two lovers imagining their union, we are also witnesses more generally to how love and imagination mix to survive the too long periods of delayed gratification. Watching two people yearn to be with one another and not get together is heartbreaking, honest, and what much of life is given over to, the waiting and the hope. That is true of sexual desire and of all other kinds of desires in life, be they for a better life, more understanding, or less pain.

The man's description of the desired woman has brought him to the brink of physical longing, but not quite to arousal. He is undone by the yearning, make no mistake, saying to her baldly, as we noted in the last chapter:

> You have ravished my heart with a glance of your eyes,
> with one jewel of your necklace. (4:9)

Still, even this confessional, exhausted statement at once illustrates both the man's yearning and his distancing, for who in a heated state of arousal is really still paying attention to the jewelry? Desire gets reckless on the details as it progresses to excitement, hence clothes that were so carefully chosen for a key date end up strewn about the floor in a matter of minutes. This man is undone by the glance of her eyes, to be sure, but he is nevertheless still describing her physical attributes.

It is not that the man is more circumspect than the woman. It is, instead, a difference in the kind of expressions of desire; it is a qualitative difference in perspective. For the man does go to considerable lengths to describe the woman's physical arousal. He lacks neither the words nor the courage for such description, but he does not invest them to articulate his own state of arousal. He describes his lover as a lush garden, filled with all sorts of fruits and spices, and with plenty of water—first a spring, then a well, and finally the "waters of life" (4:12-15). This is the garden he most definitely wants to enter, but he views it as locked. This threefold water source—spring, well, waters of life—is partly poetic parallelism. Parallelism is a device used in Hebrew poetry whereby several synonyms of a noun are paired with a second term for emphasis. In this case, three terms for a water source are paired with the term "garden." The parallelism emphasizes water with its use of these three terms and is not literally suggesting three different sources from which it comes.

Still, Israel, geographically, is a semiarid region, and so any mention of a surplus of water in a biblical text is suspicious. Any surplus of water always has to be the result of human achievement and is never a natural occurrence. And this is the case here with the description of the woman as a lush garden. The multifaceted irrigation has been generated by human means, namely, a male lover who has elicited considerable female arousal.[1] For this woman is sexually excited to the point that she unleashes "waters of life" in her arousal, and in the process betters her garden—herself—with these waters.

There may even be a faint allusion to her desire for oral sex. In 5:5, her fingers are dripping with liquid myrrh as part of her aroused wetness. In 5:13, she says of him:

> His cheeks are like beds of spices . . .
> His lips . . . distilling liquid myrrh.

The man's cheeks are full of spice-like fragrances he elsewhere used to describe her vulva (4:13-14), and his lips have the very same spice mixture she used to describe her vaginal wetness. If this can be anything more than poetic coincidence, it may imply a memory of a previous oral encounter.

The male voice, overall, is gifted with detailing the ripening, lush, scent-filled, wet arousal of his lover—the woman's gushing readiness—but it remains solely an account of her arousal and not his own. And her arousal remains for him only fantasy, as he views even such a ready, lush, tantalizing garden as locked (4:12). What is striking about this description, in addition to the blunt championing of an aroused woman, is the lack of any reference to the man's own mounting excitement, even through his being denied entrance into the garden. He concentrates instead on describing her arousal with this threefold water source and impressively offers nine different spices to try and capture her personal, excited scent (4:13-14). There is, though, nothing about his own arousal, mounting, or penetration. There is no image at all of his physical excitement, say, as the key that could unlock the garden, or the hoe that could satisfy it. There is no phallic referent at all throughout the Song, and so it seems to be a poetic choice to allow the focus to remain on the female in a state of arousal.[2] The male is not forgotten or eclipsed by the woman. Rather, he never gets to the same aroused state as she does, so the phallus is truly unimportant for once. This focus on the woman's state of arousal, then, is physiological rather than ideological, since she is the lover shown as further gone in excitement than is the man.

This attention to her may not be such a clear-cut triumph for feminism, though, since it still leaves an aroused woman on display for eight chapters in a book to which males have had the primary access. Althaya Brenner goes so far as to suggest that the omission of the penis just draws more attention to it. She argues that its absence amounts to a spiritualization, where penis can transform into phallus, as the signifier of the real power and authority.[3] Her premise, in effect, is based on a kind of Wizard of Oz factor, where what is unseen is more terrifying and powerful than the wrinkled old mortal behind the curtain. And so it is with the absent penis here. It becomes more powerful by its absence. Brenner correctly notes that while there are descriptions, presumably of a woman's genital area, as a moist and scented garden, there is no corresponding metaphor for the male pubic area. She interprets this difference to be the result of one-sided protection of male genitalia.

While it is certainly the case that there is no phallic referent in any descriptions of the male's increasing physical arousal, there is not really a concentration on genitalia for either lover in the Song. The woman's arousal is portrayed in general terms of ripening, but it is not genitally explicit.[4] Instead, it remains clouded in the mystery and richness of metaphor. Her vulva is symbolized by the garden and the vineyard, but not in exacting fashion. There is one occasion in which the text might be referring to the woman's genitals:

> I had put off my garment;
>> how could I put it on again?
> I had bathed my feet,
>> how could I soil them? (5:3)

Now the term "feet" functions in Hebrew to denote feet, but it is also a euphemism for at least male genitalia (Isa 7:20; Ruth 3:7). In the present instance, the woman could well be speaking literally about her feet. Just as she disrobed, she would also naturally wash the feet of a day's buildup of dirt before retiring for bed. She seems to be weighing in her mind whether she wants to get up after having already and fully readied herself for bed. But it is also possible that she is using a double entendre here and, if so, is being fairly risqué. For the next verse has the lover's hand thrusting into her opening. If feet are serving double duty, then the plural "my feet" indicate her vaginal lips surrounding the opening into which she envisions he will thrust. Nowhere else is "hand" thought to be a euphemism for penis, but in this text, it is possible that both body part terms—feet and hand—are being used in innovative, risqué ways.[5]

We recall from chapter 4 that the man's separation from the woman is prolonged by his view that the woman is inaccessible, fortified, and locked, while the woman's desire is prolonged due to the man's absence. Since the male views the woman as inaccessible, his speech must remain at the level of longing. He could experience frustration at points, but his excitement is left in abeyance until it inevitably diminishes. He wishes he could get with her, he yearns to be with her, yet he sees himself locked out of that option. Such foreclosure clearly circumscribes his desire. It remains fervent, but does not get to yield to bodily arousal.

Since the woman views her lover as absent and absenting at key moments, her yearning, too, is prolonged, tortuous. At the same time, though, it is also propelled into arousal, since his presence is always expected. She pines for him with more hope than he can muster, simply given their difference in attitudes. She pines much closer to the edge of actually having him, since she views it as a possibility, and the language shifts to accommodate just how feverish her want has become. The woman actively tries to satisfy her longing by searching for her lover and dreaming of him. When she cannot get to him, with her arousal already piqued to the bursting point, she takes some pleasure in his absence, by herself. In this dream sequence, erotica undeniably at full blush, the woman's yearning blossoms into bodily arousal. For a demonstration of the power of Scripture, one should read the following passage slowly and aloud:

> I slept, but my heart was awake.
> Listen, my lover is knocking,

"Open to me, my sister, my love,
for my head is wet with dew . . ."
My lover thrust his hand into the hole,
    and my insides yearned for him,
I arose to open to my lover,
    and my hands dripped with myrrh,
my fingers with liquid myrrh,
    upon the handles of the lock.
I opened to my lover,
    but he was gone. (5:2-6)

There is really no need for figurative language here, for the poetry is palpably erotic. The possibility for both the man's head "wet with dew" and his hand being more than just these named body parts is in the air, of course. Indeed, perhaps the indecision behind metaphor choice registers again the heady abandon she feels in trying to describe the scene of one's own wet dream. If his "head" and "hand" are after all potential phallic sites, they occur within her dream sequence interchangeably, when her hurried point is surely "whatever . . . get in here!" For the ancient Greek, as Foucault noted, slumber was seen as a time when one is laid vulnerable to desires that ought to be resisted.[6] The night is important in this Song as well.[7] It invites sexual desires and teases them awake until the woman herself cannot sleep. But for the Hebrew poet, the desires are not resisted at all. Just the opposite!

Here too, in the woman's own account of herself, a lock figures in the description of a desired/desiring woman, as it had for the man when he viewed her as "a garden locked is my sister, my bride, a garden locked, a fountain sealed" (4:12). But notice the telling difference. The man views the lock as a barrier rendering his beloved inaccessible. Hence, his desire, his longing, has an element of futility to it, of surrender to its impossibility. He can give up, ease up on his search, linger in his want, in desire's holding pattern, never once asking to gain entry. But for the woman, this lock is not a barrier at all, as she anticipates his having already "thrust his hand into the hole." The lock on the door is shut, but only because she is too open, too excited, to manage unfastening it in time. Her hands are too slippery to get to the lock before her lover disappears. Her excitement is not frustrated at all; instead, it is so developed that it has diminished her very motor skills. Sexual excitement has overridden efficiency and fumbled the chance for sex as he flees too quickly.

Obviously, the man need not have been discouraged by her lock at all! Its (eventual) opening, in fact, signals the next stage in her bodily arousal. Notice in the passage quoted above that "open" occurs three times and is undoubtedly a double entendre for the door and the woman. This is one double entendre an Israelite would surely know. Exodus 22:16, for example, speaks about the consequences of having "opened" a virgin, and "enter" as a term for sex assumes the notion of the woman with an opening (Gen 16:2; Deut 25:5). The initial, mounting wetness in this erotic dreamscape gives way to the woman's further opening. The woman's lock is wet, her hands are dripping, the scent of myrrh abounds, as she opens in response to him: "I arose to open to my lover" (5:5-6). She has not barred her lover at all. Instead, he has left prematurely.

This passage, in essence, is a biblical wet dream of a woman. It is also an allusion to autoeroticism, the Bible's sole scene of masturbation, with the woman's hands and fingers involved, dripping with her own wetness, and the man vanishing. This copious moistness and repeated opening is the woman's desire and probable climax. The description of dripping fingers, wet on an opening lock, followed by still silence, is a not-too-cloaked reference to a woman's orgasm. This is quite startling and unexpected, especially for biblical fare. It is worth noting at this point that a woman's orgasm might have been more important in antiquity than we might assume. Even though procreation is not an attested goal in this Song, a woman's orgasm was considered instrumental for successful conception, at least in the West before the Enlightenment.[8] It is possible, then, that attention was paid in antiquity to a woman's orgasm, at least as insurance for procreation. This attention might have even resulted in male envy on occasion. Ovid, for example, cites a tradition about the prophet Tiresias being blinded as punishment for having said that women enjoy sex more than men.[9] The sentiment is revealing for an ancient patriarchal society. The power of the male is asserted by means of Tiresias's punishment for having uttered something so awful, but it is drastically compromised by the nature of his prophetic insight. For such a tale to even make sense, there must have been some male curiosity in the sexual pleasure of woman.

For now, what I wish to pursue is how the woman's arousal is described with this allusion, appropriately of liquid, moisture, and plenty of it. While that is an apt depiction of the physiology of a woman's sexual excitement, there is still the question of how her arousal has affected her lover and the audience. For an ancient Israelite, the abundance of liquid would inevitably summon up his own frequently taxed, latent, oral desires, given the semi-arid context in which he made his living. An advertisement for bottled water or Coca-Cola is much more tempting and alluring in places like the Middle East than it is in less arid places. It can truly stir the desire of bodily thirst to the point of pain in arid, hot climates. In like manner, the description of a woman's wet dream inevitably stirs the reader's sexual interest and elicits increased saliva as a response.[10] Reading this Song means coming to participate in at least this oral pleasure of a mouth newly moistened. This effect would be more pronounced in antiquity when the Bible was read aloud.

THE ORALITY OF DESIRE

Octavio Paz has maintained that poetry itself is basically "the testimony of the senses," and so it should not be all that surprising that the Song's images elicit reactions in the reader, as they are palpable, visible, audible, olfactory, and kinetic. This erotic Song, in other words, evokes the excitement it sets out to detail. The language of excitement goes beyond descriptive to evocative in the dream sequence above, to be sure, but this also happens throughout the Song. Much of the visual pleasure is obvious in the language of flattery, where the lovers describe the various aspects of the other's physical beauty. Scents, too, become a vital treat in the stirrings of desire. Much attention is given to the naming of various spices. We saw earlier that when the man set out to describe the woman's scent, he marshaled nine different spices to help capture it and still could not. This abundance is an exaggeration beyond what any typical garden would contain, and many of the spices are considered exotic to ancient Israel.

The garden was the site of fruit cultivation, namely, the production of pomegranates, grapes, apricots, and olives. Alongside these, herbs and spices might also be grown, such as cinnamon, cardamom, and myrrh. This garden is not a functional one, but is a symbol of the woman's allure. It (she) is not a real garden, but a musty, complex, idealized one teeming with scents. In fact, as Roland Murphy notes, the style of comparison is odd here, for it is a comparison of a woman to a scent-filled garden, yet the woman herself goes unmentioned.[11] It is almost as if the man's descriptive efforts have distracted him from his beloved.

Both lovers take pleasure in the scents of the other. The woman finds pleasure in being close to him, remarking simply: "his cheeks are like beds of spices, yielding fragrance" (5:13). Her compliment reveals her proximity to him, in that she is close enough to his face to detect a scent. It is possible as well that the verse reflects the use of some type of ancient cologne. At any rate, she takes pleasure in his scent. She waxes even more poetic about his scent in 1:3, where cologne does seem to be indicated:

> Your anointing oils are fragrant
> your name is perfume poured out.

Here, she clearly enjoys the sheer smell of his anointing oils and turns that into a metaphor praising his name and the effect it has on her. Hence, scent and sound commingle as sensual pleasures in the lover's presence.

The woman's proximity to her lover is again apparent when she sighs:

> My beloved is to me a bag of myrrh
> that lies between my breasts. (1:13)

This, I should hasten to add, is a biblical compliment, for he brings her great olfactory pleasure. Myrrh is an aromatic gum from tree bark that was imported to Israel from Arabia and India. It was early on highly prized in trade in the ancient Near East, and so was a lavish gift of the wise men who visited the baby Jesus (Matt 2:11). It was also used for incense, embalming (John 19:39), and to perfume garments and beds (Ps 45:9; Prov 7:17; Esth 2:13).[12] By calling her lover a bag of myrrh, the woman expresses her multiple enjoyments: that of his scent; that he is prized as a bagful of the valued aromatic; and, not to miss, that he is clearly on top of her. Hence, here, scent is also doubling as a symbol for sexual pleasure—what it is like for her to have him on top of her. Scents, then, are vital pleasures in their anticipation of sexual union. The other senses are awakened in desire as well; notably the sense of sight, as they trade so many compliments, and hearing, when the sound of the other's voice and name brings these two lovers pleasure. But by far the dominant sense depicted in the Song is not touch, but taste. The pleasures of the mouth come into play far more often than the other senses. Oral pleasure dominates in the Song for the depiction of sexual excitement and the anticipated enjoyment.

The horticultural metaphors for sexual excitement differ, as we noted, from cultures using grain-farming images for the sexual plowing and producing of children, with the woman as field. They offer a unique precision within Israel itself if we take a further close-up of the image of a woman as the garden itself. Since the garden becomes the site for the woman's sexual arousal, it is worth the time to understand exactly what a garden would mean to the ancient Israelite. Typically, the biblical farm consisted of a garden, a field, and an area for stockbreeding. The villages were on hills, so the farm itself was divided, with the house on the hill, the field down in the valley below, and the gardens either on the side of the house or terraced on the hill slopes. Hence, when the farmer came in from the fields, he would reach his garden and the woman tending it as valued elements of his homecoming. He would likely look forward to seeing both the garden and the woman, as they represent the end to his day's labors, and the possibility, at least, of enjoyments after his labors.

The garden, then, had a dual association with a woman: one was contextual, as she would be nearer the garden, perhaps even overlooking its care; the other, more sensual, as she offered the man a lush variety of scents and tastes. She herself, like the garden, was a delight to "harvest," in contrast to the dry harvesting of grain. And it is easy to see why this might be so. A garden is not as rare as an oasis in the desert, to be sure, but it does provide for each farm the welcoming site of home and delicious pleasures that come only seasonally. Hence, in the ancient world, gardens were prized as virtual oases for the breaks they offered from hard, dry farming. Fruits were the prized part of the farm because they offered the rare, seasonal sugar and juice, so tasty and refreshing to the parched conditions of the ancient Palestinian farmer.

Pomegranates, apricots,[13] grapes, and wine are the fruit products mentioned repeatedly throughout the Song, more so than in any other biblical book. They are symbols of succulent enjoyment, markers of sensual pleasure. Fruit in any form was a delight for the ancient, poor farmers, as it offered a break from the grain-based diet. It was not a crop necessary for survival, but it enhanced their quality of living in ways we probably cannot fully appreciate. Its contribution for variety alone, in a regimen of basically bread and porridge, is significant. Fruit gave alimentary pleasure and also came to represent other sensual delights.

Since fruit is symbolic of delicious pleasures, it became metaphoric for the lovers' sexual delights in each other. So, for example, under an apricot tree (her lover), the woman proclaims, "with great delight I sat in his shadow, and his fruit was sweet to my taste" (2:3). Or, while embracing, she would give "to drink, the juice of my pomegranates" (8:2), and let him "eat its choicest fruits" (4:16). So too, when he speaks of climbing her like a tree, "may your breasts be like clusters of the vine, and the scent of your breath like apricots, and your mouth like the best wine" (7:8). Here grapes, apricots, and wine are all summoned for the extravagant, sumptuous feast both lovers imagine their lovemaking to be. As readers of poetry, we can intuit something racy in these phrases even if we cannot analyze precisely what in a woman's breasts is specifically like a grape cluster, since to be exact, they might be better likened to melons or apricots. Horticulture simply and powerfully summons the oral excitement in sexual pleasure, then and now.

Wine is the ruling metaphor for sexual pleasure in the Song, of course, in the comparative assertion, "your love is better than wine" (1:2, 4:10), in the less direct metaphor, "let us be drunk with love" (5:1), and finally, in the woman's imagined seduction with pomegranate wine (8:2). It is fairly evident that wine and sexual pleasure are linked by their sweetness and by their shared intoxicating properties. The metaphors of wine and love share a dual degree of correspondence in their taste and their effect. It is also true that the pomegranate wine may add something about the difficulties of love. The fruit, as mentioned in chapter 4, is red. Inside it shimmers and is filled with seeds. In 4:3 and again in 6:7, the woman's cheeks are compared to pomegranates, complimenting her ruddy complexion, and suggesting as well the incipient arousal in her blush. Something of love's difficulties may too be indicated, given the difficulty of extracting the seeds, as well as the juice's tartness.

The predominance of fruit imagery for sexual pleasure is at once a natural and shocking metaphorical association. Fruit offers delights in manifold ways for the senses: of smell, "the scent of your breath like apricots" (7:8); of touch, "I will grasp its branches. May your breasts be like clusters of the vines" (7:8); of sight, "your cheeks are like halves of a pomegranate" (4:3); and of taste, "I will eat my honeycomb with my honey, I will drink my wine with my milk" (5:1), and "your love is better than wine" (1:2; 4:10). It is evident that the multiple sensory pleasures offered by fruit make it an apt metaphor for the sensuous pleasures of loving a woman especially, with the senses working on full, delirious overload. It is perhaps not surprising that the sense of taste comes to dominate above others.

Fruit has general properties analogous to a woman. It has taut, delicate skin, pulpy and yielding flesh, and pungent, fresh scents and tastes. These are associative rather than literal qualities, which fruit shares with a woman, of course. One does not break skin (often) and consume flesh in lovemaking. The Hebrew term for "female," however, is *neqebah*, from the root *nqb*, to bore or pierce, so the meaning of opening a woman up is clearly evident with this term, and with the use of "opening" a virgin (Exod 22:16) and "entering" for sex.[14] Lovemaking, though, generally involves much more than intercourse, even in a culture with such telling terms for having sex with women. One does lick, linger, taste, and delight in the play and sloppy dance of tongues, lips, necks, bouncing breasts, and hardening dark nipples, themselves like pomegranate seeds, with the vaginal lips and vulva growing with excitement. These sensations of pleasure in a woman contribute to making lovemaking a delight for all the senses, just as a garden or vineyard full of fruit would be to an ancient farmer.

The succulent, heady enjoyment of fruit in the Song summons the sheer orality of sexual desire; the fact that we salivate in arousal, and that kissing is an urgent first act. The Song is smart on desire's force as it knowingly pleads "let us be drunk with love."[15] The pleasure is decidedly oral and goes well beyond mere tasting, to ingesting, and to the excess of intoxication. These two lovers are not dabbling in desire; they are overrun by it, rushing mouth first toward it. The excitement of desire is an orgiastic inundation of all our senses with taste at the forefront, and this is why food and sex are so often associated in our imaginings of sensual pleasure. Both food and sex stimulate the mouth and cater to the orality of pleasure. Aphrodisiacs are not simply sexual stimulants to enhance or guarantee successful lovemaking. They were never that clinical or goal-driven, like today's Viagra prescriptions. They enticed the senses by awakening and celebrating them.

Lovemaking becomes a feast for the pleasure of the senses in general and is not connected solely to penetration. A recent cookbook called *Intercourses* well illustrates this association.[16] It comes complete with succulent recipes and color pictures to drive home the point that our mouths dance and delight in both food and sex. If aphrodisiacs were only guarantors of successful copulation, we would not bother with the pictures and the celebration, just the chemical properties. Oral pleasure is in part why we even believe in aphrodisiacs, and why we will always prefer to eat chocolate in matters of love, rather than manufacture an aphrodisiac patch for convenience. Grapes, for antiquity and today, easily become an apt vehicle for oral pleasure because they offer taste sensations and sweet juice; the mouth is overcome and surprised by the breaking of the skin, the sweet, tart tastes, and the flow of juice for refreshment. They might well have been ancient Israel's chocolates, the literary trope for sexual pleasures.

All this is to say that our mouth is a vital erogenous zone, and the Song gives irresistible testimony to the ancient knowledge of this. Our ways of describing sexual pleasure include always the sense of taste, in acts of kissing and oral sex. Oral sex itself is nowhere explicitly mentioned in the Bible, apart from the possible allusion in Song of Songs 5, discussed earlier. But we need not assume that the biblical people did not engage in it simply because they lacked a rather stilted clinical term for it as we do. After all, lovers themselves do not typically speak so woodenly of "oral sex" and "genital contact." Oral sex may simply have been included as one of the delights of the mouth in lovemaking and celebrated throughout the Song within metaphors of drinking and tasting.

The orality of sexual desire is evident throughout the Song and is broad enough to encompass varying experiences of pleasure. Movements of the mouth in the pleasant sensations of drinking and eating are manifest on the sexual level as well. Indeed, the Song starts out with the mouth. The woman asks that her lover "kiss me with the kisses of his mouth" (1:2). She wants his mouth on hers, and she wants it repeatedly. This is no random place to start a Song about desire. The mouth is the first boundary in the crossing toward intimacy, typically the first site for the exchange of bodily fluids. Kissing is a transgression of a social distance and so initiates the possibility that other barriers can come down. In fact, part of the excitement comes through the crossing of boundaries. Hence, the woman starts the ball of desire rolling in the Song and really does not let up. You do not have to be a Freudian to perceive the mouth to be a primary erotic zone, but it may be worth a moment to sketch briefly Freud's idea of why.

Freud believed that sexual desire began not in adolescence, but earlier, in infantile experiences with bodily pleasure, which revolved primarily around the oral and the anal orifices. Oral pleasures were formed from sucking on the mother's breast. For Freud, all of the adult experience that we take from kissing, sliding tongues, oral sex, and the sucking of breasts (for a woman's lover) are really recapturing the earliest pleasure of nursing at our mother's breast.[17] While I do not wish to explore the merits of Freud's entire theory here, I do welcome his attention to the fierce oral nature of sexual desire. Then as now, kissing is the activity that most closely evokes all the oral sensations of early infantile sexuality: the sucking, warmth, and chewing on the mother's breast. And for Israelites, weaning occurred around three years of age, so it would make sense that the oral urges were well developed. Succulent, melting, juicy food and drink such as chocolate, grapes, pomegranates, strawberries, and wine all stimulate sensuous pleasure in our mouths—teeth, tongue, lips, saliva are all triggered into increasing excitement. For these reasons, these foods often make their way onto menus for seduction.

The orality of pleasure in Freud's scheme is also about the exquisite value of ingestion. Since our earliest oral pleasures also brought nourishment, satisfaction, the slaking of thirst, and calm, our sexual desires come, too, with a need, a hunger for satisfaction. Desire is born in the gap between enjoyed pleasure and its absence. Hence, for Freud, sexual desire was initiated with the desire for the mother's milk in the slipping threat of losing the nipple. Oral desire is a harder, imprinted desire, linked to survival, and it stays with us. If Freud is right that our sensuous desires begin here, then his notion might well explain the sometimes humorless urgencies of our sexual desire. We won't die if we don't reunite with our lover, but our desire can feel that fierce in our chest. We hunger for love or want to drink our lover up. These sentiments express the voracious quality of desire, the raw need, and the persistent memory of oral pleasures.

Freud's idea of the origin for desire at our mother's breast also helps to explain our close association of food with sex, and, of course, likewise accounts for the centrality of the woman's breasts in the sexual desire of her lover. The need for the breast transfers into adulthood as sexual desire, and oral pleasure entails both contact with the mouth and mimed attempts at ingestion. We still nibble and suck breasts in our expressions of sexual excitement, with traces of our earlier, desperate desire. The oral movement is an instinct that persists, akin to how cats continue to knead in expressions of contentment, long after they nurse at their mother's side. Our mouths become more sophisticated and (hopefully) nimble in sexual pleasure, but the desire is, in part, literally infantile.

The male lover in the Song details exquisite and repeated longing for his beloved's breasts:

> Your breasts are like clusters,
> I will climb the palm tree
> and pick its fruit.
> To me your breasts are like grape clusters. (7:7-8)

He is so excited by her breasts that he mixes metaphors with a date palm tree and grapes without concern, as if to say: "whatever, they are sweet, supple, ripening, and what I desire to feel, to pluck." His language is now finally slipping in its precision as hers has under desire's intensity.

Breasts come into play again at the end of the Song where Freud's association of suckling and adult desire might be indeed glimpsed, when the woman says to her lover:

> I wish that you were my brother,
>> that my mother nursed you at her breast,
> then if I met you in the street,
>> I could kiss you and no one would despise me. (8:1)

This passage is notoriously difficult to interpret. It seems to prefer incest as a means to sanction the lovers' desire. It has led interpreters to surmise that the lovers' liaison is outside of societal acceptability. It might also be an unwitting Freudian slip. The woman may desire to have her own breasts sucked (in public?), but transfers that to the safer pleasure of a mother's breasts that two siblings could share. In some ways, she is rushing her male lover through the Oedipal element of desire, where he originally desired his mother. She is assuming the incestuous, subterranean force of his desire toward her and is redirecting in whatever way can get them together. I do not mean to attribute Freudian sophistication to her words, but rather am trying to glimpse the primal urges within them. If they were siblings, then they would at least enjoy the intimacy of sharing their mother's breast, and so could easily share a public kiss. Social customs of modesty might have prevented other such public displays of affection, though these are nowhere evident in the Bible.

This final chapter of the Song moves from a fantasized brother to the woman's blood brothers, and her breasts come up once more. There is an embarrassing economic efficiency to the woman's brothers when they worry:

We have a little sister and
    she has no breasts.
What will we do for our sister,
    on the day when she is spoken for? (8:8)

Have they not been listening to this Song at all, where her breasts are praised no fewer than four times (4:5; 7:3, 7-8)?[18] It is my contention that no, they have not been listening. They are virtually clueless about their sister's desire and assets. While most of the Song has been devoted to a woman in lust, this last little vignette of the mercantile brothers casts her back into the traditional perspective of the family males needing to marry her off and secure a good marriage price in the bargain. Her breasts then become a commodity that can make the deal easy or difficult.

This turn in the Song illustrates a traditional, conservative custom encroaching on the lover's desire in the final chapter: first, in the apparent restriction against public displays of nonfamilial affection, and again in the brothers blunted concern for their sister's nonexistent breasts. Throughout the Song, her breasts have been the focus of attention too, but for their suppleness, movement, taste, and sheer enjoyment. They have been delightful and enticing. The contrast of perspectives between the desiring, hungry lover and the brothers just makes the brothers' worries look absurd and is, perhaps, a wry satire of patriarchal marriage customs.

Much of the man's anticipated pleasure revolves around the woman's breasts. His expressed hope that her breasts be like grape clusters is the most direct he gets. He wants to climb the woman and feel those breasts in his hands and mouth. Her breasts are mentioned in the Song eight times (1:13; 4:5; 7:3, 7-8; 8:1, 8, 10), though not always by him. Still, whatever else might be said of the male lover, he is clearly an ancient "breast man," or all readers/men are presumed to be by the writer(s).

Elsewhere, the man anticipates other oral pleasures of fruit consumption that clearly serve as double entendres for sex. When he enters her garden (her), he will "eat its choicest fruits" (4:16), and continue by eating "my honeycomb with my honey, I drink my wine with my milk" (5:1). Earlier he had described the woman's mouth as distilling nectar, having honey and milk under her tongue (4:11). Now he enters to enjoy these tasty treats of lovemaking, honey, milk, and added for extra measure, the wine that their love is better than, anyway. He intends not simply to taste, but to indulge in all the liquids available. His largesse during sexual excitement is evident when he extends the pleasure to all: "eat, friends, drink, and be drunk on love" (5:1). No longer alone, he turns to a presumed third party in his friends, or in readers themselves, and offers an invitation to become intoxicated with love. Following his description of feasting in sex with the woman, this directive is a seeming invitation for an orgy, a sharing at least vicariously in the delights of love's excitement. The man's invitation signals his endearing inability or unwillingness to contain himself and his joy.

This magnanimity happens elsewhere in the Song as well. The woman has the same expansive spirit in her love. After making her second pass at him with "draw me after you, let us make haste," she slows down, opening up the scene to others:

> We will exult and rejoice in you;
> we will extol your love more than wine,
> rightly do they love you. (1:4)

Whoever "they" are, she compliments them on their mutual taste in her lover! What grandeur! This is big of her. A mere four lines into the Song, after pleading for the "kisses of his mouth," she is already sharing her joy in his delights. The Song's testimony to love, in fact, is surprisingly nonmonogamous in spirit. The lovers' willingness to share their joy is, of course, a by-product of love, that giddy, continued breakdown of boundaries, with the other and with the world at large. One feels like telling the whole world when one is in love, and one hopes to enlist other aficionados willing to praise the lover endlessly. So here, quite naturally, the woman is merely assuming her ancient right to dish sessions of, "Isn't he just the best?"

Still, however, their enjoyment extends beyond the contours of their relationship, as it invites or refers to third parties. Their love is so bountiful in its fruitful and delectable yield that the lovers can afford to share it, or at least its joy. Joy can transgress the monogamy otherwise stringently legislated in the biblical legal materials. Such a perspective in the Song is a remarkably expansive, even subversive insight for Israelite society. And it is, too, a telling largesse. For in ancient Israel, the only lover who can abide more than one lover (and who, in fact, insists on the love of all the people) is their God. But he is also a jealous God, commanding monogamous fidelity from the people, his lovers in a good year (Exod 20:5).

The verbs here, of rejoicing and extolling, are frequently liturgical, gestures of pious worship for God elsewhere in the Bible (Exod 20:24; Ps 16:9; Isa 9:3). God is often the beneficiary of these emotions or causes them in his people. That they are used of the woman's lover is, of course, a compliment to the man, a bold and virtually blasphemous one, since worship goes to the one God alone. That she can risk blasphemy in a book that neglects or forgets to mention God, anyway, is perhaps not as daring as it could be, but that she can transfer liturgical language onto the sexual plane suggests the possibility that the transfer may not be one-way. In other words, if she can yoke liturgical language to her sexual desire, is it also possible to see the spiritual responses of praise and extolling as full-bodied, sensual, even verging on the sexual? The suppleness of the terms here includes spiritual pleasure as well.

We could well be meant to feel her sexual desire and anticipated joy of when she and her friends can extol the man who makes her come so alive. We could also, however, start to glimpse in this desired, yet vanishing and elusive lover, something of the nature of faith itself in the unseen God of the Hebrew Bible. If this woman, in other words, can risk the blasphemy of describing her sexual excitement in liturgical terms, can the Song itself not also be risking by describing spiritual desire in mundane, sexual terms? That kind of theology would work miracles on a certain kind of audience, one invested in and content with life's mundane pleasures, who maybe have not figured out or wondered what a God would mean outside the strictures of official religion with its temples, holy texts, and laws. What if God or the search for him occurs in the mundane, in the love and laughter of sex itself, in the enjoyment that simply cannot contain itself in one human couple? What if this aroused woman is not displayed only as a witness to erotic pleasure, but is instead the passionate, blunt lover of God, the absent? She is always having to search, ready and willing to praise even in the absence. She is there through the frustration and delay and the embodied yearning, because this is a testimony to a kind of faith, her hope that she will eventually unite with her lover.

She will "extol his love" with her friends. She will praise him, just as the psalmist praises God, in the temple of ancient Israel, and today in churches and synagogues that still use the psalms. No one steps outside of these religious environs and "extols" anybody anymore. Maybe they should. Maybe this woman did, just by stealing some religious joy and applying it for the street language of love and lust. Extolling his love recalls her praise of two verses earlier, that his "love is better than wine" (1:2). With such lavish praise, curiosity is naturally aroused as to this lover's identity. Yet the male lover stays nameless, as does she, and so identity is cloaked, undisclosed, and therefore forever open. The lover could be Solomon, he could be a shepherd, he could be both. He could even be beyond the human plane of lovers, a symbolic other for all desires. At least here, he is worthy of a communal worship, as she and her friends "rightly love you."

At any rate, both lovers are joyous enough to invite others into their pleasure. And for the male, this pleasure pivots around oral imagery. He invites the others to eat and drink, as he has, and to "be drunk with love." His pleasure beckons toward indulgence, summoning others to join him. Once more his oral delight is apparent, as her kisses inundate him:

Your mouth is like the best wine
　　flowing smoothly,
　　gliding over lips and teeth. (7:9)

This image, of course, makes no literal sense. Even the deepest kiss can only get so far past lips and teeth and still be considered a pleasant sensation. Instead, the image signals the profusion of pleasure brought on by her kisses, a pleasure obviously oral and involving the same wholesale sensations that drinking wine brings. This utterance is, in a sense, his response to her own plea for his kisses in the Song's opening: "Let him kiss me with the kisses of his mouth." Her excitement, remember, was evident by the plural, by the unnecessary qualifier "his mouth," and by her switching pronouns from "his" to "your." Now we get to see his take on kissing, and he does not disappoint. Neither of these lovers envisions kissing as mere foreplay. Instead, they linger in its extravagant delight for tongue, lips, and mouths.

Both lovers take obvious oral delight in the images of fruit and sex in the Song. They both drink wine and compare it to their love, eat fruit, and bask in the sweetness of the other. The male's attestations of oral pleasure, however, are more frequent than are the woman's. In fact, past the comparison of wine and their love which both lovers make, her oral pleasure is quite limited. She pleads for his kisses, gets to eat his sweet fruit (2:3), and enjoys his lips which "distill liquid myrrh" (5:13).

The man is able to take more pronounced oral pleasure in part because the focus in the Song is on an aroused woman. He, then, presumably, would want to enjoy her taste in as many ways as he could fathom. Her anticipated pleasure in him is more diffused among her senses. She strongly delights in him visually, as we saw in chapter 3. And, earlier, we see her pleasure when she imagines him as a bag of myrrh between her breasts. Lastly, her anticipated pleasure is expressed in her twice-repeated wish:

O that his left hand were under my head
　　and that his right hand embraced me. (2:6; 8:3)

This is an allusion to lovemaking, including even intercourse. The lovers are prone, with his hand under her head and the other embracing her. Both times, she utters this wish after invitations to make love, once on his initiative (2:4), once on hers (8:2). Wine and fruit will be enjoyed in both scenes for sustenance and as symbols of sexual delight, but it will be the man who will drink and enjoy luscious fruit more than she will. While his voice is not as direct or bold overall as hers has been, especially in this third type of discourse of desire, he is not timid. He is more pronounced in his oral pleasures, she is more pronounced in direct invitations to sex. She is better at arousal itself, indulging in and describing it, and this is where his oral pleasures lie.

The Vineyard

> Let us get up and go to the vineyards,
>   and see whether the vines have budded,
> whether the grape blossoms have opened
>   and the pomegranates are in bloom.
> There I will give you my love. (7:12)

For the woman, the vineyard is the most important location for sexual pleasure. It is where she dreams of their eventual meeting; it is where she invites him, as in this passage, to come receive her love. For him, too, the vineyard is vital, for he envisions her as a stately tree full of grape clusters. And vineyards are the origin for the wine found throughout the Song. It is the site for both their lovemaking and the wine, so they can quite naturally compare the two.

The lover, we recall, viewed his beloved's breasts as grape clusters, the lovers yearned to be "drunk with love," and love was compared to wine and found superior. The pleasures of lovemaking are associated throughout with the oral delights of fruit. Horticulture offered an apt vehicle for sexual excitement for the host of reasons explored above. It offered yet another, in the vineyard as the site for lovemaking. It is the couple's preferred spot, described in their longing rather than realized.

A vineyard is a natural locale in a Song with so much grape and wine imagery. Historically, the vineyard's association with coupling in this Song may derive in part from the presence of women during the festive grape harvest in ancient Israel. Joyful, dancing daughters and wives (Judg 21:20-22) would have made the grape harvest a natural setting for love imagery. So, too, would the fruit's own qualities at the peak of its ripening. For when ripe, the darkened grapes hang heavily on the vine, engorged with juice, and in triangular clusters. Women would be harvesting these fruits, cementing an association in the imagination and want of onlookers.

A ripe vineyard offers a powerful, subliminal seduction to those entering it. It works over the senses in diffuse yet dizzying ways, until you are not quite sure why you feel aroused in the middle of a farm. But you do. It is only nature, yet not harmless. A vineyard has the unexpected power to loose sexual longing, much as flowers can with their pure and obscene charm.

In the Song of Songs, the woman owns her own vineyard, and it is more valuable than all of King Solomon's grape harvests. In 1:6, she had lamented that she had not worked her own vineyard because her brothers forced her to labor for them. Her labor in vineyards is assumed. At 8:12, she is back in possession of her own vineyard, and she is content, even to the point that she dismisses all that mighty King Solomon has. Her vineyard in this book functions as a metaphor for her sexual power itself. And, on that level, she compares favorably to all that Solomon had, presumably his "thousand" wives and concubines (1 Kgs 11:3). On both levels, the sexual and the agricultural, the value of a vineyard is apparent. The vineyard is both valued above a king's wealth and controlled now by this woman. Her presence in the vineyard is, at any rate, a valued given for the poet. Her proud ownership of the vineyard is a reversal of fortune in the Song, too. For in the beginning of the

Song, she had to serve under her brothers' rule in vineyards to the detriment of her own.

When the vineyard becomes the metaphor for the woman's sexuality and for her vulva, then the ubiquity of wine in the Song (1:2; 1:4; 4:10; 5:1; 7:2, 9; 8:2) becomes a celebration of the woman's arousal itself, as the product of the vineyard. It was copious moistness in her wet dream and water in his visions. Now it becomes also the wine. Wine signifies not only the aphrodisiac likely to have been present at any Israelite banquet, but also the woman's product. With this particular metaphor, then, arousal has handily overtaken yearning. Yearning is intensely physical for this woman, and her descriptions now enter its most urgent space. And, in chapter 8, she has entered it alone.

At this juncture in the Song, I suggest that it is no longer about two lovers yearning to unite. By the last chapter, the woman stops her search and claims ownership of the vineyard with emphatic Hebrew construction, "my vineyard, which is mine" (8:12). By doing so, she asserts her autonomous sexuality; one not defined by a man who, as it happens, cannot be found, and one more valuable than all of Solomon's royal vineyards (8:12). The vineyard, like the garden, is a metaphor for the woman herself, her sex, and it is all hers; even a king's wealth cannot touch it. With this expression, she comes to take possession of her sexuality, desire, and body, so that in the end, this Song is not really about mutuality and balance between the sexes.[19] It is about one woman's experience of desire, the entire spectrum, from aesthetic appreciation to bodily arousal, and finally to ownership.

Horticulturally speaking, the metaphoric association of a woman with a vineyard is adroit. It well describes wanting and/or being an aroused woman. First, a vineyard produces heady liquid and sweetness that is powerful, even destabilizing. Grapes were the prized crops of a farm, since they were sweet and could be made into wine. This portrayal of a woman as a vineyard is a positive portrait of the woman, not as mere property of a farm, but as a delight in herself, for herself, "my vineyard, which is mine."[20]

Second, the properties of the fruit itself suggest genitalia and sexual pleasure. Grapes and grape clusters are dark purple, triangular, surrounded by foliage, engorged with juice at the height of their ripening, with supple, taut, yet vulnerable skins. They have a provocative, yet innocent eroticism, and elicit out into the open the very private memories of a woman's genital arousal. They require tender care in cultivation and close, persistent attention to gauge exactly when the height of ripening occurs. Hence, they are apt vehicles for describing two tenors metaphorically, namely, the physiology of female arousal, and the lover's oral delight in tasting, drinking, and exploring/cultivating her.

Third, the horticultural metaphor here turns on a biblical pun. Using fruit and its juices for woman's desire, the song plays off and subverts the procreative functionality of sex expressed elsewhere in the Bible's command to "be fruitful and multiply." Here in this Song, breeding and the harvesting of (if lucky, male) children has no place, and all the fruitfulness describes only the woman's arousal and pleasure. The woman in this Song is fruitful indeed, but in ways the Priestly writer never could have dreamed. We turn now to a discussion of the role of this woman in relation to other biblical women in desire.

6

Woman's Voice in the Canon

"A Mare among Pharaoh's Chariots"

LOCATING FEMALE DESIRE IN ANDROCENTRIC TEXTS: CONSTRICTIONS AND ESCAPE VALVES

The male lover, by way of a compliment, compares his beloved to a "mare among Pharaoh's chariots" (1:9). This meant that the latent force of the woman's sexuality had the power to throw a powerful army into confusion. The man both admires and fears the power of what such a mare can do. And so she is a mare among Pharaoh's chariots, able to throw him, too, into the confusion of desire.

In effect, the desiring woman's voice in the Song has a similar alluring and frightening potential for the biblical canon itself, able to throw it off its androcentric orderliness and hegemony. Male bias is the dominant voice present in the canon; it proceeds undeterred and is received as authoritative, as the way things are. The woman's voice challenges that bias, because it is a threateningly different one. She enters the canon on her own terms and with her own power intact, not domesticated, neutered, or erased. This assertive, startling portrait of a woman voicing her want has obvious appeal for feminist interpreters. I want now to explore this woman's role in contrast to the few desiring women found elsewhere in the Hebrew Bible. Though outnumbered, the mare is never endangered by Pharaoh's chariots. Instead, the risk in the metaphor lies solely with what this woman could do by her mere presence. The question of this chapter is what effect she can have, unbridled, free and female, on biblical androcentrism.

By now, it should be obvious that this Song is affirming, even boldly so, of human sexuality. Given the taciturn nature of other biblical materials on sex, the Song is startling, refreshing, even flamboyant. Both the anticipation and the pleasure of sex are celebrated, lingered over, and nowhere decried. Sexuality and desire are not viewed as problems to repress or punish; nor are they sources of shame.[1] More striking still, they are not areas to be legislated in any way or controlled through patriarchal customs such as the bride negotiation through the father, marriage dowries, bride prices, and the like.[2] In fact, the father is conspicuously absent in the Song, and the woman's home is referred to as her "mother's house," instead of the traditional "father's house." Her brothers stand in for an absent father, but they function as caricatures rather than realistic proxies.[3] They worry about the fate of their little sister to attract a mate due to her nonexistent breasts (8:8).

This is an instance of biblical humor, really. The brothers fret about her small breasts as a liability for love as transaction, while the lover enjoys her abundant breasts. There is a subtle dig at those brothers. For, if we know anything about this woman's physique, it is that she has bouncy, firm, delicious breasts, with nipples cool and hard as gazelle noses, that her beloved longs to taste and feel. It is a study in the contrast of love—one fueled by desire and delight, the other by patriarchal, fiscal arrangement, bartered between male heads of households. We glimpse the woman's fate under patriarchal custom here, and then see it overturned by her own assertion and affirmation that she will call the shots.

Patriarchal custom is overturned in the last chapter, and it is mocked: the men are clueless about the female assets they negotiate over all the time. The love between these two lovers is not a transaction at all, but a felt experience. The woman is allowed to speak of her own pleasure, to want it, and repeatedly: "Oh that his left hand . . ." And there is not even time or interest to be married or properly coupled. Sexual yearning is celebrated in its own right. It is sung for its own sake, and because it is, the lover's sensual pleasure is ours, too, through the listening. Lastly, her desire is not vanquished at the end. It is understood and affirmed by the woman, not any male recipient.

Plenty about this Song is refreshing and lively.[4] The mere presence of such a powerful, expressive woman merits further discussion in the present chapter. Elsewhere in the Bible, the internal worlds and perspectives of women receive scant attention. Biblical literature in general lacks attention to the internal thought worlds of its characters, and differs in this from ancient Greek literature.[5] But even with such characteristic silence, the women suffer disproportionately to the men. Women are present and active, but the narrative space devoted to the male characters vastly outstrips whatever attention is given to the women. Even when women are present, they are so primarily for male purposes: to marry, to violate, to avoid for reasons of purity, to sleep with, and so on. In other words, they are viewed "through a filter of male experience."[6] The study of women's lives in antiquity is done through recognizing that their lives are refracted through the gnomic utterances of men.[7] We have to pay attention to how women are refracted through these androcentric texts.[8] Women have not been quite erased by the male viewpoint, but they have suffered distortion.

Women were part of the community of ancient Israel, but lineage, inheritance laws, and the census were all configured through the males only. Who begat whom was really about motherhood, of course, but in the Bible, the lists of the "begats" consisted of men. Ruth and Esther, it is true, are two books named after women, but this hardly compares to the thirty-seven other Hebrew Bible books where male characters overwhelmingly dominate. From such a society, it cannot be too surprising that so much biblical material is offered from the male perspective.[9] And this is also why it is unjust of some feminists to insist that it could have been otherwise. It could not have been, and it is both anachronistic and antihistorical to insist that such a culture not be what it was in fact—patriarchal.

The Song of Songs lacks this characteristic androcentrism, and it clearly stands out for its primarily *female* perspective. The woman is the more willing and articulate of the two voices about desire. And she closes the book by championing her own autonomy and sexuality above and beyond her lover's. Her lover, in a real sense, never showed up or stayed long enough to bask in love's pleasure. He briefly taunts her to come find him in the pastures (1:8), and once invites her to come eat and drink in the garden (5:1). His presence in the Song is a coy, unresolved stasis. His desire is somewhat *arrested,* never going beyond the flirtations and invitations, while the woman's is *arresting,* coursing through the eight chapters, burgeoning like grapes the entire time.

She, under these conditions of his absence and fleeting presence, effects a change from pining for him to a self-mastery and championing of her desire, apart from its object: "my vineyard, my very own" (8:12). She does not learn to survive his absences. Rather, desire has brought her to her own celebration of self and sexuality, undefined by another. She has tracked yearning's progress in her body and heart throughout the Song. It is not, then, a Song about a frustrated or tragic love, or one that petered out over time, but is instead about a self-transforming love in a voice booming by the book's end. To put it in Freudian terms, object cathexis, that is, the attachment to an object, is vanquished, but love and desire are not. In not so Freudian terms, Falk describes the paradox of erotic love dealt with in the Song. This woman has undergone a

> conflict that intensifies passion, painful separation that heightens the pleasure of union, intimate bonding with the other that gives the individual courage to stand alone.[10]

This means everything for a book in the Bible. Conflict, painful separation, intimate bonding, and the courage to stand alone are all vital psychological features of life, as they are also elements of faith in a God. God is the one being we are called to love, heart, soul, and might (Deut 6:5), yet can never see or cathect. The Song is offering instruction for journeying through love beyond the limitations of customs, both patriarchal and psychological. Such wisdom can certainly have value on the human plane. It pushes us past various psychological blocks and fixations. But it offers, as well, inadvertent theological instruction to readers of the Bible, who are thinking about God whether he is mentioned or not.

The voice of a desiring woman is clearly a bonus for the feminist, but it is also an unwittingly adroit witness to biblical spirituality. For the desire-filled journey of faith has to entail negotiating the absence and episodic presence of the beloved other, the unseen God. Believers searching for God have to endure his apparent absence in a way that does not conquer or diminish, still less defeat, human desire. Any cataclysmic, orgasmic consummation with an unseen presence is, of course, out of the question, except for the mystics who try to do precisely this. Still, the search and desire, the giving of one's heart, soul, and might to God remain the faithful person's truest yearnings. This woman's journey for a union where she can give her all in love imitates, on the sexual level, the spiritual quest for God.

While it is true that this woman's voice speaks for the majority of the time and that this is biblically unprecedented, some caution about a feminist triumph is nevertheless indicated. Scholars such as Phyllis Trible, Marcia Falk, and André LaCocque are too quick to champion this Song as a feminist tour de force[11] or paean to gender mutuality.[12] Marvin Pope even goes so far as to crown the Song of Songs the "golden text for women's liberation."[13] These assessments limit the Song's contribution to a discussion of sexual politics.

The present work, by contrast, is a study of the desire in the Song. The woman's voice merits much of the attention, since she dominates. My intent in focusing on that woman, however, is not primarily for feminist gain. Rather, it is born of a curiosity, even a sad *yearning* to understand a biblical text, the voices it encodes, and the values it hopes to reflect, clarify, and arouse. We miss something if we just see this Song as feminist pay dirt. We force gender to the center of attention, when desire is the central theme of the Song. Desire courses in and through the body, male and female, and arches beyond bodily, even sexual limits. Hence, the Song's contribution, more so than it is feminist corrective, is this idea of embodied desire. It achieves that feminist corrective as well, but it extends further beyond issues of gender.

There is an "antipatriarchal bent" to the Song with the woman and the daughters of Jerusalem so prominent.[14] So, given the predominance of an androcentric viewpoint in the Bible, one scripted by males for a presumed male audience, what feminist or liberating stance can this woman's voice actually serve? Would not a woman writhing in desire simply undergo another kind of objectification—not of sexual conquest by a male character, but of voyeuristic fantasy by a male audience? In other words, her assertive, growing sexual excitement could well be tantalizing to the male audience, in much the same way that lesbian sex scenes are in well-selling issues of *Penthouse* today. The latter's purpose, certainly, is not to bolster any sensitivity for gay rights, but is mere titillation, and the woman in the Song is under a similar risk. Daniel Boyarin suggests that what we get is a kind of "ventriloquy," what a man would like to hear about a woman, rather than her subjectivity.[15]

Bataille's view on women in erotica is harsher still:

> Not every woman is a potential prostitute, but prostitution is the logical consequence of the feminine attitude. In so far as she is attractive, a woman is prey to men's desires.[16]

He would say of the Song, then, that insofar as the woman is attractive and turned on, she is prey to men's desires, though this time outside the text, by the audience.

Changing the audience alleviates some of her objectification. We need no longer presume an exclusively male readership as scholars did for past centuries. And if the Song is merely offered as a voyeuristic display of a woman, then the ending is a bit subversive, even disturbing. It champions her self-possession rather than worship of or desire for the male, and this would undercut the pleasure for a male voyeur. He is likely to feel robbed when she says, in essence, "keep it, my vineyard is mine" (8:12). This closes her off from the aroused audience, and I think, would aggravate male anxiety.

It is, of course, apparent that having a woman articulate her desire is going to elicit multiple reactions from any audience. Titillation is a part of reading erotica, anyway, for both males and females. For anyone who still has a pulse, the eroticism is simply too palpable to ignore. Perhaps the rabbis gave a gift by allowing this Song into the canon, and did so with a knowing smile. They would still have had to be prepared to defend its inclusion as "holy," however, as more than titillation.[17] I want to suggest, therefore, that titillation is one benefit to reading the Song, but is not its sole gift. There are, in fact, other reasons to go ahead and use a woman's voice on desire.

Using the vehicle of a woman's voice enabled the writers to focus on autonomy beyond all social constraints, be they about gender, wealth, or privilege. Autonomous affirmation as seen here—as she, in effect, goes up against Solomon in all his wealth and splendor, *and bests him*—is itself an unusual theme in the Hebrew Bible. The Bible's concern throughout is for a corporate Israel. Even Solomon is a hero of wisdom for the concern he demonstrates for the people. This tribute to self-ownership gets obscured in strictly feminist expositions of the Song. The Song is about the triumphant owning of one's autonomous voice and sexuality. It is not an inversion or reversal of gender roles, where a woman simply gets to play the male, dominant role.[18] André LaCocque argues that it is just that, a role reversal, with the woman subversively flouting patriarchal custom.[19] His interpretation, though, perpetuates the notion of woman as other. It is just that now she gets to be the bad girl other, the (later) Madonna of ancient Israel, where we can objectify and cast all of our sexual ambivalence on her. We can applaud her freedom and mock her safely. The Song is not a gender payback, nor is it a reversal or subversion of our sexual stereotypes, a kind of textual cross-dressing. It is neither that reactionary nor campy in tone, because it offers substantial insight into desire.[20]

This is because the focus, as we noted above, is not primarily on gender. As a discourse on human desire, it goes further. It signals a coming to expression of that complex, myriad human issue in any language, from any gender, beyond conventions, stereotyping, awkward silence, and outing; not of genders but of desire in speech itself, owned by an individual. The Song blasts past genders toward human desire, and feminist interpretations limit the Song's potential through the ideological lens of gender analysis. It is an assertion, a victory of the autonomy of sexuality. This explodes the stereotypes of both heterosexual partners, since the woman's voice has just reconfigured desire, changed it all around. Nothing is what it seems, but desire remains, is championed, and is not foisted off into its socially circumscribed channels.

The woman's voice becomes the instrument for the assertion and celebration of one's own personal power and delight in one's surroundings. Sexual stereotypes are always roles that can chafe against the soul's true yearnings. Playing them out maintains the social fabric, but it also lulls us into being partial actors, with our desires co-opted by society's expectations, losing the very basic point that one of the reasons we fall in love is for the sensation of freedom from any binds. The lightness and the terror of sexual yearning acutely qualify it as an inchoate force akin to spiritual desire. Love, after all, stretches us beyond the categories, the expectations, and the roles. It even stretches us beyond ourselves if we care to go, to growth, to claiming and pushing the self further, to the point of pain. As important as sexual roles were for a patriarchal ancient Israel, they had limits that the writers recognized. In the Song, we hit them. Sexual desire can be constrained to a point, but not always, and not desire in general.

It is possible that the woman's voice was used simply as a way to provide the woman's side of the story. As such, it constitutes an innovation in biblical tradition. In this understanding, then, we get a window into a woman's perspective on desire through the woman and the daughters of Jerusalem. This idea has led some to posit the possibility of female authorship.[21]

The question of biblical authorship is a vexing one, since the sources for most materials are anonymous. The stories, laws, wisdom traditions, and even historical accounts of the monarchy are all provided without named authors. Even the material in the prophets is thought to be transmitted into writing by someone after each prophet. The Gospels, even, only acquired names in the second century C.E., so that we cannot even know who really wrote Mark, Matthew, Luke, and John. A similar convention, of pseudonymity, that is, using the name of a well-known figure, is at work in the Hebrew Bible when, for example, the Psalms are attributed to David, and the wisdom books of Ecclesiastes and Song of Songs are attributed to his son Solomon. The superscriptions naming these kings as authors are thought to have been added much later. Anonymity and pseudonymity were established literary conventions for ancient Israel and leave definitive authorship uncertain.

With such conventions in place, then, both the name and the gender of the author are unknown. Since biblical texts come from and reflect such a patriarchal world, though, scholars infer male authorship. We further posit that the writers were most likely court scribes or priests, those who had the time and skill for writing. Further, with the collection of traditions, a similar group of professional men likely oversaw the transmission and collection of the materials into written texts. Given this state of affairs, then, it is unlikely that a female author is represented in the Bible, but it is not impossible. To insist that it is engages a kind of fallacy of origins, wherein context dictates all possible options. Holding too fast to this reasonable assumption precludes the opportunity for an exception. Sappho, after all, wrote within the patriarchal society of ancient Greece. She was a lesbian poet of the sixth century B.C.E. who used Homeric conventions in new erotic ways, and stood in stark, if fragmented, contrast to male poetic tradition. Based on this analogy, is it not at least possible that a woman could have penned the Song of Songs? The question of female input in the Bible is worth posing here, on the level of both writing and oral tradition.

Women and most men during the biblical period were not literate, simply because literacy was not a necessary skill for their daily lives. They had, perhaps, a basic understanding of the alphabet, and knew how to sign or recognize their names for the purposes of trade and taxation. We find jars, for example, with personal names and sometimes the name of a geographic region. And we find pottery pieces called *ostraca* with personal names written on them, along with a region and sometimes a commodity, such as wine or oil. These names, where recognizable, are of men, but there is one with the name "Jezebel" written on it, with the possibility that it could be the queen of northern Israel by that name, Jezebel, the wife of Ahab. A rudimentary literacy might have been in place for farmers as well.

Overall, though, literacy was not widespread. We do not even know if Jesus was literate. He knew Scripture, but how he came to it is left in the silence of his early years. He could have learned biblical traditions orally in synagogue just like every other non-scribe or priest. Luke, alone of the four Gospels, has Jesus reading, from an Isaiah scroll in synagogue (Luke 4:16-20). Since Luke sees his own written work as teachings for the Gentiles to read, however, he may be imputing literacy to Jesus.

Although female names do not otherwise appear (yet) in the archaeological evidence of writing, women may still have played a role in literacy. They had the primary responsibility for the education of their young.[22] The Hebrew alphabet was only twenty-two letters long, something a farm wife could have taught her children. She would, at any rate, certainly have transmitted life lessons and agricultural wisdom to her children. Women, then, undoubtedly had a hand in what later became the book of Proverbs, which is a collection of domestic, agrarian sayings, a kind of ancient farmer's almanac of folk wisdom, whether or not they wrote anything down. And it is worth remembering that originally, the laws and narratives in the Pentateuch went through a long oral phase before they were written down. In such a stage of folk culture, men and women are typically involved in the oral transmission of stories and customs.[23]

Surprisingly, writing is not mentioned all that often in the Bible. Jeremiah has a scribe who uses a stylus and scroll to copy a sermon (Jer 36:2-4, 27-28), and Ezekiel ate a scroll for prophetic effect (Ezek 3:1-3). But these terms for writing apparatus are otherwise rare. Daniel sees the Aramaic writing on the wall, but he did not put it there (Dan 5:5-17), and God had written out the Ten Commandments earlier with his own finger (Exod 31:18). In two cases, women are mentioned writing in the Hebrew Bible. Jezebel, the queen of Israel, writes out instructions in the king's name in order for Naboth to be framed (1 Kings 21); and Esther, also queen, writes a decree about the holiday of Purim (Esth 9:29). These queens could be literally writing, or merely dictating to a royal scribe. But that they are depicted as writing or dictating suggests that their literacy is plausible. It does not stand out as an odd, exceptional detail or in any way detract from these stories. In fact, the queens' ability to write is essential in both plots. It is how Jezebel's wickedness is revealed and how Esther initiates a new holiday, celebrating the victory in the story.

It is feasible and even likely that the everyday women in ancient Israel would have shared folk culture, not only of the wisdom represented in Proverbs, but also in stories, etiologies, various practical pointers on being wooed, and on handling their personal dreams and desires. There could well have been informal conventions about singing the praises of one's beloved, such as we see in contemporary Arabic songs called *wasfs*. Since marriage was typically not a choice for the woman, praising one's intended may even have taken on special importance in women's circles, as a kind of readying or psyching-up custom. Praises for one's lover could represent a ritual of hope, a kind of good omen the women would sing before they married. The collective wish fulfillment would act as an apotropaic against a possible bad mate.

Falk argues that since the Song is of a "nonalienated and nonnaive stance"[24] about love, it is probably from a woman writer. But it is also true that this perspective could just as well have come from a male writer. There is nothing *essentially* feminine about the Song's views of desire that requires female authorship. To assume there must be is sexist, for we impute our stereotype that women are more defined by relationships and care more about love than men onto this ancient Song.

The daughters of Jerusalem in the Song might represent the woman's social nexus, those in whom she could safely confide her love and desire. Women in ancient Israel did some chores together, such as fetching water at the well (Exod 2:16-19), where they would likely converse on daily matters, trade tips of home maintenance, share grievances, and the like. It is plausible that they would also share perspectives on what a good man is, even if they had no choice in their betrothal. They easily could have sung of their marital wishes, or had games of poetic skill in description, as outlets for their fantasies and creativity, which they wryly enjoyed while men were not present. This is entirely speculation, of course, since none of these features are recorded anywhere. They either did not exist or were considered too mundane and unimportant to merit recording.

Two things bear mentioning. First, ancient women certainly had perspectives on desire, even if these are nowhere recorded for the historian. They had lust, crushes, yearnings, and even wet dreams, even with their marriages arranged. They could have held these desires as silent introspection, or harmlessly shared them as catharsis with their confidantes in the village, be they sister, neighbor, or friend. Women met at the well, at harvests, at festivals, during the exchange of goods, and in war when their men were away. I am betting they opened up to one another.

Second, Israelite women were undoubtedly fully alive as people, and the Bible offers only refracted glimpses into their daily lives. Hence, it is not anachronistic to think that they had desires. Here is where a historian's task gets difficult. Since there are no records, we have to infer them in order to reconstruct a social world, rather than render it anemic of desires. Although authorship cannot be established for the Song, its basis in a folk tradition argues for women's participation in its creation.

Once we leave behind the question of female authorship, we are still left with the purpose of having a woman's voice be so dominant, free, and expressive in the Song. Although a woman's contribution cannot be proven, there are still ample feminist benefits to this portrayal of a woman. These are, perhaps, even guaranteed by the Song's anonymity. For she cannot be reduced to one individual's agenda. She gets to speak for generations beyond her author, much as art breaks well beyond any artist's intention. We could think bigger than authorship and envision her speaking for all women, all people who desire. This woman participates fully, bodily, and undergoes a transformation through the soul-drenching, chest-splitting pressures of yearning. Yearning is not easy, flowery, or for the timid. It requires the bravery of a warrior. This is why the militaristic imagery is not so much a male tag, that is, something he uses more than she, or that she uses as a demonstration of sporty role reversal. Gender itself is subsumed by yearning. It equalizes both of the sexes, and the militaristic imagery gets at desire's struggle. It is fun and thrilling to lust. It is also exhausting and flirts with the limits of sanity and serenity. You can become undone; you can indeed be slain by desire. The woman is not slain in the end, but she certainly struggles and is wounded by desire. Armor of some sort is not such a bad idea, really. It comes in the form of experiential wisdom in this Song. As we shall see in the next chapter, the Song is not only celebrating the delights of desire: it sketches, too, the costs and challenge to the human soul. This woman has been there, done that, and we all stand to gain from her journey.

She endures the struggles of desire and is transformed under them. She is clearly a survivor. In her own Exodus, she sets herself free from the bondage of the social constraints of patriarchy, a king's power, and those of desire's own making, namely, obsession and pain, into sexual, emotional freedom. She does not enter the promised land, but instead *becomes* it, as she and her lover farm for her bodily delights in love. Her body is the locus of a Holy Land. Such triumphant affirmation is clearly pleasurable to readers of the Bible who were not at all expecting a desiring woman to be their guide through yearning. It stands in marked contrast to other biblical portraits of a woman in desire. It calls to mind the most well known, other story of a woman desiring in a garden—Eve—which did not end so well. Other portraits occur in prophetic literature, namely, in Hosea 1–3, Jeremiah 2, and Ezekiel 16 and 23, in which the woman is punished for her desire.

BIBLICAL WOMEN IN DESIRE

Woman's desire occurs elsewhere in the Hebrew Bible, but never fares as well as it does in the Song of Songs. When Eve is cursed in the Garden of Eden, God informs her that he will "greatly increase your pains in childbearing," curiously adding, "your desire shall be for your husband" (Gen 3:16).[25] A very elderly Sarah laughs at the thought that she will "have pleasure again" with her husband Abraham and bear a son, Isaac (Gen 18:12). Her exclamation hints that intercourse for her has been enjoyable and is still missed. Leah, Jacob's neglected co-wife, desires a night with her husband enough to pay Rachel, the other wife, for it with some mandrakes, a supposed aphrodisiac. It is true that procreation is the point of this narrative about two women in a virtual baby race, resulting in thirteen children (Gen 30:14-21).[26] Still, Leah's desire for her husband is evident, especially if she would surrender an aphrodisiac to her competition in order to get some sex herself.

The desire of Potiphar's (unnamed) wife is articulated, burning, and frustrated in Genesis 38. Day after day, she tells the "good-looking and handsome" Joseph, "sleep with me!" but he declines. Since Joseph is the virtuous ancestor of this Israelite tale, Mrs. Potiphar remains stalled in a voracious temptress role. Her voiced desire is eclipsed by her role as foreign sexual aggressor. Elsewhere, woman's desire is used symbolically to illustrate principles of wisdom and obedience, as we shall see. But it has been Eve in the garden that has generated the most discussion of sexuality, desire, and women, and so it is to this story that we now turn.

Eve is the first human to desire, when she sees a tree "pleasing to the eyes and . . . to be desired to make one wise" (Gen 3:6). There is nothing about sex or temptation in the story, except that when Eve and Adam do eat the fruit, "the eyes of both of them were opened and they knew that they were naked" (v. 7). Eve was in a lush garden, full of food without labor. God strolled within it and chatted with the humans, and the humans were unselfconscious about their nudity. Paradise indeed! Everything was pleasant, and it appears that the first couple had it all. One problem with this paradise is that they did not know they had it all. Another is that they really did not.

Desire is born in an experienced lack. Eve wants something she does not have, so the couple does not have it all. What she desires, however, is not the chance to disobey God or tempt Adam, or even to become godlike. Her motives are not a matter of guesswork, but are provided, which is otherwise a rarity in Hebrew narrative. She eats the fruit because she sees that

the tree was good for food, and that it was a delight to
the eyes, and that the tree was to be desired to make
one wise.

—GEN 3:6

Where is the villainous, scheming vixen in this account? One
of the brutal ironies in the story is that God's command for obedience—not to eat from the tree—comes before the humans can
really exercise it, before they know the difference between good
and evil. At best, they were bound to fail or be left in blind obedience under a divine "because I said so." Such an existence
would have been ignorant bliss, but not human life at all.

God's prohibition not to eat from the tree of the knowledge of
good and evil was a test of obedience, but it had the effect, as prohibitions often do, of *eliciting desire*. Day after day in the garden,
the humans would struggle not to want the one tree, much as we
struggle not to rubberneck at a car wreck, look straight into an
eclipse, or turn around when someone says, "Don't look now!"
None of these impulses are desires, really, until they are prohibited.
Then, alas, they become very interesting. Something very human
is glimpsed in this story about desire, something beyond good and
evil, beyond morality and the impressive formation of any super-
ego. Some vital art of human desire is aroused around limits, and
so we go a little above the speed limit, read something banned,
practice underage drinking, or flirt with someone we have just
been warned about. The first couple ate the forbidden fruit.

Like God, we have our own tests and explorations to conduct. *He* tests by placing a limit: one tree is prohibited. *We* test
the limits once we know where they are. We, in a sense, investi-
gate: why this tree, which is pleasant and yields wisdom? Where
is the danger in that? If we are made in God's image (Gen 1:26-
27), then we will always be attracted to the boundary between
what part of us is God's image and what is not, and desire to explore it. Desire, for a believer in biblical spirituality, is basically
the mediator for being a creature made in the image of God, but
nevertheless separate from him.

The story of the Garden of Eden might well be a story of nostalgia, a longing for some earlier and easier life that we lost. If so, that is revealing, too, of the ancient writers' own desire, of a lust for something no longer here, a lust toward a lack, a way to stretch beyond limits. The Garden of Eden may be the symbol for the pleasures of an easier life or the psychological wish, as Freud would say, to return to the infant stage when everything was taken care of for us. Eve and Adam wanted something more than they had; they stretched their limits, but did nothing wrong. Contrary to their reputation, they did not mess up, but did just what humans will do. Desire is the inevitable human impulse toward one's limits. With that comes risk, knowledge, and self-growth. A command to stay in stasis, even for preliminary divine screenings for obedience, infantilizes humanity and is cruel.

The story includes part of Eve's curse, as noted above, "Your desire shall be for your husband." Why is this a part of the divine judgment? Why does this even need to be uttered, since the woman was created from the rib of man anyway? Her longing could easily have been depicted as a physiological given, the response, in effect, of her status as Adam's phantom, yet pro-acting, limb.[27] And just who else is Eve going to desire, anyway? By conscripting Eve's desire, the writers reflect a male Israelite anxiety that their women could go elsewhere, if not in reality, at least in their dreams. And further, by not having a corresponding curse on Adam's desire, they let male desire roam free, unpunished, and hinted that women were objects for their desire.

Women likely were eye-catching objects of desire for ancient Israelite men. The endearing Jacob impulsively kisses Rachel and then weeps for joy when he first meets her (Gen 29:11). The women in Gen 6:2 elicit the attentions of the sons of God. Their powers of attraction draw these divine beings from the sky, resulting in divine–human couplings. And in another disturbing account, Abram is so sure that Sarai's beauty is going to get him killed by the pharaoh, he pimps her out to the pharaoh by pretending that she is just his sister (Gen 12:10-20). Sarai is notified of his plan, but she is not consulted. Otherwise, though, women in narrative stories are not singled out for objectification. Various individuals are known for their beauty, but this cuts across both genders. Among those in the biblical pageant of the good-looking are Sarah, Rebekkah, Rachel, Bathsheba, Vashti, Esther, Joseph, Samson, David, and Absalom.

Eve exercised desire for both wisdom and fruit, and this desire was then cursed by being redirected to her husband. That this story came to associate woman and sexuality with sin is a notorious postbiblical development. Eve became the scapegoat for a culture's anxieties about the body, sexuality, and women. The history of interpretation of the Garden of Eden has a long, dramatic, and psychologically revealing tradition in the West as a result of different strategies of dealing with and discussing the body in ancient rabbinic and early Christian formulations. The influence of the church fathers and the neo-Platonic dualistic tendency to see the body as the house of the soul, the thing which really marked the human, led to projections of shame and belittlement that biblical texts involving or implying sexuality.

The most famous textual victim was, of course, Eve, whose fruit-eating exploits earned her, under Augustine's stylus, best unsupported role in the fall of humanity. The notion of the woman as temptress with potentially destructive decision-making abilities has long and forcefully influenced the West.[28] The Christian legacy about sexuality has been tremendously influential and largely, fatally, scripted by Augustine. It has been dire, costly, and damning for notions of sexuality, of woman,[29] and for where God stands in all this mess of being human. But even before that, most Christian thinkers viewed sex as sinful.[30] Paul connected sexuality and knowledge (Rom 1:26-27), constrained desire to marriage (1 Cor 7:2, 5-6, 9, 37-39), and then advised celibacy (1 Cor 7:6-7).[31] A general disdain toward the body and woman hardens with Paul and continues with the early church fathers. Jewish interpreters were different from the church fathers in that they tended to interpret the sexuality in the Garden of Eden as an essential, normal part of humanity.[32] It was Augustine who went the furthest and interpreted the Garden of Eden story, with Adam hiding behind the fig leaf, to be about sexuality and shame.

With this move, sex was reduced, first of all, to genital sex. It was uncontrollable, as Augustine argued: the fig leaf obscured the movement of Adam's sexual organ in desire, and it was antithetical to authentic spirituality. Augustine believed that sex would be a part of paradise, but the fall added compulsion to it.[33] The woman is seen as other and as the site for these problematic desires competing with one's spiritual desires. He even turns the woman into a field awaiting the male seed, though these are not the metaphors used at all in this horticultural garden story.[34] What was behind the fig leaves could no longer be controlled by one's will and so was now viewed as a site of shame, hence "pudenda," from the Latin verb, "pudere," "to make or be ashamed."[35]

The movement of genitals as a sign of shame, though, explains Adam's need for clothing. But it does not help to explain Eve's, since her genital excitement would take different forms, not visible even without clothing. But this does not concern Augustine, who is busy treating Eve to a sinister combination package of erasure and blame. At this point, as Margaret Miles notes, female nakedness became a cipher for sin, sex, and death.[36] Anti-body and antiwoman sentiments are yoked, and they dog Christianity from this point on.[37] The woman's naked body, in Elaine Pagels's deft image, became a palimpset—erased and rewritten on—on which subsequent attitudes were inscribed.[38] And sex is driven into something that is shameful and needs to be covered. This natural desire and function would eventually even become something worthy of confession in the Middle Ages.[39]

Augustine managed to link desire, sex, and shame in a slam dunk of guilt-inducing interpretation. The biblical problem, of course, is that desire is the only element mentioned in the text. Sex is nowhere evident, and shame is a rather strong inference to draw from the couple's newfound awareness of their nakedness.

Something has clearly happened, and it will incur God's wrath, but whether this is shameful is unclear. In fact, it might not be. After cursing them, God sews new loincloths made of animal skins, guaranteed to last. Whether this gesture is a way for him to participate in their shaming or to take care of them is a fairly significant theological point, and I incline toward the latter explanation. Further, I would suggest that anger itself, even the divine anger here, need bear no connection to human shame.

Woman's Desire in Prophecy

The image of the woman as sexual partner to God is given in four prophetic texts (Hosea 1–3; Jer 2:24; Ezekiel 16 and 23). These are all judgment texts, describing when the relationship has gone sour and God feels entitled to violent punishment and name-calling of the woman. His intimate spouse, all too quickly, becomes a whore deserving whatever she gets from him and from enemies he would put in her way. Women's desire in all four texts is viewed as wayward and infuriating to God. It is even ungrateful, since the women have apparently spurned no less a lover than God. From the prophets' point of view, she had it coming. The woman in each text stands for the disobedient people. In three accounts (Hosea 1–3, Ezekiel 16 and 23), God will strip the woman bare, humiliate her, and make her learn the error of her ways. It is unfortunate that we are only getting this intimate theological portrait at the end stages of a divine–human marriage. For the notion of God having wooed and married his people would offer powerful images for intimacy with God. Note, for example, this nostalgic prelude to the woman's punishment:

> You grew strong and tall and became a young woman.
> Your breasts were well-formed, and your hair had
> grown, but you were naked.
> As I passed by again, I saw that the time had come
> for you to fall in love. I covered your naked body with

my coat and promised to love you. Yes, I made a marriage covenant with you.

—EZEK 16:7-8

In these texts, the relationship has deteriorated, and love has turned to inhumane bitterness. In Hosea 1–3 and Ezekiel 16, God calls his partner a whore. In Jer 2:24, things are only slightly better, as God chastises her for being loose and running around in heat. With Ezekiel, though, all hell breaks loose and God is actually setting up a gang rape (Ezekiel 23) and a gang murder (Ezekiel 16) in his fury at the woman. These are awful moments for theology and women, meant to be shocking illustrations of the people's downfall. There is, of course, no talking to this kind of abusive husband; there is only the faint wish that he will stop.[40]

With such devastating wrath, there is not much room to describe the woman's desire. She is harangued into silence, and anyway, her desires are what got her this punishment.[41] So, in Hos 2:13, she is chided for having chased after her lovers. We see both the eagerness and the multiplicity of her desire. A similar charge is evident with the Jeremiah passage, since it likens her to a wild camel in heat, running all over the place. In Ezekiel 16, she is charged with sleeping with everyone who came along (v. 15) and even paying for their services (v. 34). Her desire, then, is promiscuous, voracious, and even desperate. In Ezekiel 23, she is simply described as being "full of lust" (vv. 5, 12), even going after carved images of men to have sex (v. 15). There is nothing positive about desire or the woman (that is, the people) that God himself has chosen. Violence, degradation, and rage become the divine responses to desire, sex, and women. These curious and cruel accounts of God's wrath are beyond the confines of our study of women in desire. We can see only how clipped, frightened, and distorted the woman's desire is in these misogynistic fantasies.

An insight of Foucault's might help us here. He put forth the idea that a puritanical preacher who denounces sexual excess can arouse himself and his congregation in the process. This would enable him to pay lip service against sexual pleasure, all the while getting sexual pleasure himself from the words and images he was using. We witness an example of such lewd sanctimony with these prophets. In Foucault's view, it is not so much that the prophets protest too much, it is that they do it so vividly that it occasions suspicion. The descriptions are so sexually vivid that they detract from the theological point being made against turning away from God. Ezekiel uses the image of donkeys and stallions having intercourse with the woman (Ezek 23:20), and this is meant to illustrate her infidelity. But it is too shocking, too over the top, and we are distracted by the sexual, bestial images. At best, we become suspicious of the prophet's psychology, at worst, we become suspicious of God's. For calling someone a whore or wanting them to be gang-raped lays bare a hostile attitude toward women and sexuality.

Women and their desire obviously suffer terribly in these prophetic instances of the marriage metaphor. In the case of Eve, she and her desire occur within the biblical story of the Garden of Eden that leaves out all mention of Adam's desire. She is mangled less than her biblical sisters in the prophetic marriage metaphor, but postbiblically, she has certainly borne the blame for the fall of humanity. And her desire has suffered in the process. Where it had been proactive and a mark of some self-possession in the garden, it gets harnessed to her man by God's curse. Postbiblically, her desire comes to matter not at all, as she becomes a cipher for men's uncontrollable, sinful desire. She is not a whore, but because she elicits male desires, she is to blame for them in Christianity. There is nowhere to go from here but up, and happily this occurs with the Song of Songs. It even acts as a corrective to the prophetic nightmares of a love gone awry, with its restoration of respect, joy, and a woman's voice.

The male lover is bouncing around the countryside and on top of her (the hills) with no less a name than Solomon, Israel's wisest king. Yet she, a nameless, dark, excited woman, is the heroine of the book. She journeys through desire, unhampered by male dominance, urban rules, or patriarchal customs, and still has enough left over in the final chapter to praise her own sexuality. It is truly a tour de force and a triumph when anyone can reach that stage. Against all the odds of her culture, against the legitimacy of King Solomon and a pack of brothers trying to marry her off, she stands and sings not of them, not in humility to God's greatness like Hannah (1 Sam 2:1-10) or Mary (Luke 1:46-55), but of her very own beauty. She is too sexy for the rest of them.

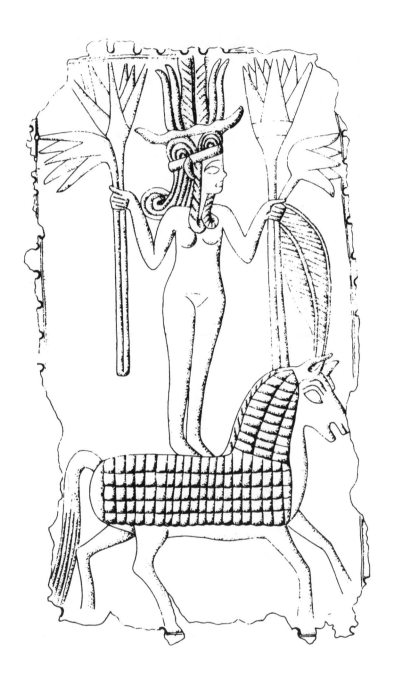

7

Passion Fierce as the Grave
Death and Desire

HITTING UP AGAINST LIMITS

> For love is as strong as death,
>> passion fierce as the grave.
>> —SONG 8:6

In addition to her account of her own journey through desire, the woman of the Song offers philosophical perspectives on the nature of desire. The above verse, the Song's most famous line, is one such observation, and this chapter will center on these general assessments of desire. Up to this point, we have been discussing the flirtation and arousal in the Song's languages of desire. We have seen how vividly and urgently two lovers express their desire while remaining separated from each other. These renderings have proven to be exciting, endearing, even salacious and blunt. They have had the effect of making the experience of desire seem all but irresistible. The upshot is that a Song about desire winds up making its readers yearn for desire itself. We have also seen a powerfully articulate woman sing of her desire in marked, stunning, and even triumphant contrast to other biblical traditions on woman's desire. The Song has proven bold on these counts and it continues to be so when probing into desire's risk. In truth, it is a sophisticated and daring exploration into yearning that transcends the limitations evident in androcentrism, but it also transcends past concerns for gender, whatever they may be, and ventures past the mere titillation that erotic literature provides.

This writer travels through and beyond desire's object in sexual union, into the emotional toll it exacts on the lovers, and then reaches out to the limits of desire itself—to where its pain, risk, and uncontrollability are felt. The Song strikes these somber chords about desire amid the frenzied excitement of love's passion. It then would stop us short and educate us further on desire's complex character, before we get the chance to slip off, contentedly aroused. This complexity of images is truly testimony to the writer's mastery. He or she is not stopping just with desire's sexual and empowering surges, as Hollywood so often does in its cult of lust. We do not see the lovers burn with passion and eventually get to explode in each other's arms, though their desire is pulsating throughout the Song. Nor does the writer stop with only the dangers of desire, as does the tragic tradition in Western culture, for example, *Romeo and Juliet, Tristan and Isolde, Dangerous Liaisons, Fatal Attraction,* and so forth. Lustful excitement and danger are two facets of desire, but neither offers a complete description of its impact. This Hebrew poet exerts a matured realism to hone desire's complexity. This is the difference: the Song is not about the satisfaction of desire. It is about desire's passion, and that means that it involves suffering. Passion derives from the Latin term for suffer. It is an emotion, yes, but with enough intensity to hurt. It becomes what Bataille termed a "violent agitation."[1] We turn in this chapter to the Song's testimony to desire's painful intensity.

The descriptions given over to desire's intensity in the Song serve as cautionary notes on desire and bespeak a healthy respect for the power unleashed by desire. When the woman finally asserts that "love is as strong as death," her sentiment is no cliché or glib assurance about the worthiness of desire as death's only real contender. Instead, given the considered skill of the figurative expression throughout the Song, we know that she means for this simile to be freighted with multivalent meanings. Love and death are, for the desiring woman of the Song, *equal* forces of life. The subtextual contest between love and death in the Song, in our psyches, has been a draw, not a victory. This poet, to be sure, is aware of desire's potency and costs, along with its rewarding pleasures.

The Song affirms the paradox that human desire is the life force and is associated with death itself.[2] It cradles this psychological ambiguity adroitly, without melodramatic despair or the muscling in of denial. And this is truly no small accomplishment. Ambiguities today, and since the onset of Platonism, tend to be carved by dualism, and so the dangers of desire can become excuses for disdaining it, especially in early Christianity. The Song beckons us to learn from desire in its full force. Along with the excitement and the transformation of desire, the Song offers cautionary instruction.

It is worth noting that the cautions of the Song toward desire differ considerably from those found elsewhere in antiquity, particularly in Greco-Roman traditions, where they are primarily about the moral risk to one's soul. In a paradigmatic example from the *Odyssey*, Odysseus has to navigate past the Sirens, who are depicted as irresistible women singing an alluring song that has victimized many a sailor before him. He has to be tied to his boat as the only way to resist his own desire, once it is ignited by the Sirens' song.[3] Odysseus is viewed as wise, and this scene is an illustration of that wisdom. His only hope in the face of desire, though, is his premeditated leashing of it and himself before the temptations begin. Merely declining does not seem to be an option here. This scene reveals much about classical attitudes toward desire (and women), namely, that it harbors danger by rendering its victim helpless under its spell. It is not at all surprising, then, that the Greeks brought us the idea of Eros (later Cupid in Latin), who was out and about inflicting people with the wound of love. In Virgil's *Aeneid*, Cupid strikes Dido with her fatal attraction for Aeneas. Once struck, we know that she is helpless and living on borrowed time. Her desire is unsurvivable.

Given the chaotic confusion and self-destructiveness wrought by the emotion of desire, the classical world fought for a solution, or better, a managed-care option for its desires, and came up with reason. The Greek philosophical tradition placed desire *under* the care of rationality. Hence, Odysseus did just what desire calls for; he bested emotion with a reasoned plan. Under this classical influence, Foucault argues, desire became for the West largely something to manage, dominate, and even defeat.[4] Sexual appetite was viewed as something to control, and that control then bespoke a virtuous individual. A loss of control was, correspondingly, a sign of laziness, of not having steeled oneself firmly enough with reason.[5]

By contrast, for the Hebrew poet, desire is not dangerous because it *may* cause an individual to lose control, to slip from the supposed superiority of reason. Instead, the loss of control is a given: "love is strong as death . . . its flashes are flashes of fire." Desire burns out of our control, by its own design, and yet that is no reason to avoid it. The Hebrew writer might see the classical attempts to secure reason's mastery over desire as futile and misguided. Flames and the grave have, as it were, a life of their own. Desire's muscled, tried independence is seen by the Hebrew writer as an essential and not correctable facet. It is most vitally an utter, thrilling *loss of control*, a giving over to the sensation of want, a foregrounding of that exquisite, aching sense of yearning, while *everything* else blurs, falling to the wayside. In a real sense, it had better be out of control, or it is not desire.

That sobering reality, that one is helpless in desire, is acknowledged in the Song. For the classical tradition, that loss of control gave rise to reason's attempt to conquer or vanquish desire.[6] There is in the Song, however, no attempt to domesticate desire, to rid it of its risks, either through moral legislation, shaming, or reason's mastery. Instead, the loss of control stands as one facet of desire along with others in a complex, mature portrait. These two lovers are neither hedonists—out for pleasure for its own sake—nor neophytes, simply naive and bent on pleasure no matter the cost. Nor are they doomed to tragedy for having ignited desire. But they have taken a courageous risk and ventured into something beyond their control. The lovers are portrayed in a daring free fall, as lustful, open, diligent, and maturing through desire's process.

Their journey through desire is an education between them and for them, the woman voicing more of desire's lesson than does the man. It is she who offers the cautionary wisdom on desire, and she does so in two essential ways: first, through the important speech comparing love with death, and second, by means of a refrain she uses throughout the Song: "do not stir up or arouse love until it delights" (2:7; 3:5; 5:8; 8:4). Her wisdom has an authority by virtue of her eyewitness account in undergoing desire. The refrain itself takes on added legitimacy as it is threaded throughout the narrative of her experience. Her journey through desire becomes an educational one for herself and for the bystanders: the daughters of Jerusalem, to whom she addresses her insights, and the reader of the Song.

It is in this way that the Song truly is Israelite wisdom literature, with the participants, and by implication, all those who read, gaining instruction. Tradition has always regarded the Song of Songs to be wisdom literature, due primarily to the mention of Solomon, the king above all others known for his wisdom (1 Kgs 10:23). The educational content of this wisdom literature, however, has not often been fully explored. The wisdom is gained from the journey of two searching lovers with all its highs and lows. The poem is at once celebratory and rueful on desire. It truly offers an education about the wholesale effect desire has on one's emotions, perspectives, and sense of self within the world. Desire envelops people, coloring and reorienting their world and their worldview. Any force that all-consuming has the power also to wound, through exhaustion, disintegration, or despair, dangers for which a person might likely be ill-equipped.

Desire's Power

Death is what lurks inside the Trojan horse of passion, as this Song reminds us in what is its most famous passage:

> For love is as strong as death
>> passion fierce as the grave.
> Its flashes are flashes of fire,
>> a raging flame. (8:6)

The first two lines are a classic example of Hebrew parallelism, where the second line is meant to reiterate, and perhaps supplement, the ideas present in the first line. Hence, "love" and "passion" are essentially the same notion, and are paired respectively with "death" and "the grave," also meant to denote the same notion. So the question here is what do love and death, passion and the grave, share as strongholds on life? The Song has been about love throughout, and this is its first mention of death. The equation is unexpected; a poem about human want winds down to a comparison of want and the cessation of life. In chapter 3, we spoke about the sheer difficulty in speaking of love at all, about how quickly one is forced to one's knees in humility, abandoned by language, and left to discover and stutter out new metaphors. Has the same necessary innovation occurred here, whereby the author is struggling to say something new about desire's fierce grip on life? Is this a morbid, cynical stance on desire, or is it somehow a life-enhancing one?

These sentiments are at once majestic, inspiring, and, upon reflection, terrifying. Love and death, whatever their differences, clearly share the trait of a totalizing strength. They are both relentless and implacable from the individual's perspective, and they exact a weighty toll on whatever emotional and spiritual resources that individual can muster. We stand reassured that love can last, yet we are also reminded that it bends to *no* control on our parts. The similes betray the fierceness of desire as well as some healthy ambivalence about its power. And there is some reassurance that death finally has a worthy opponent or competitor in love. There is even, perhaps, the fledgling hope that passion could take what Hosea had earlier hoped for, namely the plague out of death (Hos 13:14) or in Paul, the sting (1 Cor 15:55).

But in this comparison, love does not conquer death. It is a worthy contender, to be sure, but no victor. Hence, the verse is not simply a celebration of the power of love,[7] for this would privilege the love of the comparison, while ignoring, for the moment, its paired complement, death. Neither does it represent a kind of sarcastic disregard of societal norms, with love and death enlisted to demolish them.[8] Instead, however love is understood, it must stand in comparison with death. The Song forces us to confront the association of passion with death. Jonathan Dollimore notes an important benefit to exploring this association in his book on the subject, entitled *Death, Desire, and Loss in Western Culture*. He noticed that, "by acknowledging an 'obvious' connection between desire and death, the commonplace encourages us to forgo thought about it."[9] We will not do so in this chapter.

"Love" (Hebrew: *ahabah*) has been the term used throughout the Song, and so its use certainly comes as no surprise here. "Passion" (Hebrew: *qinah*) is, however, used for the first time, and so its use requires some explanation. In Hebrew, *qinah* is used to denote sexual passion and jealousy, and means "intense devotion."[10] "Passion" is used in the Bible to describe a husband's jealousy (Prov 6:34) or competing emotions (Eccles 4:4; Isa 11:3). But as an adjective, "passionate," it is used exclusively of God. The Second Commandment is a prohibition against worshiping other gods, describing Yahweh as "a passionate" or "jealous" God, the terms in Hebrew being synonymous. "Passion" includes the sense of intensity and exclusivity in Hebrew, and the inability to share or disperse one's emotions or tolerate receiving divided loyalties. Fidelity is clearly honed in the term "passion" in a way that is not the case for "love." God is passion-filled, not intermittent in his emotions, and so the people cannot afford to be intermittent in their emotional response to him. Note also, here, that the presence or existence of other gods is assumed.

God's intense passion is described elsewhere with the image of a fire: "for the Lord your God is a consuming fire, a passionate God" (Deut 4:24). God's desire, too, is likened to a consuming fire, much as human desire is here likened to a raging fire. Passion in the Hebrew Bible, whether it be divine or human, is unstoppable and pure in its intensity.[11] For Yahweh, the God of monotheism, it had better be indivisible as well, or else it is not pure. The monotheism being commanded at Mount Sinai requires a fidelity and totality similar to sexual monogamy on the human plane, hence the prophets' use of a marriage metaphor for the divine–human relationship. At best, maybe what humans can do is steal the passion in our fear about death and reinvest it toward love.

It is an odd paradox, but sex and death are often associated in Western tradition. Literature devoted to desire and sexuality will eventually get around to or hint at the presence of death with a consistency that is at once jarring and obvious. Passion comes to highlight one's mortality, and mortality animates one's passion. So Dido is inflamed with such a passion for Aeneas that she literally cannot live without him and commits suicide as he leaves Carthage. For Lucretius, desire inflicts humans with "love's deathless wound."[12] Later, there are the Western tragic couplings such as Romeo and Juliet, and Tristan and Isolde. We have romanticized the association of desire with death, and continue to do so today. Just look at James Cameron's film *Titanic*. This, after all, was a film in which we already knew the ending, yet record-breaking numbers turned out to watch two lovers dance on one of their graves. In our entertainment, at least, we like this association, even if it remains unacknowledged. And it most often does remain unacknowledged.

These traditions are not haphazard. They give dramatic testimonies to the power of love, even up against the brink of extinction. And, too, there is even an association of passion itself with death. So the French can speak of orgasm as "a little death."[13] Hamlet could yearn quite specifically and famously for death in erotic terms: "'tis a consummation devoutly to be wished."

Love and death share some qualities inherently that make their association recur in literature and in this Song. These are mutability, loss of autonomy or control, and annihilation or loss of self. Desires are always changing, never fixed, especially once consummation can occur. The mutability is itself partly what we desire and what keeps us alive. Lucretius noted early on the necessary fickleness of our desire:

> So long as the object of our craving is unattained, it seems more precious than anything. Once it is ours we crave for something else. So an unquenchable thirst for life keeps us always on the gasp.[14]

In other words, passion of the burning, dramatic, self-risking kind cannot sustain itself for long under the conditions of union. Mutability is an inherent part of love, as it is of life in general and of the death we all face. The physical features the two lovers praise so lavishly in the Song will age, wrinkle, dim, sag, weaken, gray—every one of them touched by time. The lovers' longing itself undergoes change within the Song, as we saw in the transitions inherent in the language of desire. Change offers a foretaste of death. It is as implacable as death. It is as fiercely present in life, as nonnegotiable. It commands or scares us into living life at full throttle rather than postponing our joy.

The woman's desire is undergoing a transformation within this final chapter, where she dispenses with the lover who is absent anyway, and proclaims instead her own sexuality. While she has pined for him with ardent love throughout these eight chapters, by the final chapter, her desire changes in tone. She will end the Song by inviting him one last time to hurry up and join her:

> Make haste, my beloved,
>   and be like a gazelle,

or a young stag
upon the mountains of spices! (8:14)

But somehow the desperation is gone. By this point she is no longer expecting a response, and so the book ends without one. What she does do is reclaim her sexuality and her passion for herself: "My vineyard, my very own is before me" (8:12). She is now sole owner, the brothers no longer having the land rights they presumed to have with her in 1:6, where she complained about not having time for her vineyard.

Her vineyard makes this important reappearance at the end and is now in her hands. She may still desire her lover and want for him to come to her, but she has taken the vineyard, her site for making love as well as a metaphor of her sexuality, off the market and claimed it as her own. Her desire, by the end, has undergone considerable transformation. What had been controlled by her brothers she wrested from them and claimed for her own, and even had the gumption to compare to Solomon's vineyard. There is pure joy in her celebration of self here, for she rests content with her sexuality, not needing even Israel's wisest king. And her comparison is oblique. For what Solomon had one thousand of is women in his considerable harem (1 Kgs 11:3). She knows she is their superior, that her own sexuality is more valuable than a king's wealth of opportunity. This is indeed a change. Whatever else it signals, we suspect now that any further ventures in search of her lover will be wholly on her terms.

This is one of the paradoxes of the Song; it has been about the intense sensual yearning between two lovers and has ended with the woman alone, yet resolved and strengthened. Falk points out that all along the Song has been expressing the various paradoxes of erotic love, and this is surely one of them. It tackles three essential paradoxes of such love, which she lists as: "Conflict that intensifies passion, painful separation that heightens the pleasure of union, intimate bonding with the other that gives the individual courage to stand alone."[15]

Part of the attraction of desire, of sexual coupling with the other, is to explore and experience the limits of self, to push oneself—body, soul, and might—beyond known limits. Desire seeks out the liminal edges of a soul, propelling the being toward them in a mixture of excitement and fear. There is little comfort about being in desire for this reason. It harbors small and large rips throughout the self. Desire is a liminal dance between the experienced and known out beyond the self's boundaries toward another. That is, it is as much a yearning for the other as it is a yearning to transcend oneself. We want to find ourselves in love with the other.

And oddly, in part, this has little to do with the other. It is an impulse to lose ourselves, to erase or soften the boundaries of identity. It is self-destructive in the way that growth requires. That is what love is at first, a softening of the boundaries—letting someone in and, just as important, letting ourselves out. We surrender control to the force of desire and float along. We are even conscious and tolerant of the fact that love has taken control, and so speak of it as having been "swept off our feet." In part, then, we desire this loss of control even as we fear it. We like the sensation of losing ourselves in love, assured that it is temporary. We abandon ourselves, our egos, to desire, and this mimics the eventual loss of self in death. Desire makes us sense what Bataille calls the "swift movement of loss within us."[16] That loss will only be grander at our death.

Desire, then, is partly about self-transcendence or loss of self, the urge toward annihilation of identity. It shares this with death, obviously. And this is why it is passion, suffering, and is not easy. It hurts ontologically to risk boundaries. It is a risk toward change, whether by growth or disintegration. Augustine saw this risk as bad. For him, one of the unsettling aspects of sexual union was that we forget ourselves: "So intense is the pleasure that when it reaches its climax there is an almost total extinction of mental alertness."[17] This view clearly reflects his concern. Of course, it also lets us know that the man has certainly been there!

Is such a temporary loss of self such a bad thing for a human to experience, on the sexual and spiritual plane? It seems to me that it loosens the individual from the bondage of self, and it loosens reason's tyrannical hold on that self. Our experience of life, of spiritual growth, can both be expanded through this means of losing our self. Love and death are associated by this experience of limits and the loss of ego, which are desired. From Bataille's description, it is easy to see why our desire to lose ourselves would have spiritual dimensions:

> The desire to go keeling helplessly over, that assails the innermost depths of every human being is nevertheless different from the desire to die in that it is ambiguous. It may well be a desire to die, but it is at the same time a desire to live to the limits of the possible and the impossible with ever-increasing intensity.[18]

In more biblical language, we might speak of dying in order to be reborn. But the Song and Bataille's quotation are about the desire this side of dying or losing oneself, not its accomplishment.

Camille Paglia, with characteristic candor, notes that we have become too blind or comfortable in our idealizations of love and have lost sight of some of its ardor:

> The current discourse about sex is too genteel. Freud's severe, conflict-based system has lost popularity to a casual, sentimental style of user-friendly psychological counseling that I find typically Protestant, in the glad-handing Chamber of Commerce way."[19]

Love, she seems to be saying along with the Song, is not user-friendly. In passion, one is both winner and victim. That is why good erotica cannot just be a success story, told pithily in paperbacks. We have tons of best-selling books on the sexes, on sex, but not a lot about the fever of yearning. There are no clever titles that capture yearning. Longing involves a loss of autonomy, of self-control, and so the woman in the Song lost it. She remains nameless throughout and is shown wandering the streets at night twice (3:3; 5:7).[20] Once, she is beaten by the guards for it. In sleep, too, she undergoes a more pleasant loss of control with her wet dream.[21] Death, too, forces a loss of control and can also catch one unawares, like a thief in the night. Desire's pull and surprise can be just as sudden and wrenching.

What we term a "fatal attraction" is really only desire taken to an extreme. It constitutes, of course, a woeful object choice, but it is *fatal* by virtue of its paralyzing infection in us, rendering desire inevitable. We are afraid of fatal attractions because we sense the quicksand-like grip they would have and because we know that they come from within us. There is really no outside foe to fend off. The danger lies within our heart. That means, paradoxically, that we are drawn to them at the same time that we fear them. With a somewhat dubious pride, we may know to avoid lovers who would boil the family rabbit, à la Glenn Close in *Fatal Attraction*. But we are not so sure what our own desires could do to us if given free rein. On less extreme levels, many of us probably have flirted with loves where we have felt addicted, lost, or even frightened, unable to stop. These hurried excursions lay bare desire's frightening potency, and we often use a fatal simile for such attractions: "drawn like a moth to a flame."

For Georges Bataille, there is an uneasy knowledge gained in the experience of desire, for the security of distancing ourselves from a fatal attraction is in some senses a false one. As he points out, "The stirrings within us have their own fearful excesses; the excesses show which way these stirrings would take us."[22] The human being glimpses in regular (nonfatal) attractions the extremes to which he or she could nevertheless go. In fact, for Bataille, these excesses are a chilling sign to remind us that "death . . . stands there before us more real than life itself."[23] What he means is that, in desire, we will risk our emotional or physical health, beyond reason, and we may even come to find our dis-ease itself alluring. We might, in other words, *like* the uncomfortable state of yearning we are in and risk more to feel it more intensely.

Passion Fierce as the Grave 171

I take it that this might be why women would have fantasies of rape that bear no resemblance to what they would want in real life. We live with the ever-present fear or memory of rape, and so the fantasy may be a sign, not of our having been co-opted by male-dominated images, but of expressing the excesses, the "get it over with" of annihilation that fear has fought so long to keep at bay. If Bataille and the Song are correct that the association of desire with death is more than haphazard, then fantasies simply become an expression of desire's excesses and are not wishes at all.

Near death, we are often most intensely aware of and present to life. The imminence of death brings out what Bataille nicely termed the "incandescence of life."[24] We are closest to life at its most organic as the approach of death levels all other concerns and troubles. So, too, our senses are heightened. "Paradoxically," Ackerman notes, "it is in that moment of annihilation that we become most open to life."[25] In love, too, we stretch to slow or still time. We try to hold each moment, knowing that it is futile, it will pass. It is a bittersweet sensation.

Here I believe the Song has worlds to tell us. For while we consider ourselves casually, trendily sophisticated about sex, we actually have a considerable amount to handle. We are heirs to the sexual revolution of the sixties and are victims of the AIDS epidemic, which has cruelly literalized the association of sex and death in our generation. So much for sexual freedom. It was a brief reign in which guilt was conquered through therapy, drugs, and the discarding of religions, but now the fear of survival looms. The strategy for negotiating sex and death is not avoidance (asceticism), conquest (Greek metaphysics), or despair (Romanticism), but respect for desire's truly existential power.

These associations—of mutability, annihilation, and loss of autonomy—gave rise to the thought, at least in the West, that what one finds desirable is on some level death itself.[26] Sexual desire is not driven by the specific lover, but by the longing for escape or transcendence beyond one's own identity. Death itself becomes a lure because it offers transcendence of the self, albeit through its negation. Also, death acts to intensify passion.[27] It adds to the pleasure and pain of desire. So the erotic, in Freud's terms, is the life force and contains a death wish. We are caught in this web of wanting and not wanting consummation, and eroticism works to resolve the apparent opposites of life and the pull of death.[28] And we learn what we already know from this Song, that those opposites are only apparent ones.

This lure may be why the Tristan myth of a doomed love hurtling toward death is so pronounced in the West.[29] On some level we long for death, but that is too obvious and awful to admit, so this myth acts, in Ackerman's phrase, as a kind of "emotional hieroglyph." It is too threatening to admit that we desire death, so we watch doomed love stories—whether Wagner's *Tristan and Isolde,* or, most recently, Cameron's *Titanic*—*and are enraptured by them.* Leonardo DiCaprio became a teen idol for his role as a Popsicle for love, and so youth could worship death.

In a sense, this, too, is what the erotic can do; it enables us to feel our limits and, for a brief moment, to go beyond them. It allows us to go over the edge, say, by fantasizing about a dangerous situation, and then return unharmed. Contained danger is the point of such a fantasy, with erotica acting as a kind of roller coaster for the heart. But the next moment is just as crucial. Most of us will feel more alive, thrilled, and at the same time humbled by the glance beyond ourselves. We are humbled by what we are capable of risking, of wanting in fantasy. "Ecstasy," in fact, means precisely the state of an intense emotion beyond one's limits, from the Greek *ex,* "out of," and *histanai,* "place."

Desire rocks and upsets stasis, the rut of our lives. Some people will go toward the self-destruction implicit in any self-expanding desire, be it a sexual or spiritual transcendence. They will long for the annihilation glimpsed in ecstasy. But most of us return or bring that love in for a landing into our lives. We make the attempt to incorporate that passion into the rest of our lives without settling or killing it. We do want it both ways, the passion and the stability of routine. The negotiation of desire in daily life is as delicate as surgery, and sometimes it works. It is the no-man's-land between infatuation and commitment. Desire lures us in and toward the other in a lifelong passion ending only with our death. This is true for relationships and for spirituality. After the giddy, thrilling newness is over, now what? The wisdom offered here is not for desire's dismantling or its quenching. It is instructions for living with the condition.

There is a toughened element of joy in this Song, namely, that the joy love brings also brings the grief of death. Human joy contains the fomenting of grief, through both the loss and the heightened emotions that are ushered in. Joy is a part of life, as is the pain that comes within it and unalterably in its wake. As the fourth-century church father Gregory of Nyssa noted, as long as people "look upon the tombs of those from whom they came into being, they have grief inseparably joined to their lives even if they take little notice of it."[30] Love and death, joy and grief, pleasure and hardship are all part and parcel of human existence for the Hebrew writers, church fathers, and for us.

The Song, in its association of love with death, however, is not as pessimistic as Ecclesiastes, the other wisdom book attributed to Solomon, and the other text that the Rabbis disputed for inclusion in the canon. For Ecclesiastes, there is a time to be born, a time to die, a time for joy, a time for grief, a time for making love, and a time for not making love (Eccles 3:2-5). These are all just the natural cycles of human life. And everything that Ecclesiastes tries to make sense of about that life comes to naught, as mere "vanity of vanities, all is vanity" (Eccles 1:2). In the end, all of us wind up dead, whether we have been righteous or wicked. Death becomes the criterion against which to judge a life or make sense of it. And the author cannot. All he can utter against the backdrop of certain death is that one should

> enjoy life with the woman you love all the days of your
> vain life that are given you under the sun.
> —ECCLES 9:9

He champions a pleasure not unlike that in the Song, a loved woman, but the tone is altogether different. His advice sounds defeated and weary, not erotic or joyful at all. There is, overall, a resignation to Ecclesiastes' existential probe of life and death that is lacking in the Song of Songs.

The truth about desire is that it is present, coursing within us, and can turn our world upside down in ways that are delightful and sickening, joyous and troubling. It can pull the soul right out of itself toward growth and confusion. It is overwhelmingly potent, hence attempts to control it are understandable. It can overturn society, and this is why legislation so often surrounds it.[31] As a society, we share a polite convention, to agree to tame our desire, all the while recognizing the lie, namely, that it is not tame at all. The Song, then, is not hedonistic in spirit, for it contains a wise, cautionary tone of desire's force.

In the Song, the tough power of love and of death still reigns. The woman offers with brave candor her instruction for humans participating in the thick of life's enigmas, instead of the detached cynicism of Ecclesiastes. The writer of Ecclesiastes seems at times to have surrendered his passion, left life's pleasures behind him, and is in the process of leaving behind their riddle. Where he has blanched at life's enigmas, the woman of the Song has relished them. There is a skill and readiness to approaching desire or tracking its development, once it has taken hold of the individual. Like death, desire will require all, and like death, it will likely be a lifelong fascination and fear.

Climax

Modern commentators on the Song of Songs see this passage equating love and death as the culmination of the poem. Pope, Murphy, and LaCocque even consider it the "climax" of the Song.[32] Murphy asserts that the passage can "neatly summarize" the desire of the lovers for abiding love. This sounds good because it offers a synthesis or recap in the book's final chapter, but it undermines the creative achievement of this poet. Nothing about this poem is neat, and nothing about desire can be "neatly summarized." Desire is a mess. LaCocque suggests that the conjunction of love and death is really shorthand for a sexual climax.[33]

These commentators, it should be stated, all happen to be male. That they see or impute any climax to the Song is undoubtedly gender-influenced. For Pope, the passage must be a climax because its theme is universal. But why would universal appeal qualify a verse as a book's culminating wisdom? What of the Song supports this verse as its most important passage? One would expect an increase in tension and excitement building up to this momentous insight that love is as strong as death. Instead, it comes out of nowhere. While love is mentioned throughout the Song, passion and death are making their first appearance in 8:6. If anything, the equation comes as a surprise rather than a culmination, and so, as climaxes go, it has been premature.

In addition, why does a book of erotica need a climactic moment when other biblical books such as Psalms, Genesis, or Isaiah do not? Why, in other words, assume a climax unless the reader's own desires have been stirred in the reading of this text? These men are aroused by the Song's content, and so look for a culminating moment, where their interpretation at least can find some (displaced) relief. Searching for a climax to any biblical book is too chancy, given their multiple and anonymous authorship and long history of transmission. And it imposes onto the text a pattern drawn from one's sex life, and this can only distort its meaning into wish fulfillment. Biblical interpretation, in general, tries to minimize the baggage interpreters bring to the text. Here it has failed on what may seem like a small point, that male interpreters have read a sexual movement into the text. Surely their projection is understandable, given the salacious content of the Song.

Their innocent male projection has, however, at least two serious consequences to our understanding of the Song. First of all, why assume one climax for this book rather than several?

The Song is, after all, primarily of a woman in a state of arousal, and it is her physiology that might better serve as metaphor for interpreting textual high points. The presumption of one climax to the book is androcentric and violates the perspective of the Song. Interpretation no longer illumines meaning; instead, it distorts it. The woman is speaking these verses, and her account of love and death is tempered and somber, not triumphant and releasing. We, therefore, ignore the text's tone and voice by deeming it a climax. She has already shown us one of her climaxes or near climaxes in the wet dream of 5:1-6, and this passage bears no resemblance to that bothered, dreamy night. Assuming a climax undercuts the Song's very treatment of desire, which has been devoted to excitement, longing, and waiting rather than satisfaction.

Second, who gets to decide what details in a text are significant worthy of showcasing and which are not? Which verses get to be highlighted as culminating, which are incidental, and at what cost to the text's complexity? In other words, if we start looking for textual climaxes, we will reduce and distort biblical books to meaningless snippets, where we can "neatly summarize," for instance, that the Song of Songs is about death and love.

Fire and Water

> Its flashes are flashes of fire,
>   a raging flame.
> Water cannot put it out,
>   no river can drown it. (8:6-7)

Fire and water are the two elemental and not strictly agrarian images used to depict desire's power. One of desire's inevitable risks is precisely the loss of control. Desire's metaphor is of a raging fire that "many waters" and rivers cannot quench (8:7). In antiquity, fires were a truly frightening prospect, for their swift destruction was often unstoppable, in Israel all the more so, given its scarce water supply. This is indeed a telling metaphor of desire's force and the poet's fear. Desire is understood to be unstoppable, even with a fantasy of unlimited water from the woman's sexual excitement (that is, "many waters"). Fire and water go together, then, as metaphors depicting the heat of longing and the anticipation of pleasure. This imagery is not peculiar to ancient Israel. The Roman philosopher Lucretius noted that with passion

> There is hope that in that very body that set us afire,
> the flame may be put out.[34]

The image of passion as a flame has become a cliché. Bataille insists that the fear component is necessary for effective eroticism, and fire houses that element in desire. The danger in erotic yearning is that one can be engulfed by it. Eroticism, he argues, aims to strike at "the inmost core of the living being, so that the heart stands still."[35]

The Hebrew poet even stresses the dominance of fire over water by stating that "no rivers can overflow" desire. This statement is more than naturalistic image. The poet is clearly dreaming now, for Israel simply has no mighty rivers capable of overflowing. The Jordan itself reduces to a thin stream in places. It does not have the water sources of great rivers, such as the Nile or the Euphrates. In effect, the poet is mustering all the known water sources of surrounding regions that do have mighty rivers, namely Egypt and Mesopotamia, and is still coming up short before desire. At any rate, the Israelite does not have this kind of water source to drown the flames of desire, and so fear is glimpsed in this pitiable fantasy. By needing to draw on resources not native to Israel, the poet feels utterly helpless before desire. It has been lit by human intervention, but now rages on slightly and forever beyond human control. It has the potential of true chaos.

Danger is evident elsewhere in the Song in the mention of wild animals and foreign lands by the man. As we saw in chapter 4, these were used to portray the woman's inaccessibility. They also evince some of his fear toward her. Simply put, we start to suspect that the male really wants her at this safe distance. And the woman is beaten up by the city guards (5:7), yet continues her search for her lover. These dangers, though, are qualitatively different from that of desire as a raging flame. They are about measured risks, whether he will go to animal dens or foreign lands to get her (no), or she will search the city streets where she may get mugged (yes). A raging flame is vastly beyond one's attempts at risk management. It is a disaster waiting to happen and then proceeding unchecked as chaos.

Water, as we saw in chapter 5, was a vital metaphor for female sexual excitement. Many waters played a frequent role in the Song, for pleasure and its enjoyment, and for female sexual excitement. It kept the woman lubricated for further opening, irrigated her vulva/garden, and offered the lover additional oral pleasures in sex. In the present verse, however, much has changed. Water becomes desire's inferior opponent as "all rivers cannot quench love." This suggests a rueful acknowledgment that were the lovers even able to get together and make love, they could not quench their desire. There is no satisfaction; desire has been a bit of a card trick, leading to a satisfaction that cannot occur. Eight chapters later, desire still burns, perhaps just out of control.

The information about destruction is new, as is the use of water. Celebration is tempered by realism about desire's insatiability. Consummation will not bring satisfaction, only temporary relief, but it leaves a slow burn of want going. It is a wistful, mature take on desire. There is no escaping the burn of desire as there can be no escaping death. These are, for the poet, the inevitable tough realities of life. They cannot be avoided, but neither are they good excuses to delay pleasure. The wisdom lies in recognizing that the enjoyment of pleasure, even if unabated for long stretches of time, will not quell desire's force. Such a Song, then, is not simply a celebration of love.[36] It recognizes that since passion has a force like fire and the grave, it ought to be approached cautiously, and with the lessons of those who have been there before us. One approaches with a timeliness befitting the powerful forces of life. Timeliness is, in fact, a key strategy for desire in the Song, and it is to this cautious advice that we now turn.

Desire's Timing

With so much power, unrest, and danger at stake in desire, it is not surprising that the woman offers another cautionary sentiment besides the equation of love and death. She does this with a refrain. A refrain or chorus in poetry is a verse that is repeated to highlight a leitmotif.[37] The refrain of this poem is always uttered by the woman and occurs three times, with a fourth occurring in a kind of shorthand. The refrain of 2:7, 3:5, and 8:4 is:

> I adjure you, O daughters of Jerusalem . . .
> do not stir up or arouse love
>   until it delights.

The woman in the Song advises that these women exercise caution and respect a timeliness to love. This from someone out yearning for her lover, unable to take her own advice. She is past the point to heed these words, since her desire has been awakened. She may well be lamenting her plight. For desire has bought her all sorts of experiences, but no union with her lover. The longing she feels is fierce and unsated. Nevertheless, she commands the women to wait. It is her ancient rendition of "Do as I say, not as I do."

An adjuration is a command or enjoining solemnly, as under an oath. The refrain is weightier than advice. It functions as a directive delivered from the front of desire, and it is not optional. We and the women of Jerusalem are not meant to take it or leave it. The Hebrew meaning of the verb for adjure is "to swear solemnly." This is, then, a solemn direction that needs to be heeded.[38] These vows are solemn and relational. Basically, an adjuration is a human command in the Bible, in contrast to those given by the divine. The woman of the Song is authoritative and commanding, holding her own with a God and with patriarchs (Gen 24:37), leaders (Josh 6:26), and kings (2 Kings 11:4), who otherwise play this role. She is acting her part as image of God, instructing her fellow humans to make sure that they are ready when desire is aroused, and not to dabble halfheartedly when it is. Her authority in matters of desire has been born of her experience, and so she is trustworthy.

The recipients of the adjuration are always the daughters of Jerusalem, her friends or group, never the man. We said earlier that the daughters of Jerusalem act as a chorus in the Song, but overall say very little (5:9; 6:1).[39] Some interpreters have seen these daughters as not very helpful or empathetic to the woman.[40] But this thrice-repeated adjuration indicates that they are not meant to be interactive and equal to this woman. She is issuing a command; she is instructing them on desire as an authority, not simply sharing opinions with her group. The daughters are not meant to be real or her intimate circle of friends. These two lovers are fairly isolated with their desire, with his pasture friends only mentioned once and her brothers portrayed as clueless.

These daughters of Jerusalem are keyed in, they are spoken to, and as they are mentioned elsewhere, we sense that they are present listening throughout the Song. They serve a literary function, providing a sounding board for the woman's musings and polished commands on desire. They are witnesses to her journey and foils to bounce off her views. It is atypical in the Hebrew Bible for characters to think aloud or even have thoughts,[41] so this too is innovative. And the emphasis on "Jerusalem" is important. In Hebrew, "daughters" is also the term for "villages" around such a central city. Hence, "daughters of Jerusalem" can function as a symbol for all women, those in Jerusalem and those in the satellite villages around the capital city. Cities themselves, Jerusalem included, are always grammatically marked as feminine in the Bible.

In this instance, then, the desire of a woman in Jerusalem is not left a private affair, but is offered to a wider populace in and surrounding Jerusalem, including us. It is no longer a tale of private lust. Locating the action in Jerusalem and mentioning Solomon are ways to legitimate the material as authoritative, central to the Israelite identity. They are both mentioned, for example, in Ecclesiastes, another wisdom book. One significant difference is that the speaking voice in Ecclesiastes is attributed to Solomon. Here, the woman remains the authoritative voice. Neither Solomon nor a male lover commands this oath.

The first time the refrain occurs, she has just described enjoying the pleasures of lovemaking to the point of being sick with love and needing sustenance (2:3-5). As an apricot tree, her lover has proved stately, comforting with shade, and sweet to taste, sustaining. Being sick with love, she calls for sustenance and yearns for his embrace again (vv. 5-6). There is some ambiguity about this sustenance in verse 5: "Sustain me with raisins, refresh me with apricots." Is she in need of food for energy, or more metaphorically, additional lovemaking from a man she has just compared to an apricot tree? Has her appetite simply increased from the enjoyment of sexual pleasure, or is she depleted from their exertions? His fruit is likely both, more sex as well as the means to replenish her energy and juices.

The adjuration for caution comes at this point, spliced at the end of this exhausted, giddy plaint. Can the woman be serious here? For what reader can get through this description of a delicious, fruit-filled romp and then swear to exercise caution with desire? Physical exhaustion from sex is typically a consequence we are willing to abide and is certainly not enough to caution us from desire. Her refrain puts quick brakes on the entire tone of the Song. Of course, the shift could be the accidental by-product of editing. But it occurs again right after a description of fruit ingestion and the wish for his embrace (8:2-4). In both instances, the enjoyment of fruit as a trope for sex is followed by a wish for an overt embrace, then this solemn refrain. Hence, minimally, an editor saw a certain logic even if these were originally variant traditions.

The second time that she recites the refrain is when she is bringing her lover home after a search, presumably when the anticipation of sexual pleasure would be at its most intense (3:5). After all, she has finally found him. Caution certainly would not have the upper hand here either. Three times, then, the cautionary refrain occurs close to the peak of sexual excitement. The next adjuration differs. In 5:8, she begins with the formulaic "I adjure you daughters of Jerusalem," but instead of the caution about awakening desire, she has a different message. She says instead, "if you find my beloved, tell him this: I am faint with love." It is a warning still, but not in the way the daughters have come to expect.

Here, apparently, the woman is worn out by the search itself and made faint by love. Her message, then, is specific to her plight, a longing approaching despair, with a disappearing man and an enervated woman. She demonstrates rather than describes the desperation of desire.[42] Exhausted by desire, and now looking for volunteers for a search party for this guy, her very example tells the daughters to exercise caution around desire. She dispenses with the formulaic politeness and just commands them to relay a message. Her adjuration is no longer for the women's benefit, but is now a personal errand. And the daughters of Jerusalem are quick to protest the shift here, asking, "What is your beloved more than another beloved, that you thus adjure us?" (5:9). The other three refrains have been instruction that the daughters could apply to their own potential or real situations. This one, however, is too specifically about the woman's lover. They cannot appropriate it as wisdom for living. They pipe up and wonder quite naturally what is so special about the woman's beloved over those of others. She is not shy answering, and provides a seven-verse litany of just how fine he truly is, comprising her aesthetic appreciation of him. And it works; the daughters join the search (6:1). They are enlisted by the woman's desire rather than instructed about their own.

Nevertheless, the formula of the refrain here sets up the expectation for the cautionary command, even if it is not explicit.

"I adjure you" and the naming of the daughters serve as a prompt where we fill in or anticipate the refrain without actually seeing it repeated. Hence, by way of shorthand, the woman's point is made. The advice has become predictable. The shorthand is akin to when we cut off a friend or mother before they give their characteristic advice with, "I know, I know." These daughters know, they know, that she is going to tell them to be cautious. Though the refrain differs here, the caution would seem to be most appropriate, for in the preceding verse (5:7), the city guards have just beaten her up as she was looking for her beloved. The woman is desire's beaten victim, exposed and abused in the public sphere into which she went searching. The passage depicts her low point, when, spent, she cannot even manage the refrain, but just warns the daughters.

Finally, the fourth occurrence of the refrain, mentioned above, is in 8:4. The caution is evident and supported by context, since it precedes the passage equating love with death (8:6). One can presume at this point that if these women of Jerusalem are still hell-bent on rushing toward desire, then they have not listened to a word the woman has said or witnessed the struggle of her desire throughout these eight chapters.

8

Spiritual Yearning

CANONICAL INCLUSION

We have explored the varying stances on sensuous yearning in the Song of Songs, and have now a solid appreciation of its imagery, its construction of gendered voices, and its homage to the mystery of human passion. And, too, so much probing into sensuous desire has alerted us to the erotic forces and their repercussions within our own lives. Personal memories and hopes are tapped open, alive, titillated by reading the Song of Songs. At its best, reading the Bible leaves few excluded. Reading the Song yields a renewed sense of the erotic as a human energy, a life-enhancing response to the world. This, after all, is the "luminous side of eroticism, its radiant approval of life."[1] We are far from both the exploitative tedium of pornography and the plodding stridency of preachy fundamentalism.

At this point, it is worth reflecting on how this Song contributes to the Bible and why it was considered worthy of inclusion by the ancient rabbis, whose criterion was simply that each book be holy. There are really two different but related questions here. To ask what the Song is doing in the Bible in the first place is a *historical* question; to ask what it could do for the Bible as a whole, and for readers today, is a *spiritual* question, and the one

I am asking in this chapter. My interest is less in how it came to be included in the Bible; it is already there. Instead, I wish to engage the tougher issue, that of taking Rabbi Aqiba at his word, that the Song of Songs not only fits but is the very Holy of Holies, the inner sanctum of Scripture. What does the Song add to the spiritual dimensions of the Bible, and in so masterful a way that Rabbi Aqiba deemed it the inner sanctum of God's very presence? Though my concern in this chapter is primarily with the spiritual fit of the Song in the Bible, a word about its historical inclusion is nevertheless in order.

The Hebrew Bible became a collection of writings, a canon, by the last part of the first century C.E., so roughly around the time the Gospels were being written. There is no explanation of how the process of canonization occurred, however.[2] We know that the first five books of the Bible, the Torah, were the earliest materials to be fixed as a sacred collection, sometime in the fifth to fourth centuries B.C.E., and the prophetic materials became fixed by around 200 B.C.E. Large parts of the materials had been written or orally transmitted much earlier, but their collection into a fixed body of writing occurred sometime during the last centuries before the common era. The last biblical materials, known as the Writings, are considered the latest to achieve entrance into the canon, and of these, we have rabbinic discussions over the canonicity of, for example, Ecclesiastes, Esther, Ruth, and the Song of Songs. Happily, these all made it into the canon, along with the uncontested materials such as Psalms, Job, Proverbs, and Daniel.

The Song of Songs won entrance into the canon in the rabbinic discussions when Rabbi Aqiba, the revered leader of pharisaic Judaism—that branch of Judaism devoutly concerned with abiding by the law of God and often a target in the Gospels— championed its cause. He asserted that

> the whole world is not worth the day on which the Song of Songs was given to Israel, for all the Writings are holy, and the Song of Songs is the Holy of Holies.[3]

This is a rather impassioned, seemingly overplayed plea for a book that the opposing rabbis thought belonged more properly in a bar, the so-called banquet house.[4] Aqiba's metaphoric pronouncement is telling. Indeed, it is almost blasphemous. For the Holy of Holies meant the inner part of the temple where God dwelled. Of course, he could have just been playing linguistically with the superlatives, that is, the Song of Songs is the Holy of Holies, but what a time to play. This was a stinging or clever pronouncement, for the temple had been destroyed a mere twenty years earlier (70 C.E.). Aqiba either got other rabbis where it hurt or offered them hope where they could never have thought to look.

I doubt that Aqiba was merely trying to displace a people's lingering grief over their loss of the temple. If so, he might better have located the Holy of Holies in the Torah itself, the giving of the Law at Mount Sinai. But he does not; he locates the inner sanctum of the Bible in this Song. Was he then just defending male pleasure at this description of a woman in a state of arousal? Was it a way to slip in some religious erotica, namely, protect it by elevating it? In Quentin Tarantino's film *Pulp Fiction,* two hit men discuss oral sex on a woman, and remarkably, show a due reverence to her vulva, calling it the Holy of Holies. Perhaps, then, something in the sacredness, the intimacy, and the fear of a woman's pleasure is struck here, and also in Aqiba's defense of the erotic Song. The *Pulp Fiction* dialogue provides a nice bookend to the intervening centuries since the Song. For the rabbis had debated whether the Song was too crude to be holy, with Aqiba countering that it was the very center of holiness. These fictional hit men, representing pretty much the end inning of Western civilization, bring back the holy in the only place reverence can still even be grasped—for them, a woman's vagina.

As an excursus on human desire, the Song is impressively well done and audacious, but is it an awkward, even forced, fit with the rest of the biblical materials? Maybe the rabbis simply lacked the nerve to do what really needed to be done and deny this ancient Hebrew writing entry into the canon. Or is it somehow integral to the entirety of Scripture?

Holiness for the rabbis was determined by whether a book was spiritually powerful and authoritative enough that anyone touching it became ritually unclean. For this reason, Torah readers in synagogues today will use a metal pointer to avoid contact with the holy words on the scroll. At stake, essentially, was the Song's status as a spiritual power-book. Notice here that the rabbis' definition of holiness is itself sensual and corporeal, relying as it does on a book's "capacity to affect the body of those who touch this."[5] The Song of Songs clearly has this qualification! It affects the body of its reader, though in ways no doubt unintended by the rabbis' criterion. It sets off all sorts of bodily and affective reactions, but not the sort holiness normally causes, namely, ritual uncleanness.

When we pose the question about what makes this text holy in terms of its canonical status, and further, makes it the holiest of Holies, according to Rabbi Aqiba, we are in essence asking about the theological freight of the Song. For whatever else the Bible is—a disparate collection of ancient myths, legends, laws, and history of ancient Israel—it is foremost a book chock-full of religious and theological content. The Song, then, presumably has spiritual content, enough to qualify as holy to the rabbis determining its canonical appropriateness.

At this point, we have reached the most difficult, most rewarding, and most vulnerable part of the investigation: the association of God with sex, religion with spirituality, human pleasure in senses and in spirit. The task is difficult because God is nowhere mentioned in the Song, nor is there any overt religious or theological content. The spiritual richness of this book has been present all along, but it is atypically so for a biblical book. It does not lead with God. Elsewhere in the Bible, in laws, narratives, prophecies, and so forth, God's involvement is clear, described, and at times even avoided. Jeremiah, for example, does not imagine what God would have to say to the citizens of

Jerusalem on the brink of their destruction. He speaks with authority, declaring that his words are God's. The Torah and the Prophets are written with God as a central character, interacting with the others. He can stroll in the Garden of Eden chatting up Adam and Eve, send messengers to talk with the patriarchs and matriarchs, command from a burning bush, or dictate exactly what he wants to his prophets. Though distant in the Psalms, a collection of communal and individual prayers, God is still their assumed audience. Throughout these biblical materials, God is depicted as a real force: in control, directing, commanding various laws, pleased and angered by the various affairs of humans. His presence goes unquestioned.

Ecclesiastes and the Song of Songs are written from the human perspective, without God as a palpable literary character, without God as an expressed given. With Ecclesiastes, the author questions everything about life, but not God's existence. Such agnostic rumblings are more characteristic of our time, whose theological claim to fame was to herald the Death of God movement, unsurprisingly in the late 1940s. The Song of Songs, by contrast, is a celebration of all things of human life, with God not mentioned. Clearly it is not a theological book like the other biblical books. In fact, for Bernard of Clairvaux, it came last of all Bible books for the diligent reader. Proverbs and Ecclesiastes, he believed, were preparation for the Song, since together they rid the reader of two evils of the soul, namely, the empty love of the world and too much self-love.[6] Having cleared one's soul of these evils, the reader was mature enough to encounter *the* text on love, which held knowledge of the whole of Scriptures.[7] There is, as well, an ancient Jewish tradition that recommends that one is only ready to read the Song at thirty years of age and after having read the rest of the canon.[8]

The Song is, in essence, a spiritual book. It is concerned with the responses of the soul to life and its pleasures. As such, it is neither secular nor religious, since these are modern categories and carriers of dualism. These ancient people did not walk

around dourly dividing their days into the sacred and the pro-
fane. They did not have this drive to carve out time the way we
do. And for this, they are not backwards. Instead, they may have
been ahead of us, who are now craving all sorts of holistic experiences. The problem for interpreters over whether this Song is
secular or religious has been largely self-inflicted.

Love is a human passion that cannot fit neatly into any categories of analysis. A passion that goes to the brink of death necessarily includes other types of love besides the sexual. And our view
of the sexual is, as well, often too reductive and biological. The sexual is more than acts, tensions, and even desires. It is, too, a kind
of existential stance within the world, the means through which we
understand and negotiate our way in that world. Further, Foucault
insists that sexuality is an "especially dense transfer point for relations of power."[9] For him, since sexuality is a stance within the
world, it is also inextricably caught up in the power structure of
that world. If so, then the sexuality of the Song is, too, a "dense
transfer point" in the Bible, for all relations, including those with
God, even as he is absent. The Song presents itself, through sexuality, as an excursus on all human yearning, power, and pleasure,
including those experienced in spiritual life. In other words, it is far
richer once we expand our vision to the spiritual.

The interpretive challenge, at this point, lies precisely in reck-
oning with the absence of God rather than trying to fill it. It
means asking what the absence of divine referents itself can mean
theologically. What theological illuminations occur when we
learn to read the absences? Allegorical interpretations that replace
the text's plain sense of sexual desire with a supposed better pious
reading do not interpret the absence. Rather, they rush in to fill
it with, at times, suspicious and unnecessary speed. Such readings betray the interpreter's anxiety and let it run roughshod
over the biblical text. They impose a spiritual agenda rather than
discovering it within the text itself. This is just as dangerous and
arrogant as tethering God to our expectations of what constitutes divine biblical presence.

Discerning the spiritual dimension of the Song is potentially the most rewarding part of the investigation. For if there can be a unity of the spiritual and the sexual impulses, then we have come a long way toward healing the rift between religion and sex, between the spirit and the body. And we catch biblical testimony to the sheer glee of being human, without caveat or reflex, religious promises to keep trying harder. Religion of the latter kind can wear one out. Sexual energy can wreak havoc, of course, but that potency itself does not make it sinful. The Song's unremitting, unabashed attention to desire provides a needed heuristic salve for those who have been emotionally splintered by religion.

I am not suggesting that the Song's payoff comes as some kind of license for a sexual free-for-all, nor as a flip rally cry for the triumph of sex over spirituality. Carter Heyward, an Episcopal theologian, seems to do just this with her theology of sexuality, which is in essence a challenge to experience the spiritual in sexual acts.[10] There is no doubt that sexual experience can surpass the limitations of two people and effect a kind of mystical communion. Such moments are profound, stilling, spiritual, and fleeting. By elevating the sexual as the primary avenue for this mysticism, though, Heyward reduces the spiritual to a salve for sexual abuse victims, in whom she numbers us all. Spirituality undoubtedly can be such a salve, but it is much more.

Instead, the reward from delving into the association of spirituality and sexuality is broader in scope. It, too, reclaims human sexuality from the wearied arenas of sin, shame, and abuse, but extends further, to embrace lustfully our whole human existence. Our take on sexuality would be a celebratory rather than a corrective one, celebratory of humans' urgings, leanings, hopes, desires—the entire emotional spectrum. This reward should not be understated, a matter of mere polite assent. For the erotic and the spiritual forces are foundational energies within the human being. If these are split or have somehow atrophied, then sounding their roots could well be restorative, ushering in a newfound surge of energy toward living.

Finally, this is the most vulnerable part of the investigation because it rests on the affective impact of the book's spirituality on a reader. Oddly, sexual excitement today is easier to speak about than spiritual excitement. But I do not want to demonstrate the spiritual effects of the book on an ancient rabbi or a medieval mystic, and so persuade by examples of ancient dead men. Instead, I want to show how the Song caught a modern biblical scholar spiritually unawares, deeply moved, and grasping for words. This task is vulnerable, then, because it is a terribly difficult and personal endeavor to talk about God. I out myself as a believer, but at the same time, I have not really said a thing.

"God" is one of the few terms we let go by without explanation, and to our detriment. Piety is a private matter, provoking strong emotions, but we rarely share or discover with each other what "God" is. Broaching the topic in the book will spark disparate reactions. You will follow my discussion, but at the same time, a whole host of personal convictions, memories, and emotions will get snagged. I can at once alienate readers who are basically here for the discussion of sex (and some newfound appreciation of grapes!) and frustrate others for whom "God" is a given, frequently name-dropped, and certainly in no need of an introduction. It is potentially embarrassing, too, because, though it was hard to explore why some ancient allusions are erotic, it is harder still to suggest that the Song can be *spiritually titillating.*

I find it vastly more vulnerable to talk openly about the passion, excitement, visceral, and uncertain yearning for God than I do of human sexual tension and its imagery. And I am a professor of religious studies! The timidity could well be an idiosyncrasy of my temperament, overall better left unshared, or it could stem from the cultural disdain for religion; a disdain that comes in the form of open hostility, discomfort, mocking, and secrecy. On a list of most embarrassing topics for social encounters that are not intimate, and even some that are, sex and religion always make it.

Some of this latent religion-phobia is well earned. We have been subjected to religious fanatics one too many times. They scream with placards about the end of the world or the damnation of various segments of the population. They are the cause of violence at one international hot spot after another. They are on TV asking too often for money in hair too coiffed to be real. Or they solicit door-to-door with pamphlets describing a feverish, unappealing faith. In my class one day, an athletic student wore a T-shirt that read: "His pain, your gain" over a picture of a bloodied, dying Jesus, basically weightlifting his cross. Is such "good news" meant to pump me up, get me through the work-out of life, or remind me that religion is savage, that God the father does not mess around and would spatter his son if need be? Either way, the cognitive and affective dissonance is too great to withstand.

The disdain is also our culture's heritage since Schleiermacher, who noted that in the post-Enlightenment world (since 1800), we had deemed ourselves too reasoned to buy into old myths of deities anymore, no matter how big, frowning, or solitary in power they were. We had, in other words, become "cultured despisers," who considered ourselves well over the whole religious thing. And yet there remains a trace of desire in the limping and furious irritation that belies our certainty.

"God" may be dead indeed, just a myth. Or the noun may be. It truly could be too big a word, alienating or tinny rather than real. Images of God get discarded and reinvented all the time, so that there is even a history of theology coming after the Bible. Today, the notion gets tweaked by feminism, by liberation and black theologies, by fresh new philosophical ideas, and through spiritual experimentation with various churches, New Age ideas, and yoga and meditation techniques from the East. There are all kinds of retreats and books on Zen and the Art of Lots of Different Things. These cultural indices reflect a spiritual curiosity, if not need. The hunt persists, we persist, with spiritual yearnings.

The Erotic and the Mystical

The crux for interpreters over the centuries has been how to view any theological message the Song might have. One possible response was to assert a hidden theological meaning, most often by means of an allegory that replaced the text's content; another was to jettison the project altogether and just enjoy and exegete the plain, sexual sense of the text. In chapter 3 I criticized the dualism that forces such options, especially since the Song's writers were not influenced by it. There is yet an additional point to criticize about this particular fork in the interpretive road, namely, our assumption that a biblical book ought to contain God as an agent, that it must contain theology in order to be religious or biblical.

There is no theology, that is, words (*logos*) about God (*theo*) in the Song of Songs. At best, the words of the Song offer *cues* rather than clues, cues of where God would go if he were to be active in this book. The Song thwarts our biblical expectations by not delivering a God in action. This absence plays a vital role for readers of the canon, however. It jolts faithful readers out of any spiritual complacency that might have arisen through the easy confidence that God is in the Bible. By the same token, since God is elusive, the Song acts as a fail-safe against any fundamentalist reading. You are unlikely to hear this Song thundered from a pulpit. And further, through the sheer brunt of its curious eroticism, it can often summon even the disinclined to a reading of the Bible.

The association between eroticism and mysticism is not as incongruent as it first appears. A mystical experience is geared toward joy just as eroticism is. It is that rare moment when prayer, meditation, or life yields joy, serenity, a light, and a fullness in presence. It is when our boundaries lift for a moment and we melt into the world. These moments are fleeting, rare, delicious, and not made up. They can occur through exhaustion, in nature, by listening to music, and in sexual union. As an example, I recall one occasion when, tired from playing tourist all day in

Oxford, I stepped into a random chapel, which at the time held no religious interest for me. I was there to cool off, sit, and get away from all the other hot, tired tourists. A woman was playing improvisational piano nonstop, and though I wasn't paying any conscious attention, the notes deliciously flooded me. Everything became clearer: the sensations of the colors in the stained windows; the tart scent of dust, the sweet, cool, tree-ness of the pew, the taste of breath. My energy soared, tears were streaming down my face, and I felt giddy to be alive. I left without labeling the experience mystical, of course, but looking back, it was as if my soul had cracked open for a moment and gotten the full spa treatment by that music.

Modern writers on desire, Bataille, Kristeva, Paz, de Rougemont, and Barthes among them, are all quick to note an association between eroticism and mysticism, and they have no biblical agenda operating in their analyses. The association between these human forces is borne precisely from desire. To recall the clear words of the poet Octavio Paz:

> Eroticism is first and foremost a thirst for otherness.
> And the supernatural is the supreme otherness.[11]

Roland Barthes sees in the search and hunger for the other and in the experience of erotic love much of what constitutes faith. He notes that "to expend oneself, to bestir oneself for an impenetrable object is pure religion." The woman of the Song has indubitably expended and bestirred herself for her lover. She is not working her religious issues out in her dating life; nor is Barthes. Instead, they both learn so much about desire that it implicates *even the holy*. Barthes concluded the following from love:

> that the other is not to be known; his opacity is not
> the screen around a secret, but, instead . . . reality and
> appearance is done away with. I am then seized with
> that exaltation of loving *someone unknown,* someone
> who will remain so forever: a mystic impulse.[12]

The experience of desiring and loving someone involves an extension of the self and the recognition that, on some deep level, the other cannot be fully known. The limits are reached and exposed by desire, so that Adam did not really know his wife at all. In sexual desire, we ache to be with the other. We insist on it, with phrases such as, "I'm gonna explode if I don't see you!" or "I'm sweatin' you."[13] We want to get as close as possible and melt into the other in an effort to break down every barrier. "The final aim of eroticism," Bataille notes, "is fusion, all barriers gone."[14] And it never succeeds, or it comes in such gaspingly short stints that we are confounded, happy, and let down—a cocktail of emotions we could not have anticipated. The first stirrings of human desire occur in the presence of another, the object of our affection. But as these stirrings grow in the joy and frustrations of love, they develop, move, and start to experiment without objects, and this, for Bataille, is when mysticism arises.[15] The nature of eroticism is given over to the delicious torture of longing. Erotica will have an object to which it yearns, but it is primarily a psychological exposé on coping with its lack. With its focus on desire over its objects, erotica actually sets the searcher up for a mystical experience.

Mystic commentators of the Song caught this association too, the affective similarity between sexual want and the spiritual quest, and used it to talk about the Song.[16] Bernard of Clairvaux, for example, did not displace his sexual unease by reading spirituality into the Song, but instead caught something in its crevices, as it were, in the subtexts and tensions in the woman's longing. He spent eighteen years interpreting it, not simply mining its depths but reaching them.[17] His interpretations offered far more than allegory, but they challenge the reader to commit beyond reading. Bernard thought that interpretation of this Song commanded a journey from the reader, a willingness to go beyond words, to eventually get bored by the titillation they offered, and to enter mystically by force and awkwardness into a power waiting, silent, and kind.[18] It is not that no one showed up for that poor woman in desire. It is that someone never left.

Contemplation of biblical texts in the mystical tradition was linked with joy and sensual appreciation and was clearly not the chore we might hold it to be. So Bernard would have had no reason to worry or repress if he found himself enjoying this Scripture, as he did. Bernard was no Luther! The vow of celibacy, properly understood, does not vanquish sexual desire, but instead is a promise to sharpen it within the spiritual journey. It is a way to focus one's passions and express them as a stance toward the world. Sexual partners become distractions, not because they are so tempting, but because they deflect the fundamental energies of sexual desire toward an object. Mysticism is trying to get toward a desire without manifest objects.[19] The notion of dying to the self is about dying to the ego and its needs, because they drag the self off from joy and drain off the very eroticism of life.

Bernard begins at the Song's beginning, and spent his eighteen years of interpretation only getting through the first two chapters and the beginning of the third.[20] By way of illustration, we shall look at his analysis of the Song's opening want: "Let him kiss me with the kisses of his mouth" (1:2).

Immediately, he makes several interpretive moves that bear mentioning. He zeroes in on the kiss as the central element, he assumes the male lover is Christ, and he personally identifies with the woman. Bernard and most mystics read Scripture by placing themselves into character. So he easily becomes the *she* here, in a pious cross-dress. He held that the Song functions as a mystical guidebook that refers to each person's relationship with God as that person prepares to become Christ's bride.[21] Right off, then, this Christian interpreter sees the kiss as Jesus and as what he desires.[22] The kiss is a tangible mark of Jesus' presence. In fact, Bernard thinks the kisses are means for him to be sure about Christ.[23] The spiritual kiss of Christ's mouth is something the Christian wants again and again. The kiss is plural, embodied, and forever desired once tasted. The spiritual kiss satisfies as it leaves wanting. It is hungered for, and for Bernard, the whole Song is about God's wooing the soul. The believer stands ready and waiting.

There is no question that this is Christocentric and reads the unmentioned Christ into its interpretation. But in so doing, Bernard does not ignore the sexual desire of the Song. He wants to be close to his savior and fully means it: "that is why I ask him, not any other, angel or man, to kiss me with the kiss of his mouth." Bernard does not shrink from describing Jesus in erotic terms. His desire is every bit as bold and insistent as the woman's is. In fact, he lauds her directness: "It is a great thing which she will ask of the Great One, but she does not flirt with him as the others do, and she does not beat about the bush."[24] Her forthrightness qualifies as spiritual directness. For the monks, believers are encouraged to be real rather than shallow, and to ask in prayer for what they want directly.

No one in the Gospels ever got near enough to Jesus to smell his breath, to want to be embraced or be drunk by love with him (some of the Song's other erotic images). It is only, and famously, Judas who gets to kiss Jesus (Matt 26:49). That kiss becomes a kiss-off. Yet here, Bernard is confident that people can ask for such intimacy from Jesus. There are occasions in the Hebrew Bible when such oral intimacy with God is demonstrated, most notably in the Prophets. Jeremiah, for example, becomes a prophet after God touches his mouth and essentially regurgitates his own words into Jeremiah's mouth (Jer 1:9). Ezekiel, by contrast, is at least entitled to full service when he must eat a scroll with divine words on it to begin his prophetic career (Ezek 3:1). Isaiah gets his lips burned before God to commission his career (Isa 6:7).

But in Gen 2:7, virtual mouth-on-mouth intimacy is achieved for the human and the divine. Having formed the first human from dirt with his own hands, God then covers the nostrils and mouth of the new creature with his own and gives the breath of life. This scene is intimate and headily corporeal, too close to watch, really, and vaguely, accidentally homosexual, even pedophilic. The images manage to convey that this story is in some ways a story about a God who comes too close. Later, the human couple tries to hide from this God and hide their bodies by dressing them with fig leaves. No doing on both counts. For God is there, strolling nearby, and he redoes their makeshift clothes by stripping them and selecting animal-skin fashion to replace the fig leaves. If he is not God, just who does he think he is, anyway? He is presuming, entitled, or just plain angry. This is intimacy with God. And it is frightening, though desired. Hence, by Moses' time, the people actively do not want to be so close to God, and so they send a representative or mediator. They are relieved, not saddened. The intimacy of God is something maybe only a mystic can bear.

Bernard wants the full force of union with God, and he sees in the Song the same gritty, wholesale determination. The yearnings of the mystic and the aroused woman are similar; their genders and objects of desire quickly become fairly incidental in terms of the big picture. He identifies with this woman. He likes the sexual, embodied desire here, because for him this quite literally gives flesh-and-blood realism to his incarnational faith.[25] Just as God became flesh in Jesus Christ, Bernard can go the full, erotic distance in his mystical response to God. The desire for God is on a different plane from sexual love, but it is nevertheless rooted in human desire, which is "voracious." He clearly imposes a christological reading onto the Song and is wholly unconcerned to explain that move, as if it were too obvious for him to bother. We may criticize him for reading Christ into the Song when he is not there. But we should also notice that he does not trade off eroticism for piety. Eroticism is not disarmed, just extended in his mystical reading. He keeps the aroused woman to demonstrate his own embodied, lustful passion for Christ.

CUES FOR THE DIVINE

There are allusions in the Song that, though not overtly theological, call to mind other biblical sites of God's presence. These allusions prod readers who are familiar with biblical material. Since the Song was written late, well after the Torah was fixed and the Prophets were known, I argue that these allusions are the skillful means by which the writer does include God. The Bible reader, whether ancient rabbi or modern biblical scholar, would get the resonances immediately and without trying to or meaning to. They serve as biblical rivets supporting the general theme of yearning, and allow it to hint at spiritual yearning, too. They are the small spiritual tacks that by themselves mean little, but within a canonical reading of the Song, that is, one conscious of its fit within the biblical collection, become theologically significant.

The curious mixture of allusions and opaque descriptions in the Song has always confounded its interpreters. It forces the interpreter to start grasping for comprehension. Some of its words are only used once, or they refer to specific features known from other biblical texts: the curtains of Solomon, Pharaoh's chariots, myrrh, En-gedi, Jerusalem. So the Song's difficulty propels a biblical search. For instance, the woman describes her lover as a "cluster of henna blossoms in the vineyards of En-gedi" (1:14). En-gedi itself is likely to mean nothing to most readers, but we can grasp the delight of the man's scent and the sexual meaning of the vineyard. The biblical literate would be able to recall that En-gedi was David's oasis, where he fled from Saul in the contest over who would be king (1 Sam 24:1). This does not add all that much and may be unintended by the author. We get the picture without it, but it is suggestive of additional nuances. For now, the male lover not only smells great and is desired for lovemaking in a vineyard, but he is also a rare and delightful relief to the woman, even a refuge; like an oasis to one caught in the desert heat. In addition, En-gedi is a real oasis, so the lover is no fantasy, as generic oases can threaten to be. He may be absent, but he exists.

The Song is full of these seemingly incidental details, and they often thwart comprehension rather than clarify a given context. They usually do not aid the reader in establishing the setting for the action. In the example just cited, for example, we still could not say whether the couple made love at En-gedi or had ever been there. Nevertheless, it is still worthwhile to examine the details of the Song for what they might yield to its overall meaning. On occasion, they suggest fairly significant allusions. In the remainder of this section, six such images that help to stud the erotic Song with spiritual possibility are discussed. Throughout this work, I have commented on the spiritual dimensions of the Song for various relevant themes and passages. Hence, the present discussion is meant only to supplement the spiritual relevance discovered in the previous chapters. Here I examine six specific details that hint at the possibility of God's presence in a text that never names him.

(1) The identity of the male lover is left obscured throughout the Song and is likely not even a constant, since king, shepherd, and Solomon are all contenders at various moments. His identity is never known and cannot be confirmed, as he never appears. It is possible that his elusive quality is intentional to the Song rather than sloppy. Perhaps the identity shifts with ease from Solomon to shepherd to some more ineffable presence. The king mentioned could be anyone; Solomon, at least, is known for his wisdom, and a shepherd, though a commoner, is also frequently the image used for God elsewhere in the Bible (Isa 40:11; Ezek 34:11-31).[26] The identity cannot be confirmed and does not really matter, since the Song is devoted to desire itself and not its object. And because this is primarily worked through the woman, the male lover can easily be a kind of shape-shifter anyway, keeping us off balance, fending off efforts at identification. Still, it is perhaps significant that it does keep changing. The mystery elicits suspicion and allows for the possibility that the desire extends beyond all objects. I am not

saying simply that the woman is really lusting after God all along. I am suggesting that this is a conspicuous amount of material to devote to the psychology of desire for it to be only about Israelite crushes. In this case, the mystery man means that we do not have to commit to any one identity. The search for him becomes relevant for all sorts of reasons and desires.

(2) As we saw in chapter 7, the woman likened desire to a fire that many waters cannot quench:

> Its flashes are flashes of fire,
>   a raging flame. (8:6)

This image effectively conveys desire's implacable power and intensity. Passion and fire are elsewhere linked with the deity, especially in Deut 4:24, where God is described as a "devouring flame, a passionate God." Fire itself is a biblical means by which to demonstrate God's presence.[27] Hence, it is a flame that does not consume the bush before Moses (Exod 3:2-4). Also, it was God's manifestation on Mount Sinai (Deut 4:12). In addition, a light on the altar was a liturgical means to signify God's presence in ritual. And when the deity banished Adam and Eve from Eden, he posted a guard with a "flaming sword" to protect the tree of life (Gen 3:24). The "flashes of fire" here connote a similar defense strategy, since the woman is cautioning others about love.

The Song, then, has enlisted an image often used of God's presence to speak about the presence of desire in life. Fire, though, is a ubiquitous feature of ancient life, and so we would expect it to receive heavy use as a metaphor. The two need not be consciously related in the writer's mind, and any resonance could well be accidental. There is one detail, however, that argues against mere coincidence. It bears mentioning particularly since it is often omitted in some English translations. The phrase "raging flame" is literally rendered from the Hebrew as "flame-yah." The final syllable is termed a theophoric, meaning that it is the divine name, Yahweh, in shortened form. These theophoric elements are quite frequent in Israelite personal names. For example, Jeremiah, Isaiah, Josiah, and Zedekiah all have the same "yah" ending, rendered in English as "iah." The use in the Song is unusual, however, because it is attached to a noun, "flame," rather than a proper name. Some scholars understand this to be a kind of idiom for the superlative indicating a most "intense flame" or "raging flame" or some such. And there is a type of superlative in Hebrew that does use the generic term for god, "el." So, for example, the cedars in Psalm 80:10 are "mighty cedars" from the Hebrew saying, "cedars of el." These scholars then reason by analogy that a similar device is operating in the present case, only with the deity's proper name.

While the generic term for god does function as a semantic device for superlatives, this verse would be the sole case where the proper name Yahweh does. And it would be a surprising use, really. Considerable care taken around the divine name in the Bible, illustrated by the Third Commandment, which prohibited the wrongful use of the divine name (Exod 20:7). It is not said "in vain" with the personal names, because these are all praising God. "Isaiah," for example, means in Hebrew "Yahweh gives salvation." "Jeremiah" means something like "Yahweh exalts." In the postbiblical period, the scribes who copied Bibles were so reverent toward the divine name that they scrambled the vowels, thus making it impossible to pronounce properly. The misguided went ahead and pronounced it anyway, and that is how we get the misnomer "Jehovah."[28] The reverence toward the divine name makes it unlikely that it was used as a mere syntactical device in the Song. As the shortened form of the divine name, the phrase would then read "flame of Yah" rather than "raging flame." It would be the only mention of God's name, and as we can see, it is pretty well hidden and cut in half. Also, it is pretty late in the Song, its final chapter, to be bringing God in, if that is what has happened here. And it does not effect a thematic change in the Song's direction in any way. It remains complete without the addition, and so it is a theophoric element totally without any kind of theological fanfare. This leads Pope to assert that it is simply "scanty evidence for God in the Song" and so is unlikely.[29] His position is understandable, for by itself it gives too little to go on and crushingly too late. It is almost a tease to smuggle such a tiny piece of a possible God into this image. Pope is right that it is scanty evidence, but he may be wrong that it is insignificant. Despite the conviction of his position, it should be noted that this is the only phrase in his 701-page commentary on the Song where he does not offer a translation, but instead leaves a blank.[30]

It is scanty evidence, to be sure. But it is possible that the talk of passion and fire has recalled the deity in the writer's mind in just as incidental a fashion as it has for the biblical reader. By conveying passion's intensity as fire, the writer perhaps unwittingly recalled God's portrayal as passionate fire and then added "flame of Yah," as an afterthought or unconscious impulse. This is not at all the scene-stealing God of Sinai or the prophets, but it is nevertheless a textual presence, slight and shortened though it may be.

God's name "Yahweh" is itself derived from the verb for existence, "to be." And hence, its use will always have, or should have, an expansive, transcendent quality to it. Originally, its breadth of meaning bordered on the ridiculous, as when Moses introduced the idea in Egypt. He had to talk the people into walking out into the desert because "I am who I am" (the divine name) sent him. Who in this scene was braver—Moses for his persuasion or the people for consenting? For he had basically said to them, "Existence dictates that we go!" And they went.

The flame of Yah becomes a fitting image to describe the passion in human existence, for its flame could spread everywhere in life. In some sense, there is no better place for God's name to fit but in this existential passage about love and death. Francis Landy argues that it is "flame of Yah" and that it is truly the "apex of the credo and of the Song," but not for its dramatic entrance. Instead, it is the crux of the Song because it is so ephemeral, because it is just a tiny suffix, an "open vowel, disappearing into silence."[31] What was scanty to Pope, and thus grounds for ambivalent dismissal, becomes for Landy significant for its very smallness.

This blurry, fleeting hint of the divine is reminiscent of God's presence with Elijah in "a sound of sheer silence" and nothing more (1 Kgs 19:12). Both are hard to detect, easy to miss, and easy to dismiss. There are these moments of divine presence, which are subtle, almost challenges to pay attention. Elijah, after all, could easily have missed the presence in a slight breeze, for who takes the time to listen to silence? Even the burning bush, a symbol of unmistakable miracle today, was not spectacular at first. It took Moses' turning aside to notice something odd about it, namely, famously, that the thing was not being consumed. Only then does God address Moses and give him world-changing instructions. But this Moses was not at all hit over the head with a dazzling divine presence. Instead, something just caught the shepherd's eye. We are left to wonder how often God had been laying that bait of his presence before it took with one attentive human. These passages are biblical testimonies to how insignificant the divine presence can appear. In like manner, readers of the Song can easily gloss over God.[32]

(3) Another instance of possible divine presence occurs when the man tenderly says to his lover, his "dove":

> In the clefts of the rock,
> > in the covert of the cliff,
> let me see your face,
> > let me hear your voice. (2:14)

The description is yet another example of the lovers' game of hide-and-seek, which they play out in the natural world of mountains, cliffs, and vineyards. But this image of "clefts of the rock" recalls another hiding scene where a face visual is also requested, between God and Moses.

After Moses has spent so much time atop Mount Sinai talking with God and receiving the commandments, he cannot resist asking if he can see God's face. God booms that no one may see his face and yet live, from which we deduce that the answer is "no." Yet he offers Moses the compromise of letting him see his back, not his face, when he installs Moses in the cleft of a rock and passes over it (Exod 33:23). In this scene, the cleft of the rock is the safe vantage point for the one who desires to see the other's face. In the Song, it becomes instead the shy hiding spot of the other. If this phantom lover could be God, then the initiative and quality of his manifestation have altered considerably. For here, he is not overbearing, booming, and protective of the human from a fatal sighting. Instead, as the male lover, he has become curious, flirtatious, and inquisitive about the other hiding in the cleft. He demonstrates a desire to know the other, the beloved. He, this time, wants a peek at the human. It would not be such a bad theological idea to have God take an interest, once in a while.

(4) Another allusion, also from Exodus, occurs in 3:6 in a passage that is notoriously difficult to interpret. The Song takes note of a mystery, asking:

> What is that coming up from the desert
> like a column of smoke?

The reminiscence from the desert wanderings in Exodus is unmistakable. Once the people left Egypt, they had to cross the Sinai desert to get to the promised land. Several times they suffered from bouts of panicked nostalgia and desired to hightail it back to Egypt. God offers reassurance by promising to be their guide for the journey. He will do so "in a pillar of smoke by day, and a pillar of fire by night" (Exod 13:21).

Whatever else this apparition in the Song is, there is desire for it. The woman wants an answer, wants to know what that "pillar of smoke" is this time, and she yearns for it.

(5) There is certainly no question that the vineyard and the garden are the sites for sexual union and, at points, symbolize the woman's sexuality and vulva in the Song. As a site, the vineyard is vital for God, too. In Isaiah 5, the Song of the Vineyard, the

prophet sings a song to his beloved, much as the present Song has done. The song is rife with viticultural images, and the beloved's identity is obscured until verse 12, when it turns out to be God.[33] In Isaiah 5, God's loving, attentive care is likened to that of a vintner, and the people en masse are his vineyard. Because vineyards were so highly esteemed in ancient Israel, it is natural that they were appropriated in biblical traditions to convey other values—here, the relationship of God with his people. The sexual tenor of the vineyard metaphor from our Song, of course, does not carry over to the divine–human relationship, but the more general tenor of passion does. The beloved God loves his vineyard, the people; so, too, the male lover of this Song loves his beloved vineyard, the woman. The Isaiah vineyard becomes an allegory, as the characters are revealed to be stand-ins for God and the people. In the Song of Songs, however, the vineyard remains a metaphor, and the lovers remain the central and vital characters. In contrast to allegory, the Song's metaphor of a vineyard is plush with meanings and retains them all.

A similar association occurs with the garden, again clearly a symbol for the woman in a state of delightful arousal. The garden is more broadly a site for the pleasures of farm life, and that tenor, namely, of enjoyment rather than sexual arousal, carries over to theology in the tradition of a garden of God (Gen 2:8-3:24; Ezek 31:8-9). In the Garden of Eden, God has all the delights of earth and chooses who can enjoy them. "Eden," in fact, means "delight," and so it is obvious that both humans and God enjoy these gardens. Sites of pleasure are enjoyable, as they are delicate. Tending becomes a protected right. In Eden, it becomes God's call to banish any partakers of misbegotten pleasure. In the Song of Songs, it is the woman's exclusive right to invite her lover into her garden, her tended, delicate center of delights. The male lover does not have a garden himself; he yearns to come into hers. Once banished, one can easily argue that the first couple initiates the first bout of yearning for something previously enjoyed, namely, the pleasures of God's garden.[34] The male lover in the

Song, too, longs for the pleasure that he has previously known with his beloved. He longs for reunion, not union. Vineyards and gardens are, in a sense, the best creation has to offer. They are worthy even of God's visitation. The metaphoric tenors of both value and pleasure are struck in the Song and are associated with God's enjoyments of these lands elsewhere in the Bible.

(6) A final instance involves various terms and materials that recall the temple. These are the mention of cedar (1:17), which is the high-quality wood used in constructing the temple; the mention of a kind of ark (3:9); and the presence of myrrh and frankincense, scents often used for incense in worship (liquid myrrh, Exod 30:23). In addition, the mention of "our house" (1:17) is odd since the lovers are not living together, and they detail most of their activity outside in natural settings. "House" itself is a term in Hebrew for both domestic dwelling and the temple, which was viewed as God's dwelling place. In this regard, the oft-repeated mention of Jerusalem might be significant. The Song uses various terms to denote joy and celebration. These occur elsewhere, of course, but are also the terms for praise and worship in the Bible.[35]

None of these pieces identify the temple in the Song. And the Song is not a cloying puzzle. But studded as these details are throughout the book, what they might faintly suggest is that the context for worship has been expanded. The entire outdoors, with vineyards, mountains, goats, hills, foxes, myrrh, and cedar, is now the locale for joy, for praise, for worship. In the postexilic world, God was no longer assumed to be located in the Jerusalem temple, so that worship, if it was to be done, was not only centralized in the second temple. God's presence is not restricted to that temple structure, but it is everywhere, radically ineffable, even in texts. All these clues for the divine in the Song are indirect, mere teases of a possible God sighting. Separately, they are far too meager to hang a theology on, but along with the theme of searching, they are suggestive of a slight spiritual pulse.

Spirituality of the Song of Songs

If we redirect our interests from theology to spirituality—what humans do in their quest for meaning—whole worlds open up in the Song. The difference is key. Theology will obviously want to talk about God. Spirituality may, but it need not, for it is concerned broadly with what the soul needs to nourish and nurture itself. For us, then, spirituality can include a wide array of activities, such as prayer, New Age healing ceremonies, obscure monastic rituals, or yoga, drumming, and meditative practices. The ancients had this need to nurture and nourish their souls as well. We should keep in mind that the people of biblical times did not have it easier—spiritually speaking—than we do, nor did they have Bibles. The quest for meaning is most apparent in the wisdom literature of the Bible (Proverbs, Ecclesiastes, Job, Song of Songs), though spirituality courses through much biblical material. These texts ponder the meaning of life, customs, and belief in God in terms that matter to the human. They provide no proofs of religious certainties or any admonitions at all, but instead offer practical, experiential wisdom drawn from life.

Hence the Song, devoted to yearning, fits in as a lesson, first on the ancient Israelite crush. Because the love in the Song does not reach its desired consummation, though, the lesson becomes valuable for all sorts of human yearnings. Sexual desire was conveyed largely through metaphors involving fruit, where fruit was the vehicle of the metaphor, and the tenor, its additional meaning, was sexual desire. As metaphors, the fruit images meant sexual pleasure even though it went unstated. Metaphors have this kind of freedom, this kind of allusive quality. With the book as a whole, the sexual pleasure, too, functions as a metaphor, not an allegory. The Song's theme of sexual desire begins to serve as a vehicle for another level of metaphoric meaning, the tenor of spiritual yearning. Again, this goes unstated and relies on the competencies of its readers. Metaphors, unlike similes, rely on some of the pieces being put together in the comprehension of the reader's mind:

they rely on common, implicit meanings. The cycle of metaphoric meanings in the Song is rich and complex, comprising the pleasures and struggles of the human in the world.

The metaphor of spiritual yearning in no way replaces the other meanings, as an allegory would. Instead, all the meanings about fruit, sex, and spiritual hunger coexist. Spiritual desire is within the metaphoric range of meanings, since the Song is about a search for a loved one who is not present. It exists at its edges, implied, not stated, and is a definite reach for readers. The writers did not sit down and chart a complicated metaphoric cycle of how they would smuggle God in with no one noticing. They may not even have intended a spiritual dimension to the Song. But because it lands in the Bible and is a search for an absent loved one, spiritual meanings come alive. The Song then begets a biblical mysticism in which human love can become the vehicle through which readers can come to understand divine love.[36]

Human desire, the wanting and wishing for something or someone not present, is a motif threaded throughout the Hebrew Bible, and was, as I suggested earlier, a motivator for the final collection of a biblical canon. The desire for life, love, and God himself pulses throughout the biblical stories. These are all, in essence, tales of yearning beyond one's limits and boundaries, either as an individual wanting more, or as a nation wanting land or to survive disaster. The biblical writers are trying as best they can to probe the marvels of life: that humans will work, get hurt, have tedious days and conversations, along with moments of dazzle, breathtaking beauty, the pure milky sound of giggling, and moments of terror, anomie, and cruelty. The yearning is palpable, even while under wraps and strained. It is covert, hidden, yet presses up against the surface of the texts, the syntax, the allusions and metaphors themselves.

The total unabashed devotion to desire erupts in this Song. The woman gives a demonstration of what loving heart, soul, and might would look like. And this could come in handy as wisdom when practicing the command to start loving God that way

(Deut 6:5). It is a love that finally transcends the need for a manifest object; it has become mystical. The woman is alone in the end; she has been stood up, but only by her expectations. Yearning is left unsatisfied, yet somehow triumphant, affirming, bursting, and accepted for itself. The woman does not collapse into self-abnegation, self-sacrifice, or delusional idealization, but starts to put it all together and know that her love is a faith in things unseen.

The poets used pedestrian details of farm life: shepherds, milk, young women, grapes, figs, vineyard pests. When describing the emotion of desire, they used ways to sustain the separation between the lovers. The separations were scripted realistically on the hot, bright, rocky landscape of ancient Israel, but they themselves were contrived, brought on to describe yearning's life span, its inner workings. Yearning ricochets off the inner psychic walls of frustration and anticipation, of foretaste, imagination, and the memory of previous lovemaking, of afternoons spent in dreamy, bothered want. Searching through the hard landscape became the Song's metaphor for the search of a lover, the search for union, communion; not daydream, but presence. It had attendant, real risks, of foreign lands, violence, and failure, yet desire fueled courage.

Spirituality may not be obvious in a given text, or, for that matter, in a life, but it is nevertheless present. In fact, the hiddenness itself has worlds to teach us by disarming our impatient insistence on empirical demonstrations of divine care. The book of Job, for example, is a steely, intrepid probe into God's apparent absence during suffering, and that is still what we often wrestle with, the randomness, indignity, and utter lonliness of suffering. This Song's unrelenting yearning in the absence of any obvious divine clue is actually what makes the book so spiritually useful and profound to the modern age, itself wrestling with a crippling absence of meaning. Faith may be faith in things unseen, but spirituality is the yearning for them nonetheless, to the point of exhaustion and solitude. Desire is this kind of humorless hunger. There is a strong spiritual pulse to this lusty Song, after all.

This erotic Song celebrates not the sexual above all else, but rather the senses themselves as the alert, twitching, multireceptive channels through which a human being gets to fall in love with life itself. It is really fabulous overkill how equipped we are for sensory input. We could smell a breast as easily as incense, taste a rock as easily as milk, feel our lover's name no less than his or her thighs, and hear the sounds of blossoms and doves. We have so many access points to the world. In this sense, desire is not so much the quest for a fuller life but an appreciation for the one all around. Desire has "a kind of naked and denuding intensity."[37] The smells, colors, and detailed visual images of the Song are there for a reason. They script a covert, yet obvious theology. The woman's senses are on high alert, feeling, sensing *every little thing* and finding each huge and delectable. As readers, our empathy gets enlisted until we too are boosted into a smarting attention where we can almost hear the grape skins burst with their juice, see the honey drip off lips, and feel the chalky scampering of lithe, button-nosed gazelles. So the details get to matter a great deal—the cinnamon, apricots, gazelles, and foxes—but not just as part of some colorful scenery. Instead, they comprise a celebration of the beauty in the created world.[38]

These details are each testimony to love's energy and voraciousness. They show a woman whose senses are awakened in love and are being simply, deliciously inundated. Gushing in her sexual and sensual excitement, she can do nothing else but compare the exquisiteness of the feeling, love, to trumping wine, the best liquid her world knows. It is not the same comparison we would make, because we are spoiled, able to select from an array of wines from the world. Her plaintive comparison is real, drenched, telling, and tied to the hardship, livelihood, and relief offered through life's not-so-simple pleasures. Wine and love are terribly complex pleasures. This ancient, biblical hymn to erotic energy elicits our own passions for sensing life right down to the cinnamon. It can work over our senses, and, in exquisite moments, go beyond them all to our gut. This sort of lively attention to the details, then, becomes a challenge to taste the creation itself and relish it.

Throughout the Hebrew Bible, God becomes less and less detectable on the sensory level in the Bible, and so the senses go on full alert in the Song. Human attention takes initiative, bravery, and life long patience. God, starting now, is in everything, just as his name, Yahweh, originally meant—in the cedar trees, the fruit, woman, man, foxes, mountains, rocks, incense, many waters, fire, and love itself. The regular mundane world has become the temple holding the inscrutable presence of God. The incense, cedar, fire, ark, and praise are all around here somewhere, but in the natural world. Nothing special, nothing new, just a different, fully felt yearning for presence. The world under spirituality becomes a creation, the command simple: check it out.

The Song is a pastiche of the story of the Garden of Eden, only with jazz-like theological improvisation. Our attention is not merely brought to the animals, hills, flowers, and fruit; it lands right in them, face first. The poet wants us to feel the teeming gardens, the vineyard, the chased little foxes, and to be drunk with love for it all. It is like Eden, the place of delight, a teeming garden of paradise. But humans ruled over animals there, and woman's desire was restricted to her husband. Now, in this garden, both assertions of power and constraint are lifted. We become participants, rolling around in gardens, faint with love, no better than or superior to little foxes, leopards, or doves, and our desires are left to roam all over the place.

The Song's spirituality calls for us to notice the wonders of a delight-full, complex life. It makes those wonders accessible to all. Biblical theophanies are no longer the privilege of patriarchs, prophets, priests, and kings, but now pulsate for simple agrarian couples in love and pained by lust. In many ways, the Song is an ancient gratitude list. It is a theology of absence, but it is certainly making do. Its condition of an absent God is not so different from our world today. God is not identifiable anymore, and so it is terribly easy to forget him, or to disdain religion and keep the heavy tomes closed. Similarly, the city guards of the Song disdain the woman on her search, first by ignoring her, then by beating her up. We each have some of that guard in us, and some of that woman. The Song is a theology of absence, but it manages, unlike us, not to sulk about it. Instead, it celebrates human, sensual life in a teeming creation.

Abbreviations

AB	Anchor Bible
ABD	*Anchor Bible Dictionary*
BibIntSer	Biblical Interpretation Series
BibSem	Biblical Seminar
BRev	*Bible Review*
HAR	*Hebrew Annual Review*
JSOT	*Journal of the Study of the Old Testament*
OBT	Overtures to Biblical Theology

Notes

Chapter 1

1. Marvin H. Pope, *Song of Songs,* AB 7C (Garden City, N.Y.: Doubleday, 1977) 89–132; Roland E. Murphy, *The Song of Songs,* Hermeneia (Minneapolis: Fortress Press, 1990) 13–28.

2. For a clear explanation of how metaphors function, particularly in biblical material, see Sallie McFague's *Metaphorical Theology* (Philadelphia: Fortress Press, 1982).

3. André LaCocque notes, too, a tradition in which Proverbs represented his moral writings, Ecclesiastes his natural writings, and the Song of Songs his more contemplative efforts. *Romance, She Wrote: A Hermeneutical Essay on Song of Songs* (Harrisburg, Pa.: Trinity, 1998).

4. How can a culture so devoted to relativism dare to make this Victorian call so freely?

5. At sites such as Hazor, Jerusalem, and Gibeon, especially. See Amihai Mazar, *Archaeology of the Land of the Bible: 10,000–586 B.C.E.* (New York: Doubleday, 1990) 478–85.

6. For the ancient Greek philosophers, too, deprivation is closely linked to privation. Michel Foucault, *The History of Sexuality,* vol. 2, *The Use of Pleasure* (New York: Random House, 1985) 43.

7. Jack Miles, *God: A Biography* (New York: Knopf, 1995).

8. Georges Bataille, *Erotism: Death and Sensuality* (San Francisco: City Lights, 1985 [1962]) 11.

9. As Bataille reminds us, we must never imagine human existence apart from passions. *Erotism,* 12.

10. The Greek philosophers early on caught the value of repetition in pleasure. Foucault, *The History of Sexuality,* vol. 2, 54–56.

CHAPTER 2

1. "Ask": *šaʾal;* "seek": *baqeš;* "delight in": *ḥaphes;* "desire": *ḥamad.*

2. By the first century C.E., the apostle Paul advises the unmarried to stay unmarried, but he too is working on borrowed time, believing the end of the world to be imminent (1 Cor 7:8).

3. Owen Chadwick, *A History of Christianity* (New York: St. Martin's, 1995) 72–73, 287.

4. The Ninth Commandment prohibiting lying against your neighbor also stands without further explanation.

5. The remaining laws, 1–5, contain expansions to explain their purposes, but not to provide direction (as does the tenth).

6. The wife in Israelite society was viewed as property and so can occur second in a list of a neighbor's six possessions. See chapter 6 for a discussion of androcentrism (male-centeredness) and sexism in biblical texts.

7. Ilana Pardes, *Countertraditions in the Bible: A Feminist Approach* (Cambridge: Harvard Univ. Press, 1992) 125.

8. For interesting and clear studies of this literature, see Diane Ackerman, *A Natural History of Love* (New York: Random House, 1994); Denis de Rougemont, *Love in the Western World* (New York: Pantheon Books, 1956 [1940]); and Octavio Paz, *The Double Flame: Love and Eroticism* (Orlando, Fla.: Harcourt Brace, 1995 [1993]).

9. Jeffrey Weeks, *Sexuality and Its Discontents: Meanings, Myths and Modern Sexualities* (London: Routledge & Kegan Paul, 1985) 127–28.

10. André LaCocque argues that the Song is too sexual to be wisdom literature. André LaCocque, *Romance, She Wrote: A Hermeneutical Essay on Song of Songs* (Harrisburg, Pa.: Trinity, 1998) 1. For Brevard Childs, the focus on a woman in love illumines the institution of marriage. *Introduction to the Old Testament as Scripture* (Philadelphia: Fortress Press, 1979).

11. Paz, *The Double Flame, Love and Eroticism* 15.

12. Audre Lorde, "Uses of the Erotic: The Erotic as Power," in *Sister Outsider* (Freedom, Calif.: Crossing, 1984) 54; Susan Sontag, "The Pornographic Imagination," in *Styles of Radical Will* (New York: Farrar, Straus and Giroux, 1966) 61.

13. Jack Miles, *God: A Biography* (New York: Knopf, 1995).

14. Pardes, *Countertraditions,* 126.

15. See chapter 6 for a discussion of these prophetic images.

16. See chapter 6.

17. LaCocque, *Romance, She Wrote,* 24.

18. David Biale suggests that the lack of words on desire and sex is due to the subordination of individual states to communal concerns.

Eros and the Jews: From Biblical Israel to Contemporary America (New York: Basic, 1992) 13.

19. For readers interested in learning more about sex in the Bible, see the brief and helpful entry, "Sex and Sexuality," by Tikva Frymer-Kensky in *ABD* (1992) 5:1144–6; Ilona Rashkow, *Taboo or Not Taboo: Sexuality and Family in the Hebrew Bible* (Minneapolis: Fortress Press, 2000); Gail Corrington Streete's *The Strange Woman: Power and Sex in the Bible* (Louisville: Westminster John Knox, 1997) examines materials from the Hebrew Bible and the New Testament with attention to the gender dynamics involved.

20. See chapter 6 for a discussion of desire and this first couple.

21. For a detailed study on the terms for love, desire, and sex, see Athalya Brenner, *The Intercourse of Knowledge: On Gendering Desire and "Sexuality" in the Hebrew Bible,* BibIntSer 26 (Leiden: Brill, 1997) 8–30.

22. Exceptions occur in the story of Lot's daughters who take the initiative and sleep with their father (Gen 19:33, 35), and in descriptions of virgins who have not yet "known" or "lain with" a man (Gen 19:8; Num 31:17; Judg 11:39).

23. This verse has enjoyed a long history of interpretation for sexual legislation in the postbiblical world. For a comprehensive study of its interpretive life by Jews and Christians, see Jeremy Cohens, *"Be Fertile and Increase, Fill the Earth and Master It": The Ancient and Medieval Career of a Biblical Text* (Ithaca, N.Y.: Cornell Univ. Press, 1989).

24. Infertility was assumed by the biblical authors to be located with the female alone. They viewed life to be within the male seed, and so, for example, Onan was killed for wasting seed on the ground instead of delivering it within the womb (Gen 38:9-10). Onanism later came to mean masturbation, since it was the production of seed without the intent or possibility of procreation. Technically, however, Onan was not masturbating. Instead, he was practicing a form of birth control by pulling out of the woman prior to ejaculation.

25. Notice that barrenness is seen as woman's problem, and its solution still lies with the male partner, though this time with a divine one, Yahweh.

26. Other examples where male desire is a prelude to sexual union include Gen 34:19 and Esth 2:14; 6:6.

27. Sontag, "The Pornographic Imagination," 54.

28. Audre Lorde considers the distinction key and sees power in the erotic because it is an expression of feeling. Pornography, she argues, is sensation without feeling and so is destructive, not healing. "Uses of the Erotic," 54.

29. Ibid.

30. Bataille asserts that no one doubts the ugliness of the sex act and stresses that the pleasure we anticipate also ushers in anxiety. *Erotism,* 145.

31. Lorde sees the defining characteristic of pornography to be using others as objects. "Uses of the Erotic," 54. Sontag holds it to be organ-rather than person-centered; the participants in pornography use each other as objects. "The Pornographic Imagination," 40. For Brenner, it includes control as well. *Intercourse,* 162.

32. Michael Fox adds that all this anticipation can bring out a youth-ful or adolescent quality to the yearning that is evident in the Song. *The Song of Songs and the Ancient Egyptian Love Songs* (Madison: Univ. of Wisconsin Press, 1985) 311. This same adolescent, impetuous energy is why LaCocque argues that the Song is not properly wisdom literature. *Romance, She Wrote,* 8.

33. Paz, *The Double Flame,* 9.

34. Fox, *The Song of Songs and the Ancient Egyptian Love Songs,* 295.

35. Hence, the eroticism of the Song does not enlist specific allusions to genitalia and coitus. Ibid., 298.

CHAPTER 3

1. Ann Astell, *The Song of Songs in the Middle Ages* (Ithaca, N.Y.: Cornell Univ. Press, 1990) 2–4.

2. Athalya Brenner, *The Intercourse of Knowledge: On Gendering Desire and "Sexuality" in the Hebrew Bible,* BibIntSer 26 (Leiden: Brill, 1997) 174.

3. Marvin H. Pope, *Song of Songs,* AB 7C (Garden City, N.Y.: Doubleday, 1977) 114.

4. Gene McAfee, "Sex," in *The Oxford Companion to the Bible,* ed. Bruce M. Metzger and Michael D. Coogan (New York: Oxford Univ. Press, 1993) 691. This is a complicated historical development that I can only touch on here. There are several excellent and readable accounts available on this period. See especially Peter R. Brown, *Society and the Holy in Late Antiquity* (Berkeley: Univ. of California Press, 1982); Margaret Miles, *Carnal Knowing: Female Nakedness and Religious Meaning in the Christian West* (Boston: Beacon, 1989); Elaine Pagels, *Adam, Eve, and the Serpent* (New York: Random House, 1988).

5. See Michel Foucault's excellent and provocative analysis on how sexual conduct comes to be seen in the Christian West as a matter of moral solicitude in his *The History of Sexuality* , vol. 1 *An Introduction* and vol. 2, *The Use of Pleasure* (New York: Random House, 1985).

6. Pope, *Song of Songs*, 89-132; Roland E. Murphy, *The Song of Songs*, Hermeneia (Minneapolis: Fortress Press, 1990) 13–28. Carol Meyers suggests that the Song's explicitness had past exegetes understandably running for cover in allegory. "Gender Imagery in the Song of Songs," HAR 10 (1986) 209–10.

7. André LaCocque, *Romance She Wrote: A Hermeneutical Essay on Song of Songs* (Harrisburg, Pa.: Trinity, 1998) 3.

8. Jean Leclerq, *The Love of Learning and the Desire for God: A Study of Monastic Culture*, trans. Catharine Misrahi (New York: Fordham Univ. Press, 1961).

9. Pope, *Song of Songs*, 17, 114; Robert Alter, *The Art of Biblical Poetry* (New York: Basic, 1985) 185; LaCocque, *Romance She Wrote*, 67.

10. For a discussion of this pairing, see chapter 7.

11. Diane Ackerman, *A Natural History of Love* (New York: Random House, 1994) xix.

12. Ibid., xxiii.

13. Michael Fox, *The Song of Songs and the Ancient Egyptian Love Songs* (Madison: Univ. of Wisconsin Press, 1985) 295.

14. Lila Abu-Lughod, *Veiled Sentiments: Honor and Poetry in a Bedouin Society* (Berkeley: Univ. of California Press, 1986) 241.

15. Tikva Frymer-Kensky terms it an idyll of romantic love unconstrained by societal considerations: *In the Wake of the Goddesses: Women, Culture, and the Biblical Transformation of Pagan Myth* (New York: Free Press, 1992) 197. In her sense, this is what love looks like underneath the legal preoccupations in the Bible. Marcia Falk calls this type of form a lyric consisting of a personal feeling, sensuality, and musicality. *Love Lyrics from the Bible: A Translation and Literary Study of the Song of Songs*, Bible and Literature Series 4 (Sheffield: Almond, 1982) 114.

16. Falk, *Love Lyrics from the Bible*, 127–35; Pope, *Song of Songs*, 56–57.

17. For a fascinating, provocative study on God's body in the Bible, see Howard Eilberg-Schwartz, *God's Phallus and Other Problems for Men and Monotheism* (Boston: Beacon, 1994).

18. Robert Alter instead breaks the metaphors down into pastoral, urban, and regal images. *The Art of Biblical Poetry* (New York: Basic, 1985) 186. Falk sees four arenas: countryside, wild landscape, interior environments, city streets. *Love Lyrics from the Bible*, 139.

19. For a beautiful study on the inchoate force of love, see Ackerman's *Natural History of Love*. Also, for the difficulty facing the biblical writer, who took on this essential human concern without known biblical parallels, see Frymer-Kensky, *In the Wake of the Goddesses*, 197.

20. Ackerman, *Natural History of Love,* 12.

21. Harold N. Moldenke and Alma Moldenke, *Plants of the Bible* (New York: Dover, 1952) 129.

22. Ackerman, *Natural History of Love,* 190.

23. Falk, *Love Lyrics from the Bible,*127.

24. Julia Kristeva, *Tales of Love,* trans. Leon S. Roudiez (New York: Columbia Univ. Press, 1987) 3.

CHAPTER 4

1. The Hebrew verb here shares the same root as the term for "heart," *lbb,* with the sense that his heart has been depleted. See Roland E. Murphy, *The Song of Songs,* Hermeneia (Minneapolis: Fortress Press, 1990) 156.

2. Georges Bataille, *Erotism: Death and Sensuality* (San Francisco: City Lights, 1985 [1962]) 19.

3. Ibid., 17.

4. Falk and Fox both note the empathy the Song elicits. Marcia Falk, *Love Lyrics from the Bible: A Translation and Literary Study of the Song of Songs,* Bible and Literature Series 4 (Sheffield: Almond, 1982) 130; Michael Fox, *The Song of Songs and the Ancient Egyptian Love Songs* (Madison: Univ. of Wisconsin Press, 1985) 295.

5. Henri Frankfort, H. A. Frankfort, John A. Wilson, Thorkild Jacobsen, and William A. Irwin, *The Intellectual Adventure of Ancient Man: An Essay on Speculative Thought in the Ancient Near East* (Chicago: Univ. of Chicago Press, 1946) 54.

6. Edith Hamilton, *Mythology: Timeless Tales of Gods and Heroes* (New York: Penguin, 1969) 47–54.

7. Simone de Beauvoir, *The Second Sex,* ed. and trans. H. M. Parshley (Harmondsworth, England: Penguin Books, 1972 [1949]).

8. Samuel N. Kramer, *The Sacred Marriage Rite: Aspects of Faith, Myth and Ritual in Ancient Sumer* (Bloomington: Indiana Univ. Press, 1969) 59.

9. See Page du Bois, *Sowing the Body: Psychoanalysis and Ancient Representations of Women, Women in Culture and Society* (Chicago: Univ. of Chicago Press, 1988), for a discussion of Greek sources and the association in Greek literature between agriculture and human reproduction. This association is also pronounced in the biblical story of the Garden of Eden in Genesis 3; see chapter 6.

10. Ibid.

11. Sherry Ortner, "Is Female to Male as Nature Is to Culture?" in *Woman, Culture, and Society,* ed. Michelle Z. Rosaldo and Louise Lamphere (Stanford: Stanford Univ. Press, 1974) 67–87.

12. André LaCocque, *Romance, She Wrote: A Hermeneutical Essay on Song of Songs* (Harrisburg, Pa.: Trinity, 1998) 50.

13. The refrain is "I want you to rock me, like my back ain't got no bones." Its final lyric is "I want you to roll me until I don't want no more." The woman's desire, then, is fully spent by her lover's efforts. She undoubtedly is not passive, but it is clearly her lover's labor that is key.

14. Fox, *The Song of Songs and the Ancient Egyptian Love Songs*, 313.

15. Ibid.

16. The following collection is a helpful, well-rounded series of essays devoted to the relation of sex and the sacred, including ethics: James B. Nelson and Sandra P. Longfellow, *Sexuality and the Sacred: Sources for Theological Reflection* (Louisville: Westminster John Knox, 1994), xiv.

17. Ibid., xiv.

18. Diane Ackerman, *A Natural History of Love* (New York: Random House, 1994) 54–55.

19. Ibid., 54.

20. Ibid.

21. Bataille, *Erotism*, 20.

22. Howard Eilberg-Schwartz, *God's Phallus and Other Problems for Men and Monotheism* (Boston: Beacon, 1994).

23. Fox, *The Song of Songs and the Ancient Egyptian Love Songs*, 313.

24. Carol Meyers argues that the heavy use of military imagery for the woman is unexpected and against stereotype, and so, about the woman's strength. *Discovering Eve: Ancient Israelite Women in Context* (New York: Oxford Univ. Press, 1988) 178–79.

25. Falk suggests that the search scenes might themselves be metaphorical ways of describing loss whenever a beloved is not near. *Love Lyrics from the Bible*, 148.

26. Some scholars see a basic gender complementarity in the Song that is uncharacteristic of biblical materials: Falk, *Love Lyrics from the Bible*, 144; Phyllis Trible, *God and the Rhetoric of Sexuality*, OBT (Philadelphia: Fortress Press, 1978) 144–65; LaCocque, *Romance, She Wrote*, 39. Still, within the Song, gender balance yields to the dominance of the woman's voice over that of the male. See chapter 6.

27. The verse itself has been notoriously difficult to translate. Literally it is something like "I did not know, my soul set me, chariots of Aminadab." Murphy, *The Song of Songs*, 176. A soul in confusion and a military presence of chariots is clear, though the battle is less so.

28. Francis Landy, *Paradoxes of Paradise: Identity and Difference in the Song of Songs*, Bible and Literature Series 7 (Sheffield: Almond, 1983) 144–45.

CHAPTER 5

1. Brenner notes the same thing for the phrase "waters of life." Athalya Brenner, *The Intercourse of Knowledge: On Gendering Desire and "Sexuality" in the Hebrew Bible,* BibIntSer 26 (Leiden: Brill, 1997) 33.

2. Michael Fox, *The Song of Songs and the Ancient Egyptian Love Songs* (Madison: Univ. of Wisconsin Press, 1985) 310.

3. Brenner, *Intercourse,* 38.

4. Fox, *The Song of Songs and the Ancient Egyptian Love Songs,* 299.

5. Marvin H. Pope, *Song of Songs* AB 7C (Garden City, N.Y.: Doubleday, 1977) 515.

6. Michel Foucault, *The History of Sexuality,* vol. 2, *The Use of Pleasure* (New York: Random House, 1985) 66.

7. In fact, Fox argues that the romance occurs at night and this suggests that it is secretive. *The Song of Songs and the Ancient Egyptian Love Songs,* 145.

8. Thomas Laqueur, *Making Sex: Body and Gender from the Greeks to Freud* (Cambridge: Harvard Univ. Press, 1990) 3. His work is a fascinating study of the changing attitudes and assumptions about sex throughout Western history.

9. Ovid, *Metamorphoses* 3.323–31.

10. Pope, *Song of Songs,* 441; Francis Landy, *Paradoxes of Paradise: Identity and Difference in the Song of Songs,* Bible and Literature Series 7 (Sheffield: Almond, 1983) 79.

11. Roland E. Murphy, *The Song of Songs: A Commentary on the Book of Canticles or the Song of Songs* (Minneapolis: Fortress Press, 1990) 160; Pope, *Song of Songs,* 493–97.

12. Pope, *Song of Songs,* 350. Maddeningly, scholars (Pope, Murphy, Moldenke and Moldenke) tend to neglect to mention the salient detail here, just what myrrh smells like. It has a rich, woody, sweet scent, and is available as incense still today.

13. Most English translations mention apples rather than apricots (2:3, 5; 7:8; 8:5). The apple was not domesticated in ancient Israel, however, until fairly recently. The apricot was present in biblical times and is the most likely candidate for the sweet fruit of this Song. Harold N. Moldenke and Alma Moldenke, *Plants of the Bible* (New York: Dover, 1952) 185–87.

14. See chapter 2 and above.

15. Marcia Falk mentions that food and drink are often associated with eroticism in literature. *Love Lyrics from the Bible: A Translation and Literary Study of the Song of Songs,* Bible and Literature Series 4 (Sheffield: Almond, 1982) 150.

16. Martha Hopkins and Randall Lockridge. *Intercourses: An Aphrodisiac Cookbook*. Photography by Ben Fink (Waco: Terrace, 1997).

17. Diane Ackerman, *A Natural History of Love* (New York: Random House, 1994) 124–25; Sigmund Freud, *Three Essays on the Theory of Sexuality* (New York: Basic, 1962) 39–72.

18. Falk believes that references to mountains in the Song also serve as metaphors for the woman's breasts. *Love Lyrics from the Bible*, 146.

19. Falk, *Love Lyrics from the Bible*, 118.

20. Her autonomous power might be one of the paradoxes of erotic love, namely, an "intimate bonding with the other that gives the individual courage to stand alone." Ibid., 150.

CHAPTER 6

1. "Sexuality" did not become a term until the nineteenth century, but it is obviously part of desire well before then. Michel Foucault, *The History of Sexuality*, vol. 2, *The Use of Pleasure* and vol. 3, *The Care of the Self* (New York: Random House, 1985).

2. For a discussion of biblical and rabbinic materials of control over women and sexuality, see Judith Plaskow, *Standing against Sinai* (New York: Harper and Row, 1990) 172–77.

3. Marcia Falk notes that males generally play more distant roles in the Song. *Love Lyrics from the Bible: A Translation and Literary Study of the Song of Songs,* Bible and Literature Series 4 (Sheffield: Almond, 1982) 141.

4. This woman's voice differs from other Eastern love literature and Western courtly love traditions. Ann W. Astell, *The Song of Songs in the Middle Ages* (Ithaca, N.Y.: Cornell Univ. Press, 1990) 10.

5. See Erich Auerbach's classic comparison of Greek and Hebrew literature in *Mimesis: The Representation of Reality in Western Literature* (Princeton, N.J.: Princeton Univ. Press, 1973 [1953]).

6. Plaskow, *Standing against Sinai,* 6; John J. Winkler, *The Constraints of Desire: The Anthropology of Sex and Gender in Ancient Greece* (New York: Routledge, 1990) 4.

7. Winkler, *The Constraints of Desire,* 4.

8. Athalya Brenner, *The Intercourse of Knowledge: On Gendering Desire and "Sexuality" in the Hebrew Bible,* BibIntSer 26 (Leiden: Brill, 1997) 179.

9. Winkler makes an interesting observation that since women did exercise considerable household power, it became socially necessary for men not to acknowledge it. *The Constraints of Desire,* 8.

10. Falk, *Love Lyrics from the Bible,* 150.

11. André LaCocque argues for a female poetess bent on subversive tactics of reusing biblical allusions defiantly. *Romance, She Wrote: A Hermeneutical Essay on Song of Songs* (Harrisburg, Pa.: Trinity, 1998) xi; Athalya Brenner, *The Israelite Woman: Social Role and Literary Type in Biblical Narrative* (Sheffield: JSOT Press, 1994) 46–56, 138.

12. Brevard S. Childs, *Introduction to the Old Testament as Scripture* (Minneapolis: Fortress Press, 1979) 194.

13. Marvin H. Pope, *Song of Songs* AB 7C (Garden City, N.Y.: Doubleday, 1977) 690.

14. Ilana Pardes, *Countertraditions in the Bible: A Feminist Approach,* (Cambridge: Harvard Univ. Press, 1992) 119; Phyllis Trible, *God and the Rhetoric of Sexuality,* OBT (Philadelphia: Fortress Press, 1978) 144–65.

15. Daniel Boyarin, *Carnal Israel: Reading Sex in Talmudic Culture* (Berkeley: Univ. of California Press, 1993) 161.

16. Georges Bataille, *Erotism: Death and Sensuality* (San Francisco: City Lights, 1985 [1962]) 131.

17. See chapter 8 for a discussion of the rabbinic decision for the Song's holiness.

18. For Falk, there is not a reversal of stereotypical male-female relations, but an absence of all hierarchical domination. *Love Lyrics from the Bible,* 118. LaCocque again sees the poetess "shedding her societal chains" and "shouting her freedom from gender stereotypes." *Romance, She Wrote,* 64.

19. LaCocque, *Romance, She Wrote,* 205.

20. LaCocque, however, does argue that it has a "carnivalesque" tone to it, where kings, bishops, and magistrates are caricatured and made fun of. Ibid., 64.

21. LaCocque, *Romance, She Wrote,* 41.

22. Carol Meyers, *Discovering Eve: Ancient Israelite Women in Context* (New York: Oxford Univ. Press, 1988) 149–54.

23. Falk, *Love Lyrics from the Bible,* 134.

24. Ibid., 135.

25. Had God otherwise envisioned multiple partners in this paradise, and did he not catch the slam to Adam in his comment?

26. Leah won hands down, with six sons and a daughter to Rachel's two sons. Two slave women, Zilpah and Bilhah, each had two sons by Jacob.

27. Thomas Laqueur asserts that a one model of sex dominated in the West from antiquity until the end of the seventeenth century. Thomas Laqueur, *Making Sex: Body and Gender from the Greeks to Freud* (Cambridge: Harvard Univ. Press, 1990) 25. In this case, then,

it would be fully natural for Eve to yearn for her bigger half, to want to become one (Gen 2:24).

28. So much so that my students in introductory classes always resist seeing that "sin," "fall," and "temptation" are all lacking in the Genesis 3 account.

29. Margaret Miles, *Carnal Knowing: Female Nakedness and Religious Meaning in the Christian West* (Boston: Beacon, 1989) 102–3. Jewish interpreters, too, struggled with sexuality and worried about the power of desire. David Biale, *Eros and the Jews: From Biblical Israel to Contemporary America* (New York: Basic, 1992) 34. There even developed a legend that Moses, as lawgiver, was celibate. Plaskow traces a change in Jewish thought where women became more associated with sexuality in the rabbinic period than they were in the biblical period, and that this became an increasingly negative association. *Standing against Sinai,* 170, 175, 177. For her concise discussion of Jewish attitudes about sex, see 170–210.

30. Miles, *Carnal Knowing,* 94. See also the discussion in chapter 3 above.

31. For an incisive and clear discussion of Paul's complex views on sex and sexuality, see Gail Corrington Streete, *The Strange Woman: Power and Sex in the Bible* (Louisville: Westminster John Knox, 1997) 120–39.

32. Biale, *Eros and the Jews,* 41.

33. Miles, *Carnal Knowing,* 94.

34. Augustine, *City of God,* trans. Henry Bettenson (London: Penguin, 1984 [1972]) 14.23-24.

35. Ibid., 14.23.

36. Miles, *Carnal Knowing,* 12.

37. Foucault, *The History of Sexuality,* vol. 2, 68.

38. Elaine Pagels, *Adam, Eve, and the Serpent* (New York: Random House, 1988).

39. Foucault, *The History of Sexuality,* vol.1, *An Introduction,* 58–63, 116.

40. For a feminist analysis of these images, see Renita J. Weems, *Battered Love: Marriage, Sex, and Violence in the Hebrew Prophets,* OBT (Minneapolis: Fortress Press, 1995).

41. Brenner views the prophets' marriage metaphor to be a "pornographic fantasy of male desire." *Intercourse,* 171.

CHAPTER 7

1. Georges Bataille, *Erotism: Death and Sensuality* (San Francisco: City Lights, 1985 [1962]) 19.

2. As does Freud, *Beyond the Pleasure Principle* [1920], in *On Metapsychology: The Theory of Psychoanalysis,* The Pelican Freud Library, vol. 11 (Harmondsworth, England: Penguin, 1984).

3. *Odyssey,* book 12. With, of course, lots of gender repercussions again in the woman and dangerous desire.

4. Michel Foucault, *The History of Sexuality,* vol. 1, *An Introduction,* 78 and vol. 2, *The Use of Pleasure,* 66–70, 79, 83 (New York: Random House, 1985); Jonathan Dollimore, *Death, Desire, and Loss in Western Culture* (New York: Routledge, 1998) 14, 22, 24.

5. Foucault, *The History of Sexuality,* vol. 2, 67, 69.

6. Ibid., 66–70.

7. Roland E. Murphy, *The Song of Songs,* Hermeneia (Minneapolis: Fortress Press, 1990) 195.

8. André LaCocque, *Romance, She Wrote: A Hermeneutical Essay on Song of Songs* (Harrisburg, Pa: Trinity, 1998) 177.

9. Jonathan Dollimore, *Death, Desire, and Loss in Western Culture* (New York: Routledge, 1998) xii.

10. Murphy, *The Song of Songs,* 197.

11. For Bataille, eroticism and mysticism share this pure intensity. *Erotism,* 253. See chapter 8.

12. Lucretius *On the Nature of Things,* trans. W. H. D. Rouse, rev. M. F. Smith, 2d ed, Loeb Classical Library 181 (Cambridge: Harvard Univ. Press, 1982)1.34.

13. Bataille, *Erotism,* 239.

14. Dollimore, *Death, Desire, and Loss in Western Culture,* 128–29.

15. Marcia Falk, *Love Lyrics from the Bible: A Translation and Literary Study of the Song of Songs,* Bible and Literature Series 4 (Sheffield: Almond, 1982) 150.

16. Bataille, *Erotism,* 239.

17. Augustine, *City of God,* trans. Henry Bettenson (London: Penguin, 1984 [1972]) 14.16.

18. Bataille, *Erotism,* 239.

19. Camille Paglia, *Vamps and Tramps* (New York: Random House, 1994) 22.

20. When the city guards are making their rounds. This is more likely and necessary at night, though the text does not explicitly say so.

21. See chapter 5 for discussion of this wet dream.

22. Bataille, *Erotism,* 19.

23. Ibid.

24. Ibid., 240.

25. Diane Ackerman, *A Natural History of Love* (New York: Random House, 1994) 110.

26. Denis de Rougemont, *Love in the Western World* (New York: Pantheon, 1956 [1940]) 46.

27. Ibid., 42–46; Bataille, *Erotism,* 23.

28. Bataille, *Erotism,* 146.

29. Ackerman, *A Natural History of Love,* 109.

30. Dollimore, *Death, Desire, and Loss in Western Culture,* 45.

31. Foucault, *The History of Sexuality,* vol. 1.

32. Marvin H. Pope, *Song of Songs* AB 7C (Garden City, N.Y.: Doubleday, 1977); LaCocque, *Romance, She Wrote,* 160; Murphy, *The Song of Songs,* 196.

33. LaCocque, *Romance, She Wrote,* 171.

34. Lucretius, *On the Nature of Things,* 5.108, 1, 6-7; Laqueur adds that classical writers would also view orgasm as the result of heat, Thomas Laqueur, *Making Sex: Body and Gender from the Greeks to Freud* (Cambridge: Harvard Univ. Press, 1990) 46.

35. Bataille, *Erotism,* 17.

36. Murphy, *The Song of Songs,* 195.

37. Ibid., 76.

38. Other examples occur when Abraham makes his servant vow to find Isaac the right wife, Gen 24:37; when Joseph is dying, he makes the people vow to bring his body up out of Egypt when they go, Gen 50:25; Exod 13:19. Also, Num 5:19; Josh 6:26; 1 Sam 14:28.

39. Fox argues as well that they speak in 3:6; 5:1; 6:13; 8:5, though the text is not clear in these instances that a change of voice has occurred. Michael Fox, *The Song of Songs and the Ancient Egyptian Love Songs* (Madison: Univ. of Wisconsin Press, 1985) 302.

40. Falk, *Love Lyrics from the Bible,* 148.

41. This lack of interiorization is even a distinguishing characteristic of Hebrew prose. See Erich Auerbach, *Mimesis: The Representation of Reality in Western Literature* (Princeton, N.J.: Princeton Univ. Press, 1973 [1953]).

42. Murphy, *The Song of Songs,* 168, finds this an expression of her desolation.

CHAPTER 8

1. Octavio Paz, *The Double Flame: Love and Eroticism* (Orlando, Fla.: Harcourt Brace, 1995 [1993]) 25.

2. For a historical study on the process of canonization, see Sid Leiman, *The Canonization of Hebrew Scripture: The Talmudic and Midrashic Evidence* (Hamden, Conn.: Archon, 1976).

3. *Mishnah Yadayim* 3.5.

4. Modern commentators tend to quote this defense to show rabbinic passion, but without much comment on its implications.

5. Ilana Pardes, *Countertraditions in the Bible: A Feminist Approach* (Cambridge: Harvard Univ. Press, 1992) 120.

6. Bernard of Clairvaux, "Song of Songs, Sermon 2," in *Selected Works* (New York: Paulist, 1987) 211.

7. Ann Astell, *The Song of Songs in the Middle Ages* (Ithaca, N.Y.: Cornell Univ. Press, 1990) 26. The twelfth century saw the wisdom books as philosophy books: Proverbs was devoted to ethics; Ecclesiastes was devoted to physics, the workings of the outside world; and the Song of Songs was devoted to holy matters. Robert Alter, *The Art of Biblical Poetry* (New York: Basic, 1985) 185; André LaCocque, *Romance, She Wrote: A Hermeneutical Essay on Song of Songs* (Harrisburg, Pa.: Trinity, 1998) 12.

8. Astell, *The Song of Songs in the Middle Ages,* 27.

9. Michel Foucault, *The History of Sexuality,* vol. 1, *An Introduction* (New York: Random House, 1985) 103.

10. Carter Heyward, *Touching Ourselves: The Erotic as Power and the Love of God* (San Francisco: Harper & Row, 1989).

11. Paz, *The Double Flame,* 8.

12. Roland Barthes, *A Lover's Discourse: Fragments* (New York: Farrar, Straus and Giroux, 1978) 135.

13. The latter means "being really into someone" which in turn means desiring the other. I am indebted to my student Melanie Telzrow for this example and its translation from college-age desire.

14. Georges Bataille, *Erotism: Death and Sensuality* (San Francisco: City Lights, 1985 [1962]) 129.

15. Ibid., 130; Denis de Rougemont, *Love in the Western World* (New York: Pantheon, 1956 [1940]) 141.

16. The most striking and frequent mystical metaphors are drawn from sex. Bataille, *Erotism,* 223–24; de Rougemont, *Love in the Western World,* 142.

17. Julia Kristeva, *Tales of Love,* trans. Leon S. Roudiez (New York: Columbia Univ. Press, 1987) 155.

18. Ibid., 153.

19. Bataille, *Erotism,* 225.

20. Jean Leclercq, *The Love of Learning and the Desire for God: A Study of Monastic Culture,* trans. Catharine Misrahi (New York: Fordham Univ. Press, 1961) 85.

21. Astell, *The Song of Songs in the Middle Ages,* 73.

22. Bernard of Clairvaux, "Song of Songs, Sermon 2," 220.

23. Ibid., 218.

24. Ibid., 232.

25. Kristeva, *Tales of Love,* 159.

26. See also Isa 49:9; 63:11; Jer 23:3; 31:10; Zech 9:16; 10:2-3; 11:1-17; 13:7-9.

27. Francis Landy, *Paradoxes of Paradise,* Bible and Literature series 7 (Sheffield: Almond, 1983), 127–29.

28. Hebrew has no "j" sound, and so wherever English Bibles have a "j," it is a "y" in the original language.

29. Marvin H. Pope, *Song of Songs,* AB 7C (Garden City, N.Y.: Doubleday, 1977) 89–132, 670–72; Roland E. Murphy, *The Song of Songs,* Hermeneia (Minneapolis: Fortress Press, 1990) 192.

30. Pope, *Song of Songs,* 653.

31. Landy, *Paradoxes of Paradise,* 127.

32. Or be denied the chance to notice, depending on the English translation.

33. See my article "God's Vineyard—Isaiah's Prophecy as Vintner's Textbook" *Bible Review* 14:4 (August 1998).

34. See chapter 6.

35. Examples include Isa 9:2; 25:9; 35:1-2; 46:10; 49:13; Zech 9:9; 10:7; Pss 32:11; 40:17; 63:12.

36. Astell notes the paradox that the way up, that is, to God, is the way down, that is, through the experience of human love. *The Song of Songs in the Middle Ages,* 100, 102.

37. De Rougemont, *Love in the Western World,* 145.

38. Landy notes that while critics cite the book's beauty, few discuss how it contributes to the poem. *Paradoxes of Paradise,* 137. See especially his chapter 3, "Beauty and the Enigma."

Bibliography

Abu-Lughod, Lila. *Veiled Sentiments: Honor and Poetry in a Bedouin Society.* Berkeley: Univ. of California Press, 1986.

Achtemeier, E. R. "Desire." In *Interpreter's Dictionary of the Bible,* ed. G. A. Buttrick. Nashville: Abingdon, 1962. Vol. 1: 829–30.

Ackerman, Diane. *A Natural History of Love.* New York: Random House, 1994.

Alter, Robert. *The Art of Biblical Poetry.* New York: Basic, 1985.

Astell, Ann W. *The Song of Songs in the Middle Ages.* Ithaca, N.Y.: Cornell Univ. Press, 1990.

Auerbach, Erich. *Mimesis: The Representation of Reality in Western Literature.* Princeton, N.J.: Princeton University Press, 1973 [1953].

Augustine. *City of God.* Trans. Henry Bettenson. London: Penguin, 1984 [1972].

Barthes, Roland. *A Lover's Discourse: Fragments.* New York: Farrar, Straus and Giroux, 1978.

Bataille, Georges. *Erotism: Death and Sensuality.* San Francisco: City Lights, 1985 [1962].

de Beauvoir, Simone. *The Second Sex.* Ed. and trans. H. M. Parshley. Harmondsworth, England: Penguin Books, 1949 [1972 edition].

Bernard of Clairvaux. *Selected Works.* Trans. G. R. Evans. New York: Paulist, 1987.

Biale, David. *Eros and the Jews: From Biblical Israel to Contemporary America.* New York: Basic, 1992.

Boserup, Ester. *Woman's Role in Economic Development.* New York: St. Martin's, 1970.

Boyarin, Daniel. *Carnal Israel: Reading Sex in Talmudic Culture.* Berkeley: Univ. of California Press, 1993.

Brenner, Athalya. *The Israelite Woman: Social Role and Literary Type in Biblical Narrative.* BibSem 2. Sheffield: JSOT Press, 1994.

———. *The Intercourse of Knowledge: On Gendering Desire and "Sexuality" in the Hebrew Bible.* BibIntSer 26. Leiden: Brill, 1997.

Brown, Peter R. *Society and the Holy in Late Antiquity.* Berkeley: Univ. of California Press, 1982.

Caird, G. B. *The Language and Imagery of the Bible.* Philadelphia: Westminster, 1980.

Chadwick, Owen. *A History of Christianity.* New York: St. Martin's, 1995.

Childs, Brevard S. *Introduction to the Old Testament as Scripture.* Philadelphia: Fortress Press, 1979.

Cohen, Jeremy. *"Be Fertile and Increase, Fill the Earth and Master It":* *The Ancient and Medieval Career of a Biblical Text.* Ithaca, N.Y.: Cornell Univ. Press, 1989.

Coward, Rosalind. *Female Desires: How They Are Sought, Bought, and Packaged.* New York: Grove, 1985.

Dollimore, Jonathan. *Death, Desire, and Loss in Western Culture.* New York: Routledge, 1998.

du Bois, Page. *Sowing the Body: Psychoanalysis and Ancient Representations of Women, Women in Culture and Society.* Chicago: Univ. of Chicago Press, 1988.

Eilberg-Schwartz, Howard. *God's Phallus and other Problems for Men and Monotheism.* Boston: Beacon, 1994.

Falk, Marcia. *Love Lyrics from the Bible: A Translation and Literary Study of the Song of Songs.* Bible and Literature series 4. Sheffield: Almond, 1982.

Fernandez, James W. *Persuasions and Performances: The Play of Tropes in Culture.* Bloomington: Indiana Univ. Press, 1986.

Foucault, Michel. *The History of Sexuality.* Vol. 1, *An Introduction.* New York: Random House, 1978.

———. *The History of Sexuality.* Vol. 2, *The Use of Pleasure.* New York: Random House, 1978.

———. *The History of Sexuality.* Vol. 3, *The Care of the Self.* New York: Random House, 1978.

Fox, Michael V. *The Song of Songs and the Ancient Egyptian Love Songs.* Madison: Univ. of Wisconsin Press, 1985.

Frankfort, Henri, H. A. Frankfort, John A. Wilson, Thorkild Jacobsen, and William A. Irwin. *The Intellectual Adventure of*

Ancient Man: An Essay on Speculative Thought in the Ancient Near East. Chicago: Univ. of Chicago Press, 1946.

Freud, Sigmund. *Three Essays on the Theory of Sexuality.* New York: Basic, 1962.

———. *Beyond the Pleasure Principle* [1920]. In *On Metapsychology: The Theory of Psychoanalysis,* The Pelican Freud Library, vol. 11. Harmondsworth, England: Penguin, 1984.

Friedl, Ernestine. *Women and Men.* New York: Holt, Rinehart, and Winston, 1978.

Frymer-Kensky, Tikva. *In the Wake of the Goddesses: Women, Culture, and the Biblical Transformation of Pagan Myth.* New York: Free Press, 1992.

———. "Sex and Sexuality." In *Anchor Bible Dictionary,* ed. David Noel Freedman. New York: Doubleday, 1992. Vol. 5:1144–46.

Goulder, Michael D. *The Song of Fourteen Songs.* JSOT Supplemental Series 36. Sheffield: JSOT, 1986.

Halperin, David, John Winkler, and Froma Zeitlin, eds. *Before Sexuality: The Construction of Erotic Experience in the Ancient Greek World.* Princeton, N.J.: Princeton Univ. Press, 1990.

Hamilton, Edith. *Mythology: Timeless Tales of Gods and Heroes.* New York: Penguin, 1969.

Heyward, Carter. *Touching Our Strength: The Erotic as Power and the Love of God.* San Francisco: HarperSanFrancisco, 1989.

Hopkins, Martha and Randall Lockridge. *Intercourses: An Aphrodisiac Cookbook.* Photography by Ben Fink. Waco: Terrace, 1997.

Kramer, Samuel N. *The Sacred Marriage Rite: Aspects of Faith, Myth and Ritual in Ancient Sumer.* Bloomington: Indiana Univ. Press, 1969.

Kristeva, Julia. *Tales of Love.* Trans. Leon S. Roudiez. New York: Columbia Univ. Press, 1987.

LaCocque, André. *Romance, She Wrote: A Hermeneutical Essay on Song of Songs.* Harrisburg, Pa.: Trinity, 1998.

Laiou, Angeliki. *Consent and Coercion to Sex and Marriage in Ancient and Medieval Societies.* Washington, D.C.: Dumbarton Oaks Research Library and Collection, 1993.

Landy, Francis. *Paradoxes of Paradise: Identity and Difference in the Song of Songs.* Bible and Literature series 7. Sheffield: Almond, 1983.

Laqueur, Thomas. *Making Sex: Body and Gender from the Greeks to Freud.* Cambridge: Harvard Univ. Press, 1990.

Leclerq, Jean. *The Love of Learning and the Desire for God.* New York: Fordham Univ. Press, 1961.

Lederer, Laura, ed. *Take Back the Night*. New York: Morrow, 1980.

Leiman, Sid. *The Canonization of Hebrew Scripture: The Talmudic and Midrashic Evidence*. Hamden, Conn.: Archon, 1976.

Lorde, Audre. "Uses of the Erotic: The Erotic as Power." In *Sister Outsider*, 53–59. Freedom, Calif.: Crossing, 1984.

Mazar, Amihai. *Archaeology of the Land of the Bible: 10,000–586 B.C.E.* New York: Doubleday, 1990.

McFague, Sallie. *Metaphorical Theology*. Philadelphia: Fortress Press, 1982.

Mead, Margaret. *Male and Female*. New York: William Morrow and Co., 1949.

Meyers, Carol. "Gender Imagery in the Song of Songs." *Hebrew Annual Review* 10 (1986) 209–23.

———. *Discovering Eve: Ancient Israelite Women in Context*. New York: Oxford Univ. Press, 1988.

Miles, Jack. *God: A Biography*. New York: Knopf, 1995.

Miles, Margaret. *Carnal Knowing: Female Nakedness and Religious Meaning in the Christian West*. Boston: Beacon, 1989.

Murphy, Roland E. *The Song of Songs: A Commentary on the Book of Canticles or the Song of Songs*. Hermeneia. Minneapolis: Fortress Press, 1990.

Nelson, James B. and Sandra P. Longfellow, *Sexuality and the Sacred: Sources for Theological Reflection*. Louisville: Westminster John Knox, 1994.

Nielsen, Kjeld. "Ancient Aromas Good and Bad." *BRev* 7:3 (1991) 26–33.

Ortner, Sherry. "Is Female to Male as Nature Is to Culture?" In *Woman, Culture, and Society*, 67–87. Ed. Michelle Z. Rosaldo and Louise Lamphere. Stanford: Stanford Univ. Press, 1974.

Pagels, Elaine. *Adam, Eve, and the Serpent*. New York: Random House, 1988.

Paglia, Camille. *Sexual Personae: Art and Decadence from Nefertiti to Emily Dickinson*. New York: Vintage, 1991.

———. *Vamps and Tramps*. New York: Random House, 1994.

Pardes, Ilana. *Countertraditions in the Bible: A Feminist Approach*. Cambridge: Harvard Univ. Press, 1992.

Paz, Octavio. *The Double Flame: Love and Eroticism*. Orlando, Fla.: Harcourt Brace, 1995 [1993].

Plaskow, Judith. *Standing against Sinai: Judaism from a Feminist Perspective*. New York: Harper and Row, 1990.

Pope, Marvin H. *Song of Songs*. AB 7C. Garden City, N.Y.: Doubleday, 1977.

Rabin, Chaim. "The Song of Songs and Tamil Poetry." *Studies in Religion/Sciences religieuses* (1973) 3:205–19.

Rashkow, Ilona. *Taboo or Not Taboo: Sexuality and Family in the Hebrew Bible.* Minneapolis: Fortress Press, 2000

Ricoeur, Paul. "Wonder, Eroticism, and Enigma." In *Sexuality and the Sacred,* ed. James B. Nelson and Sandra Longfellow. Louisville, Ky.: Westminster John Knox, 1994. 80–84.

de Rougemont, Denis. *Love in the Western World.* New York: Pantheon Books, 1956 [1940].

Roussell, Aline. *Porneia: On Desire and the Body in Antiquity.* Oxford: Blackwell, 1988.

Sanday, Peggy. "Toward a Theory of the Status of Women." *American Anthropologist* 75 (1974) 1682–1700.

Sawicki, Jana. *Disciplining Foucault: Feminism, Power and the Body.* New York: Routledge, 1991.

Shattuck, Roger. *From Prometheus to Pornography.* New York: St. Martin's, 1996.

Sontag, Susan. "The Pornographic Imagination." In *Styles of Radical Will.* New York: Farrar, Straus and Giroux, 1966. 35–73.

Streete, Gail C. *The Strange Woman: Power and Sex in the Bible.* Louisville, Ky.: Westminster John Knox, 1997.

Trible, Phyllis. *God and the Rhetoric of Sexuality.* Philadelphia: Fortress Press, 1978.

Veyne, Paul. "The Roman Empire." In *A History of Private Life. I. From Pagan Rome to Byzantium,* ed. Paul Veyne. Cambridge: Belknap Harvard Univ. Press, 1987.

Walsh, Carey E. "God's Vineyard—Isaiah's Prophecy as Vintner's Textbook." *Bible Review* 14:4 (August 1998).

Weeks, Jeffrey. *Sexuality and Its Discontents: Meanings, Myths and Modern Sexualities.* London: Routledge & Kegan Paul, 1985.

Weems, Renita J. *Battered Love: Marriage, Sex, and Violence in the Hebrew Prophets.* Minneapolis: Fortress Press, 1995.

Whyte, Martin King. *The Status of Women in Preindustrial Societies.* Princeton, N.J.: Princeton Univ. Press, 1978.

Winkler, John, J. *The Constraints of Desire: The Anthropology of Sex and Gender in Ancient Greece.* New York: Routledge, 1990.

Scripture Index